P9-AFC-518

CULTURE**SHOCK!**

A Survival Guide to Customs and Etiquette

MUNICH

Liz Smith

Marshall Cavendish
Editions

This edition published in 2007 by:
Marshall Cavendish Corporation
99 White Plains Road
Tarrytown, NY 10591-9001
www.marshallcavendish.us

Other Marshall Cavendish Offices:
Marshall Cavendish International (Asia) Private Limited. 1 New Industrial
Road, Singapore 536196 ▪ Marshall Cavendish Ltd. 119 Wardour Street, London
W1F 0UW, UK ▪ Marshall Cavendish International (Thailand) Co Ltd. 253 Asoke,
12th Flr, Sukhumvit 21 Road, Klongtoey Nua, Wattana, Bangkok 10110,
Thailand ▪ Marshall Cavendish (Malaysia) Sdn Bhd, Times Subang, Lot 46,
Subang Hi-Tech Industrial Park, Batu Tiga, 40000 Shah Alam, Selangor Darul
Ehsan, Malaysia

Marshall Cavendish is a trademark of Times Publishing Limited

ISBN 10: 0-7614-5409-8
ISBN 13: 978-0-7614-5409-0

Please contact the publisher for the Library of Congress catalogue number

Printed in China by Everbest Printing Co Ltd

Photo Credits:
All photos by the author except page 184 (Photolibrary)
▪ Cover photo: Age Fotostock/Sylvain Grandadam

Munich subway map: Wikimedia Commons/ Maximilian Dörrbecker
(Chumwa)

All illustrations by TRIGG

ABOUT THE SERIES

Culture shock is a state of disorientation that can come over anyone who has been thrust into unknown surroundings, away from one's comfort zone. *CultureShock!* is a series of trusted and reputed guides which has, for decades, been helping expatriates and long-term visitors to cushion the impact of culture shock whenever they move to a new country.

Written by people who have lived in the country and experienced culture shock themselves, the authors share all the information necessary for anyone to cope with these feelings of disorientation more effectively. The guides are written in a style that is easy to read and covers a range of topics that will arm readers with enough advice, hints and tips to make their lives as normal as possible again.

Each book is structured in the same manner. It begins with the first impressions that visitors will have of that city or country. To understand a culture, one must first understand the people—where they came from, who they are, the values and traditions they live by, as well as their customs and etiquette. This is covered in the first half of the book.

Then on with the practical aspects—how to settle in with the greatest of ease. Authors walk readers through topics such as how to find accommodation, get the utilities and telecommunications up and running, enrol the children in school and keep in the pink of health. But that's not all. Once the essentials are out of the way, venture out and try the food, enjoy more of the culture and travel to other areas. Then be immersed in the language of the country before discovering more about the business side of things.

To round off, snippets of basic information are offered before readers are 'tested' on customs and etiquette of the country. Useful words and phrases, a comprehensive resource guide and list of books for further research are also included for easy reference.

CONTENTS

ACKNOWLEDGEMENTS

With grateful thanks for their help and friendship, Uta Hacker (Author) for the intial push! Doris Guntner for helping us settle in. Sarah Keenan and Theodora Quraeshi for the fun investigative outings. Edwin Court for his experiences and expertise. Elizabeth Boyd for proof-reading and help in every way, and to Meike Maenecke. Not forgetting the members of the International Women's Club of Munich past and present, and to my husband John, for his technical wizardry.

Liz Smith

DEDICATION

To my wonderful ever-expanding family, scattered
across the world.

MAP OF GERMANY

DENMARK

BALTIC SEA

NORTH
SEA

POLAND

NETHERLANDS

GERMANY

BELGIUM

CZECH
REPUBLIC

LUXEMBOURG

FRANCE

● MUNICH

AUSTRIA

SWITZERLAND

ITALY

MAP OF MUNICH

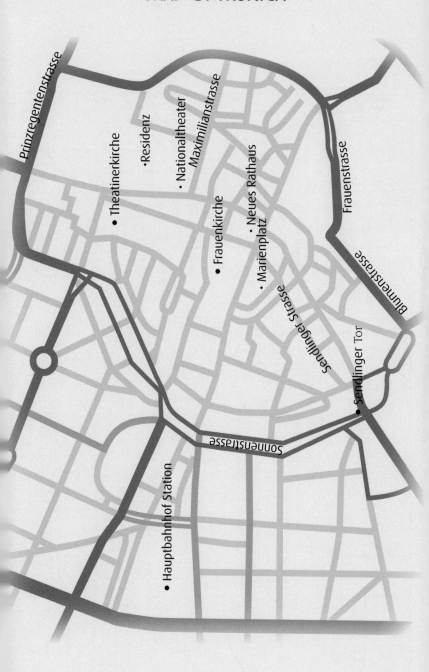

MUNICH SUBWAY MAP

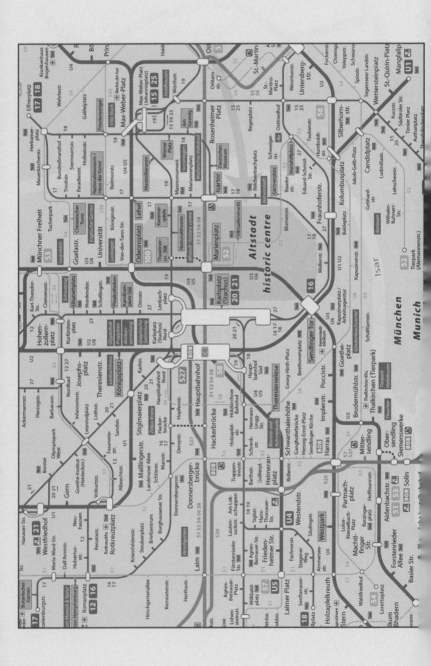

FIRST IMPRESSIONS

CHAPTER 1

'Schau mer amoi, dann seng ma scho...'
'Let's wait and see, then we'll see.'
Used when Bavarians want to end a conversation with
differing opinions and the outcome will be revealed in the
distant future.
– A popular German saying

MUNICH AT FIRST GLANCE

What does Munich mean to you? Do you think of it being an alpine city set on a mountain slope? Actually it is mostly flat. Do you think of beer being consumed in vast quantities? Well, it is regarded as the beer capital of Germany, possibly the world, and yes, during the annual Oktoberfest, vast quantities are consumed. Do you imagine men in *Lederhosen* (leather trousers) and women in *Dirndls* (a kind of pinafore cut very low)? They can certainly be seen dressed in this manner, and more so in summer at their street festivals and at Oktoberfest.

The first glimpse of a new city is often from the pages of guide books and maps. All cities sparkle in those glossy pictures, taken from advantageous angles, but a map can give a better clue to a city's history and progress. A glance at Munich's map soon shows you that it is an old city with a small, clearly defined, circular centre, dissected by small streets, from which radiate broad avenues. All this is encircled by another circular road, well within the city limits and about 2 km from the centre. About 10 km from the centre is a wide motorway, not yet circular as the southern section is missing but it does divert traffic from far away places around the congested urban areas. A train network is also evident, which has 442 km (275 miles) of inner-urban lines and 86 km (53 miles) of underground lines, so for those living in the city centre a car isn't a necessity.

Flying in to Munich airport, many people are struck by the orderliness of the countryside. The fields are rectangular, with the various colours of crops defining the edges rather than hedges. The rivers, which defy regularity, can be picked out by the attendant trees which trace dark, meandering lines through the chequered countryside. At first, the narrow country roads are barely visible, but as the plane descends for landing, you can pick out the extensive, white farm buildings, the agricultural wealth of the area, the clustering hamlets and the different shaped steeples of the village churches.

The airport has two terminals that are modern, spacious and shiny clean structures of glass and metal with a high arched roof covering the connecting courtyard, and shops and restaurants a-plenty in both areas. Announcements are in both German and English and there are illustrated symbols for buses, trains and shops negating the need for any language, as well as plenty of information desks. The train ticket machines are a mystery for many newcomers, even for Germans, but there is a manned desk round the corner—just out of sight of the machines! Whether travelling to town by road or rail from the airport, there is an impression of space, and the gaily flapping Munich flags outside the airport add a cheery note. For about six weeks in winter there is a huge illuminated Christmas tree and in summer, the uncultivated areas are aglow with dandelions—flowers that are almost a national symbol in Bavaria.

If choosing to hire a car rather than take the S-Bahn (suburban metro railway), train or taxi, be sure that you know the route of your journey and how everything operates before venturing from the airport, as there are no lay-bys or motorway services to pull into between the airport and town. I found this to my cost the first time I hired a car alone at the airport. To leave the car park, a ticket must be fed into a slot to raise the barrier, the steep slope negotiated and a gap found in the oncoming traffic, which for me was on the wrong side of the road. I couldn't get the window to close, though I had checked the windscreen wipers and headlights, both necessary on a dull February morning. I had to drive

25 km (15.5 miles) with the window open before I could stop—to find that with this model of car the switches had to be lifted up from below.

The first impressive structure to be seen on the drive in to Munich from the north is the football arena, set right next to the motorway, which at this point has six lanes in either direction. It is huge and at first looks like an enormous, quilted, silver, inflatable rubber ring. It is even more impressive at night if one of the resident teams is using it, as it is then illuminated in either red or blue, depending on the team. It is like something from outer space!

Soon the motorway is down to two lanes as vehicles turn off towards Austria, Italy, Switzerland, France and destinations beyond. If you are heading towards western Munich, the road passes more spectacular sights: some of the tallest glass skyscrapers in Munich, the futuristic BMW museum, the Olympic tower and the silver tiled canopies that cover some of Olympiapark where the 1972 Olympic Games were held. It all looks superb!

One soon realises why people say, "It's a lovely place!" On my first trip in to the city I was surprised how soon we could walk around the centre and asked my husband, "Is this all there is? Where's the rest of it?" The beautiful centre can be walked round in less than an hour, though that barely scratches the surface of what Munich has to offer. A friend who visited recently was impressed as she found it "so clean, and there are no yobs!" Some cities may have a few disreputable youths loitering around the centre but not Munich. There are many cameras monitoring the behaviour in the streets, and if there is any trouble, the police will be there before you know it.

Students can finish school when they are sixteen, but most of these then take an apprenticeship. The students who continue with their academic studies take their end of school exams at the age of 19 and it is usual for them to complete their first degree at 27, or even 30, so the student areas have an older, more sober air than in other European cities. Many of the students who live in the surrounding area return to their parents' home in the evenings.

What is immediately evident to some visitors and new comers is the smoking. Cigarettes are available from machines in almost every street, and though 16 is the official age to start smoking, some start as young as 13. A few restaurants and cafes are non-smoking, and others have non-smoking areas, though these are not often partitioned off. Larger office blocks have smoking rooms and usually there are enormous ash trays at the entrance. Most stations are non-smoking areas and in the main, everyone finishes their cigarettes before going on to the platforms, creating clouds at the entrances. People know just how long they can smoke as the trains, buses and trams are usually so punctual that you can almost set your watches by them.

Though crimes do happen, it is an amazingly safe city, where people obey the rules. It can be strange for a foreigner to wait at a pedestrian crossing until the green man appears, even though a clear view of the road shows that there is no vehicle within 500 m (547 yards) in either direction. Crossing on a red light warrants an on-the-spot fine and it sets a bad example to children. On public transport, it is hardly ever the German children who are misbehaving, especially if they are accompanied by an adult. Very often there is just one child per family, so children are given undivided attention by parents who are several years older on average than in the previous generation. My husband, John, has observed school children going meekly to ask a bus driver for a cigarette lighter that he had confiscated before alighting. Where else would a driver on public transport be so respected? The seats designated for the old and infirm are also surrendered without fuss, though this often has to be asked for. It is rare to see children dropping litter. There are lots of bins around the city and in many places these are separated into three sections, for paper, glass and other rubbish, to make recycling easier.

I'd heard from many that Germany is an egalitarian society, and it would certainly appear so in the beer gardens. On closer inspection though, most people socialise with others from the same or similar professions. Many young adults socialise after work, though generally not with their work colleagues, as work and leisure are kept apart. Social interaction is often at a sports or fitness centre—resulting in a trim workforce. Lots of people travel around town by bicycle, and the smooth cycle paths adjacent to the road are only for bikes and not to be walked on! One can see even elderly people peddling around town. For those whose sense of balance is no longer reliable, large tricycles are ridden instead. The people in the street who have beer drinking as their main hobby can easily be spotted, as there are quite a few well developed stomachs around, but this doesn't hamper their cycling. Years ago, it used to be that you could spot a foreigner by the fact that he or she didn't have a goitre, a normal occurrence in an ageing Bavarian. Enlarged thyroid glands were caused by a lack of iodine in their diet, and these days, people living in Bavaria use Jodsalz—iodine enriched salt—to counter any lack in the diet of this land-locked state. Many older people have a faint scar around their throat where they have had an operation on their thyroid gland.

If someone comes to Munich from another part of Germany, they will immediately notice a difference in both the culture and the language. Within their family and friendship groups, people from Munich are fun and friendly, but it doesn't often extend to people in the street. It is hard to smile at people or start a conversation with them if there is no eye contact first and people passing each other in the street often avert their eyes. I'm told that it is because of the general culture of not getting involved with people they don't know. It is not usual for people to open doors for others or for people to help others with a heavy case or a pushchair down a flight of stairs. It is not rudeness; it is just a different way of behaving. Similarly with customer service; here, the customer is not king! Often, a queue will form whilst the cashiers finish a conversation or go off to complete another task. Many friends thought that it was because they were foreigners that shop assistants were unhelpful or rude to them and were upset or angry. In fact, everyone is treated the same regardless of where they are from.

The tone of voice is very important in most countries, and in Bavaria it is gravelly and brusque. Outsiders may think an argument is taking place when two Bavarians are having a friendly conversation. Most people within Munich speak 'High German', but the Bavarian language is more than a dialect and many people born and raised in Munich cannot understand some villagers living a mere 20 km (12 miles) away. There is a lot of play on words in Bavarian comedy, and the use of rhyme in their sayings is quite common. But, as with the English language, jokes and sarcasm don't translate well. Most people who come to live in Munich try to learn the language. But if you were to pose a question to someone you don't know, the Bavarian answer will come back quick as a flash—leaving the questioner none the wiser. In the centre of the city, especially in the information centres, people usually speak English, especially if they are under 35 years old as they will have learnt it at school. In the suburbs, it is a different story apart from professional people. All the doctors and dentists I've met have a wonderful mastery of English.

There has been a huge difference in the last five years in the amount of English used in advertising. The German airline Lufthansa has 'There's no better way to fly' written on the sides of their buses, and 'Coming soon' can be seen on the windows of new shops. Posters often mix the two languages as in 'I can fly. smile-preis', or don't make a lot of sense as in 'Shorty sun' for a sun bed centre. The language of computers is English and generally understood but this doesn't always translate to everyday usage. To attach something is thought only to apply to a computer and no one knows what 'cc' means, though the abbreviation is often used. 'Wellness', which isn't used in England, is often used in relation to health and fitness centres here.

Until recently, few shops accepted debit or credit cards, but now debit cards can be used in most large stores. This does not usually apply to deliveries. We paid a large deposit for our new lounge suite and because of a past experience with our Bavarian removal company, I asked how we should pay. I was told that it must be cash as the delivery men don't carry any equipment to process cards. It is perfectly normal here to hand over several thousand euros in cash and for the delivery man sign the receipt.

The décor in Bavarian homes is either heavy and traditional, with lots of dark wood and heavy linen curtains or colourful, angular and modern, but both styles usually favour wooden floors with a few rugs. It is normal in a Bavarian household for people to take off their shoes at or just inside the door, which helps to keep the home clean. This was unusual for me at first but is now a way of life. Often there is a shoe cupboard by the front door where the slippers are kept and visitors often bring their own 'house shoes' with them when they come to visit. Many people keep several spare pairs of cloth slippers in case visitors forget their own. Most houses and flats have external shutters. In the old houses these are made of wood, but more often now they are metal or plastic roller shutters, and as the cooler nights close in, the shutters come down, helping to insulate the homes. They are also an extra protection when people are away from home, as are the double locks on most doors.

The winters were a shock. I knew it could get cold here but not *this* cold! The lowest our thermometer has registered here is -25°C (-13ºF), I thought only Siberia got so cold. The small local lake can remain frozen, solid enough for skaters, for weeks. Below -10°C (14ºF) I feel as if my face is being bitten. I was told by an alpine mountaineer that there is no such thing as cold, just inappropriate clothing—so I must buy more. I still prefer the summers, which can vary from cool to sizzling. The lack of wind is noticeable too, to someone who is used to it, but there can be amazing storms when the saplings are bent double, leaves are stripped from trees and rain falls in torrents. It all makes for an interesting and varied life.

OVERVIEW OF LAND AND HISTORY

CHAPTER 2

'De dümmsten Bauern ham de grässtnKardoffn.'
'The stupidest farmers grow the biggest potatoes.'
A cross between a joke and a display of envy, used when
the Bavarian economy changed from being based on
agriculture to a base of modern industries.
—A popular German saying

BIRTH OF MUNICH

The German name for Munich is München, which means 'place of the monks'. Munich is believed to be situated near the site of a small settlement dating back to the 700s that was partly run by monks (Munichen).

Several dukes ruled the land that would later become Bavaria, but it was Henry the Lion, Duke of Saxony and of Bavaria, who first established the community of Munich. At the time, the Bishop of Freising, a small town to the north of Munich, had control over a bridge that spanned the River Isar near Ismaning. As the bridge was located along the vital salt trade route from Hallein to Augsburg, the bishop was able to levy tolls on merchants, ensuring their safety when crossing the river. Henry had the bridge destroyed and another one built upstream near Munichen so that he, rather than the bishop, would benefit from the tolls. Shortly after, Henry himself moved to Munichen and awarded the settlement certain rights that would enable it to prosper, such as the right to establish markets and the right to mint coins.

Fearful of losing a vital source of revenue, the Bishop of Freising appealed directly to his nephew, Holy Roman Emperor Frederick Barbarossa, to intervene on his behalf. The king's ruling, however, went against the bishop and on 14 June 1158, Emperor Frederick sanctioned the founding of Munich by Henry.

THE WITTELSBACH DYNASTY

In 1180, Henry's fortunes took a downturn when the emperor outlawed him on the grounds of disloyalty. Emperor Frederick then handed control of Munich and the whole of Bavaria to Otto von Wittelsbach. Thus began the Wittelsbach dynasty, which was to rule Bavaria up to the early 20th century.

In 1302, Ludwig the Bavarian became the ruler of Munich, before ascending the throne as King of Germany in 1314 and Emperor of the Holy Roman Empire in 1328. Munich subsequently adopted the empire's black-and-gold heraldic colours, which are still displayed around the city today. Under Ludwig's guidance, Munich became a centre for culture and was elevated to the status of a city. As the Wittelsbach family's power grew, fierce rivalry between family members over control of the territory developed, leading to the formation of three duchies within Bavaria.

Between 1467 and 1508, Munich was ruled by Duke Albrecht the Wise, who issued a decree establishing primogeniture (inheritance by the oldest son), thus allowing for the reunification of all the duchies of Bavaria. He also encouraged and supported the arts. During his reign, great works of sculpture, painting and architecture were produced in the late gothic style. The externally austere brick cathedral, now the symbol of Munich, was built at this time and the towers completed in 1488.

Reunification of the Bavarian duchies became a reality during the rule of Albrecht's son, Wilhelm IV. Wilhem was an ardent Roman Catholic and opposed the Reformation. During his reign, St Michael's Church and the Jesuit College were built. At the time, the college was the largest contiguous building complex in Munich. The buildings can still be seen on Neuhauser Strasse today.

Wilhem the IV's son, Duke Albrecht IV, continued to oppose the Reformation by making Catholicism Bavaria's exclusive religion. His successor, Duke Wilhelm V, promoted Munich as a centre of German Renaissance art. The first casting of bronze in Munich was done during this period.

In 1598, Duke Maximilian I became ruler of Bavaria and his reign saw the appearance of the baroque style in the arts. The Duke fought on the side of the Hapsburg dynasty in the Thirty Years' War, between 1618 and 1648. As a result of the war, he acquired more lands and was given the title of *Kurfürst* (Elector). But the war eventually took its toll and the occupation of Munich by first the Swedish, followed by the Spanish army, as well as a sweeping plague, reduced the population of Munich to less than half its number before the war.

The peak of the baroque period in Munich took place between 1651 and 1679, during the rule of Elector Ferdinand Maria. At this time, Italian artists flocked to work in the city. The Austrians occupied Bavaria from 1705 to 1715. Bavaria had sided with France against the Hapsburgs and their allies in the War of Spanish Succession but had been defeated.

At Christmas in 1705, the peasants and townsfolk from upper Bavaria revolted against the occupying army and

The statue of the Virgin Mary in Marienplatz, with the distinctive towers of the Frauenkirche in the background.

marched on to Munich, only to be decimated by the Austrian soldiers outside Munich's southern city gate at Sendling.

Patriotism

One of the leaders of the revolt was a blacksmith from Kochel am See by the name of Balthasar Mayer. He was subsequently killed in the Sendling battle and became an enduring symbol of one's love for one's country.

At a peace conference in 1714, Elector Maximilian II Emanuel returned from exile in France and the Netherlands, to regain control of the whole of Bavaria. Once again the arts flourished in Munich under Maximilian II, who encouraged the French artistic styles he had grown fond of during his exile. In 1726, Elector Karl Albrecht came to power and, in 1742, was elected Holy Roman Emperor in Frankfurt, becoming known as Charles VII. For the next 20 years, artists in Munich drew their inspiration from the rococo style.

Elector Max Joseph III ruled from 1745 until 1777, bringing great artists from different parts of Europe to Munich. He ensured 30 years of stability and peace with Austria by renouncing his hereditary titles. He introduced compulsory education and presided over the founding of the Bavarian Academy of Sciences.

Power was in the hands of Karl Theodor between 1777 and 1799, and the dominance of both the Church and the royal court grew. In 1777, the whole court and its entourage, totalling almost 3,000 people, moved from Mannheim to Munich. The city's expansion meant that the city's fortifications were demolished to allow for urban development.

Although he was unpopular with his citizens, Karl Theodor left a legacy that is enjoyed by all in Munich to this day. For it was he who commissioned an American, Benjamin Thompson, and a gardener, Friedrick Ludwig von Sckell, to design the first people's park on the continent of Europe, the Englischer Garten.

In 1800, French revolutionaries occupied Munich and Napoleon used the city as his operational headquarters.

Napoleon rewarded Maximilian IV Joseph, successor to Karl Theodor who had died in 1799, for his help by bestowing upon him the title of King Maximilian I.

Birth of Oktoberfest

On 17 October 1810, Maximilian's son, Crown Prince Ludwig, married Therese of Saxe-Hildburghausen in Munich. As part of the entertainment for the wedding, a horse race and a folk festival were held in a meadow to the west of the city. The meadow became known as Theresienwiese, in honour of the bride. And it is here that Oktoberfest is still held, ostensibly to commemorate the wedding, though these days, the consumption of copious amounts of beer seems to be the overriding aim of the attendees!

FLOURISHING ARTS AND CULTURE

Architect Karl von Fischer won King Max I Joseph's competition to design a new theatre and the result was the building of the Nationaltheater, a place where the common people could enjoy musical performances. Unfortunately just five years after completion in 1818, fire gutted the theatre. A plea went out to the people to help provide funds for its rebuilding and to this end, a small tax was put on beer.

In 1815, Bavaria joined the German Confederation, which was formed as a way to stop Napoleon's advances. Then in 1818, Maximilian Joseph I proclaimed a more liberal constitution, which provided for religious equality among Catholics and Protestants. When his son Ludwig became king in 1825, he continued the political reforms begun by his father and promoted education and the arts on a grand scale.

King Ludwig I was forced to abdicate by the revolution of 1848. He had spent tremendous amounts of money transforming Munich and the citizens were unhappy with the king's extravagance. The problems were exacerbated to some extent by press censorship at a time when the people wanted more freedom of expression as well as the general unrest in Europe. The primary reason for his unpopularity, however, was the king's affair with an Irish dancer known as Lola Montez.

Ludwig's son, Maximilian II, succeeded his father and Munich continued to expand. By 1850, it had 100,000 residents, making it the fourth largest German city after Berlin, Hamburg and Breslau. Throughout the next 16 years, Maximilian II encouraged academics from the north of Germany to come and live in Munich, enhancing the city's reputation as a seat of learning. His ministers dealt with the running of the city and state while he fostered interest in architecture, founding the Bavarian Nationalmuseum, the beautiful Maximilianstrasse, the Maximilianeum (the building which still houses the Bavarian Parliament) and the Regierungsgebäude, which is the seat of government for Upper Bavaria.

The Rathaus tower and its famous revolving tableau.

In 1864, Maximilian II died and his 18-year-old son became King Ludwig II. At first, Ludwig refused Prussian chancellor Otto von Bismarck's offer to join a German federation under Prussian rule and sided instead with Austria during the Prussian–Austrian War in 1866. Austria's defeat and Prussia's moderate stance towards Bavaria eventually led Bavaria to join the German Empire under Prussian King William I in 1870.

However, King Ludwig II preferred life in the country to affairs of state and spent much of his time on his palaces and his love of music. Composer Richard Wagner became a close friend, and his music inspired the king. Ludwig had three palaces constructed, one at Neuschwanstein, the inspiration for Walt Disney's world-famous castle in Disneyland; Herrenchiemsee, a close copy of Versailles; and Linderhof, a little gem with formal gardens set amidst woodland. Ludwig's extravagance incensed his ministers, who had him declared insane. His death by drowning, in 1886, at the age of 40 was never fully explained. But King Ludwig II's image lives on in countless souvenirs sold in Munich today.

A Community of Artists

The expressionist group of painters—*Der Blaue Reiter* or Blue Rider group—was established by Wassily Kandinsky, Paul Klee, Franz Marc and Kandinsky's pupil and mistress, Gabriele Münter.

Ludwig's brother, King Otto I, was mentally unfit to assume power, so the role fell to his uncle, Prince Regent Luitpold, who ruled between 1886 and 1912, heralding yet another era of artistic development for painters, writers and architects. Theodor Fischer, who was the head of the city's urban growth office, decided to grade buildings along Munich's streets by their density and height. His vision was preserved until 1979, ensuring that few of the city's buildings were taller than six storeys and therefore smaller than the Cathedral Church of Our Lady.

The population of Munich had reached more than 500,000 when the Neues Rathaus, the new town hall, the focus of modern Munich, was completed in Marienplatz in 1903.

Prince Regent Luitpold died in 1912 and the last of the Wittelsbachs to rule, Ludwig III, reigned until 1918.

A NEW ERA FOR MUNICH

Whilst the rich in Munich developed aesthetic appreciation, the poor masses became desperate. Unemployment, disease and mortality amongst young adults was on the increase, exacerbated by the outbreak of World War I in 1914. Germany lost the war in 1918 and the people of Munich, under socialist banners, demanded a new constitution. The king escaped from the angry crowds under cover of darkness and a Free Peoples' Republic was declared, led by Kurt Eisner. Arguments raged between the factions on the right and the left of the social democrats and two months later, in January 1919, elections were held, which Eisner's party lost.

The conservatives gained control and promoted nationalism. In 1923, Adolf Hitler, the spokesman of several right-wing groups, and his troops marched into a meeting of Bavarian politicians and declared a *Putsch* (coup d'état). Although Hitler enjoyed the support of many people, he was arrested and imprisoned in 1923. He was released the following year.

No central government had control over Germany in the 1920s and the victorious countries of World War I occupied the industrial areas, contributing to galloping inflation. A new currency was introduced in 1924, and a degree of calm returned to Germany and Munich but with anti-Semitic undercurrents.

HITLER'S MUNICH

In 1929, the US Stock Exchange collapsed, launching the Great Depression of the early 1930s. Unemployment was widespread throughout the western world but it was highest in Germany, where it affected almost a third of the working population. The result was political polarisation.

In March 1933, the National Socialist Party came to power. Hitler became Chancellor of Germany with dictatorial powers, and promised solutions to Germany's problems. The state invested in floundering industries, created new industrial areas, built a motorway network, new towns and started rearming militarily.

Two divisions of the Gestapo, the secret police, were created. The Sturm Abteilung (SA) or storm troopers, led by Ernst Röhm were street fighters who wanted a Socialist revolution. The Schützstaffel (SS) were the elite unit of the Nazi Party led by Heinrich Himmler, who became Chief of Police for Munich. On 30 June 1934, the Röhm Putsch, later known as the Night of the Long Knives, took place. It was a success for Himmler; he had all dissenting members of Hitler's party either murdered or imprisoned in a Dachau concentration camp. Himmler became one of Hitler's closest aides.

White Rose Rebellion

The White Rose, a group of students from Munich University, voiced their dissent against the war and the slaughter of young Germans through a pamphlet. They threw the pamphlets down on the floor of the university's main hall, but the authors were caught and met their deaths in 1943. In remembrance of them, metal images of their pamphlets have been set in the ground in front of the main university building.

In 1935, Munich was designated one of Germany's five Führer Cities and several new buildings were constructed. In the same year, the swastika became the official German flag and in September, anti-Jewish laws were passed. Munich became the headquarters of the Nazi movement, and it was here in 1938 that Neville Chamberlain, Édouard Daladier, Adolf Hitler and Benito Mussolini signed the Munich Agreement, allowing the German occupation of Czechoslovakia. World War II began in 1939, when Germany occupied Poland.

POST-WORLD WAR II

Munich was bombed throughout the war, so when the American army arrived on 30 April 1945, it was to a city in ruins. Order had to be restored to the demoralised city of Munich. The population had been halved and many of the young men had been killed or injured.

The occupying army (the United States army was allotted the south of Germany) asked for help, and a former mayor helped with the reorganisation of the city by encouraging the population to help. The city council approved a plan put forward by councilman Karl Meitinger to rebuild the old city but to separate the old and new zones with a ring road. Debris from demolished buildings was cleared and taken to a piece of spare land north of the city, where it formed a rubble mountain. It was on this rubble that Olympiapark was eventually built and where the 1972 Munich Olympics were held.

The Christian Social Union (CSU) was elected to power in 1946, and Munich became the capital of the Free State of Bavaria. The CSU has managed to hold power almost continuously ever since, sometimes in coalition with the Free Democratic Party (FPD) or the Social Democratic Party (SPD).

Two large German corporations, Siemens and Allianz, relocated from Berlin to Munich, major construction work continued for many years and by 1957, Munich's population had exceeded one million.

Bavaria is one of the states (*Länder*) of Federal Germany. Though the state is governed from Berlin, the elected state senate, which sits in the beautiful Maximilianeum, is still solidly CSU and it has autonomy over many local decisions.

Franz-Joseph Strauss

The forceful Franz-Joseph Strauss was the best known politician of modern Bavaria. A joint founder of the CSU, he was elected its chairman in 1961, after having served as defence minister in the German government. He was the Bavarian Minister President from 1961 to 1980. He oversaw the transformation of Bavaria from an economy reliant on agriculture to being the centre of Germany's new economy. A fiercely patriotic man, Strauss was against forging closer ties with East Germany for many years but later changed his mind.

The presence in Munich of the European Patent Office (EPO) is due to a large extent to Franz-Josef Strauss. The building, which opened in 1977, is on Erhardtstrasse, on the west bank of the River Isar, opposite the Deutsches Museum. The organisation has continued to expand and now employs almost 7,000 people, including highly qualified scientists and engineers in charge of examining each patent application with meticulous care.

In 1992, the new airport located near Freising opened, bearing the name of Franz-Josef Strauss.

REBIRTH OF MUNICH

Industry re-established itself in and around the city in the second half of the 20th century. MAN has its massive vehicle works northwest of the city at Karlsfeld; BMW is located just north of the Petuelring in Milbertshofen; and Siemens' headquarters is just south of the city in Ober-Sendling, although it has branches all over the Munich area.

In 1998, the magnificently modern new exhibition centre (das neüe Messegelände) opened in Riem, on land formerly occupied by the old airport and the U-Bahn, the underground train service, was extended to service it. With its large modern halls and vast car parks, Munich is now able to host international exhibitions on a grand scale.

CENTRE OF TECHNOLOGY

The economic acceleration in the area continued as the century turned, and almost every fortnight would see a new company established within 30 km of Munich. Cisco started the IT trend in 1993 and was then joined by Amazon, Cellway and SAP, on sites near the airport at Hallbergmoos. Hewlett-Packard, Intel, Logitech, Microsoft and Oracle are just a few of the larger IT companies who benefited from having land initially designated and sponsored by the Bavarian Free State. There were an estimated 18,000 IT companies around Munich in 2000, giving it the highest density of IT firms in Europe and the fourth worldwide. The fortunes of many in the IT industry experienced a severe downturn in 2001, resulting in most companies having to impose cost-cutting measures.

Research in biotechnology has also been sponsored by the Free State of Bavaria. An Innovation and Founders' Centre for Biotechnology (IZB) was built in Martindorf, to the south of Munich. The centre attracted many young scientists who have set up new companies in the area. The Grosshadern Clinic, the Gene Centre of the University and the Max Planck Institute for Biochemistry and Neurobiology are also located in Martindorf.

Film and Publishing Centre

Munich has also become a magnet for the film and publishing industries, with its own high school for film and television. Media Works Munich, whose large orange globe can be seen from Ostbahnhof, has premises on Rosenheimer Strasse and incorporates an array of companies. The premises formerly housed a food factory and a tailoring company but now the buildings buzz with cameras. Many radio, television and film companies are also to be found in Unterföhring and Ismaning. These include Pro 7/Sat1, Premiere television, Bavaria film, Bayern Rundfunk and Antenne Bayern.

Publishing and printing are two of Munich's main businesses. With 266 publishing houses, Munich is on a par with New York City. Publishing companies such as Hubert Burda Media Holding, which publishes several magazines and a TV guide, have their main editorial headquarters in Arabella Park but send everything electronically to be printed in Stuttgart. Süddeutscher Verlag, which produces Bavaria's highest circulation quality daily newspaper, is situated to the east of Munich. Falk Verlag, which publishes maps, is located in Berg am Laim, as is the Berlin-based Bertlesmann/Springer empire. Many smaller publishing houses produce specialist books, newspapers, magazines and journals.

Construction Boom

The construction industry has seen a boom in this generation. The building of the facilities for the 1972 Olympics was followed by the construction of buildings to house burgeoning industries in the area and all their employees. As the city and its suburbs expanded, the infrastructure was improved, resulting in new shops, roads, hospitals, fire and police stations, sewage works, rubbish disposal depots and sports facilities. Plenty of jobs for architects, lawyers, estate agents, construction workers and many other related trades were created. The new architectural styles of the 20th century, as seen in the Fünf Hof Centre on the west side of Theatinerstrasse, have enhanced central Munich.

Financial Centre

Today, Munich is the premier insurance centre of Germany and the third most important in Europe after Paris and London. Allianz is the largest insurance group in the world and Munich Re is one of the world's biggest reinsurers—both companies have their bases in Munich. Swiss Re, the world's largest reinsurer also has a vast modern complex in Unterföhring. Bavaria is home to Germany's largest public social insurance group too.

Munich has the largest number of banks per capita in Germany and is the country's second largest banking city after Frankfurt. The two most important Bavarian banks are the Bayerische Landesbank and the HypoVereinsbank which together form the Girozentrale.

Highly-qualified workers from all over the world are employed around the city in many expanding industries. Munich fosters business and cultural links with seven other international cities—Edinburgh, Verona, Bordeaux, Sapporo, Cincinnati, Kiev and Harare—via 'twin city' links.

Modern-day Bavaria is synonymous with both laptop and *Lederhosen,* and unemployment in the state is the lowest in Germany. In 2001, a poll was taken and Munich was selected from among 35 German cities as the city in which most Germans would like to live.

SNAPSHOTS OF RESIDENTIAL MUNICH
Finding Your Way

Some 700 years ago, the oldest part of Munich, the Altstadt, was divided into four quarters, still clearly discernible, as they are divided along main roads. An area least visited by tourists is the quarter west of Sendlinger Tor, up to

Neuhauser Strasse. Comprising of narrow streets, it has the oldest restaurant in town, the Hundskugel. It was said that if you were born along Kreuzstrasse or Damenstiftstrasse, there was no need to stray further afield as everything you needed in life was to be found there. There are now modern blocks of apartments built on sites once damaged by bombs, many of which are owned by the Catholic Church and the city's tax offices.

The more spacious north-western quarter is home to the cathedral, the police headquarters and the Ministry for Culture. Soon after the founding of Munich, the north-east section became home to the House of Wittelsbach. The ducal family lived first in the Alter Hof, the old court, and after 1571, in the Residenz, with the peaceful Hofgarten adjacent. The former Central Mint is located in this elegant quarter, as is the Nationaltheater and the *Rathaus,* the magnificent pseudo-gothic town hall. It also has elegant shops and hotels and a few extremely expensive apartments.

The south-eastern area is the centre for sustenance, where the Viktualienmarkt, the main vegetable market, is bordered by a row of butchers. It also houses the city's museum, the new Jewish synagogue opened in 2006, a large school and the central fire station. At present, the Altstadt is the least densely populated of the central city areas.

North-west

Lehel, just north-west of the old city, used to be where the craftsmen lived. Bounded by the Englischer Garten in the north and the River Isar to the east, it had splendid, spacious apartments added around 1870. Now, as one emerges from the U-Bahn station alongside a quaint teashop nestling beneath the parish church of St Anna, it is the quiet elegance of the place that appeals. The small gardens and the monastery exude calm, while round the corner there are countless rented apartments, some in faceless modern blocks erected after the war. Maximilian Strasse, the most expensive shopping street in Munich, has several museums and art galleries housed in heavily ornate buildings.

North of Hauptbahnhof is Maxvorstadt, an educational belt of schools, institutes, financial offices, museums and galleries, which appear almost devoid of people in the evenings. Yet, incongruously, these are some of the most densely populated areas in Munich.

North of Munich

Schwabing, just north of the old city centre has been, for about 100 years, one of the most sought after areas in which to live. Incorporating the main university area and located close to the city centre, it has a lively nightlife of its own and lots of individual shops. Though 70 per cent of the area was destroyed during the last war, much of the rebuilding managed to retain the old style, giving it an established feel. Housing is mixed, from expensive detached homes with gardens, to apartments found above shops and offices. True to old planning laws, the buildings are usually no taller than six storeys. When the Karstadt department store was planned in Münchener Freiheit, it had to be reduced by a couple of storeys before building permission was granted.

Schwabing is especially popular with young singles, who love its convenient location, especially as the beautiful, spacious, almost rural Englischer Garten borders the area to the east. In summer, cafés and bars spill onto the pavements and there is a constant buzz of life.

Further north is Milbertshofen, an area of industry and apartments interspersed with lots of small green spaces. Just to the west, the Olympic village that housed the 1972 Olympic contestants is like a separate community. Its inhabitants, both students and workers, enjoy living close to the park and do not mind the occasional 16-storey blocks, the stark lines and the density of the accommodations.

Moosach, when approached from the city, has block upon boring block of apartments above shops and the one-way system around the bus and train station can be a nightmare. The main street, Dachauer Strasse, sees a constant stream of traffic, but there are some pleasant parts in the southern region. Am Hart is an area of small homes, many with tiny gardens, but there are also huge blocks of flats that completely dominate the skyline of adjacent Hasenbergl, which to the outsider may appear as a sad place where teenagers can be seen hanging around corner shops.

Feldmoching, though only divided from Hasenbergl by a field, seems to exist in another world. A small community where the houses are well-spaced, it has a tiny village green, a war memorial and lots of green gardens. In total contrast Freimann is almost entirely industrial, with the MOC Sports and Fashion Centre trying to breathe new life into it. Barracks cover a large area between Freimann and Am Hart.

The huge MAN truck works dominate Karlsfeld, which is rather cut off from the rest of Munich by vast railway sidings,

The distinctive Olympic Tower stands out in Munich.

and the wide A99. But the 304 and the S2 train line maintain the connection to the city. The district is surrounded on the other sides by open fields and has a lovely lake as a focus for summer recreation. Although Allach has plenty of industry in the north-west, it is truly countryside, surrounded by fields of flowers in the spring and summer. It has farms right along the main road and horses graze beside the little river Würm, which flows from Untermenzing, a slightly more built-up district and not quite as charming.

Hartmannshofen is right out of a fairy tale. Many of the homes, which vary from old country homes to modern villas, are set in their own woodland gardens. One can imagine a pony and trap tied up in the back yard, yet Mercedes-Benzes now glide sedately along the streets. Obermenzing too is delightful. Rough grass verges lend a rural atmosphere and the ancient village hostelry has shutters, painted in Bavarian white and blue, as is the Maypole in front. Yet it is only 300 m (1,000 ft) from the traffic dashing along the A8 to Stuttgart.

The East

The Au district, east of the River Isar incorporates Haidhausen and Berg am Laim, which were working-class areas during the early 20th century. As they are close to the city, the older apartments are now quite sought after and several parts have new developments. Rents depend on the prices set by the local council, which takes into consideration the amount of local industry and the dirt and noise from the train tracks nearby.

Bogenhausen is one of the most elegant places to live. Even the king was not allowed to have his opera house built there. Close enough to the city yet adjacent to the river, it is a peaceful, sophisticated district of old villas. Herzog Park, where many modern mansions have been built, is on the river's old flood plain. A drawback could be that the only public transport is the bus. Parkstadt is further east and the homes are not as expensive. Taller and taller apartment blocks for the proletariat have been erected towards Arabellapark and Oberföhring, though there are still pockets where detached and semi-detached houses are predominant. Johanneskirchen and Unterföhring are a mix of all types of housing, but increasingly, taller apartment blocks are overtaking these suburbs.

The straight road between Denning and Englschalking is quite like an English suburban high street with small shops facing the street and mixed housing behind. Next to it, Daglfing has lots of semi-detached houses and several developments of not too tall apartment blocks, as well as a couple of good-sized parks. Reim, the 'horse centre' of Munich, still has two race tracks and a few paddocks, though soon the horses may have to live in flats too as the construction work encroaches!

The rich community of Aschheim/Dornach obtains its wealth from the ever-expanding high-tech industrial park. Most of the recent developments have been of terraced houses, rather than high-rise flats. The hope is to have a rail link one day but at the moment, the inhabitants rely on buses or their own cars. The old farming communities of Ismaning, now with a high-tech industrial park, and Garching, with its Technical University and Max Planck Institute in the north and heavy industry in the west, were quiet sleepy towns 30 years ago. Now every plot made available by the local farmers is being used for housing or industry, and they are expanding rapidly.

While Trudering and Waldtrudering further to the south-east have many pleasant detached houses away from the main road, the area within the vicinity of the new exhibition centre is being filled with block after block of flats. In years to come, they will be softened by greenery like the developments in Heimstetten, but the price of the flats there reflects the present stark outlook.

An industrial area links Heimstetten to Kirchheim, which is a quaint, newly cobbled village with a Maypole in the middle. Neuperlach and Ramersdorf are known for their ugly high-rise flats and busy wide roads but in fact there are some rather pleasant areas of mixed housing, and some of the shabbier areas have been spruced up. The European School, originally built for the children of the Patent Office

A snow-covered park in Riem, on the eastern fringes of Munich.

employees is to be found here. The pretty old centre of Alt-Perlach with the church and Maypole remains untouched by the racing technological age.

South of the City

Sendling is and always has been an impoverished area, the home of poorer workers. On the southern boundary is one of Munich's huge power stations with its chimneys belching out (filtered) smoke. Here rubbish is burnt and heating produced for the local area. Sendling incorporates a vast wholesale fruit, vegetable and flower market, where large trucks shuttle in and out in the early hours.

Isarvorstadt is almost a town in itself, with Gärtnerplatz as its centre and Fraunhoferstrasse its high street. The German and European patent offices cover two blocks and the monastery of the Heart of Jesus almost another. The imposing State Theatre is located here, as are several smaller theatres. There are streets and streets of apartments, each with its own character but never so tall as to keep out the sun. The southern part of Isarvorstadt becomes more run-down beyond the imposing Labour Exchange, where the old slaughterhouse is hidden behind brick walls.

From here westwards, specialist clinics are to be found stretching into Ludwigsvorstadt. I'm told that if you're going to be ill, there is no better place than Munich to be in! This district is graced by the beautiful Church of St Paul and has some splendid villas, many of which have since been converted into business premises.

Mittersendling and Obersendling do not have the number of apartment blocks found in some neighbouring suburbs, but a mix of terrace houses, semi-detached and detached homes with their own gardens. Many of these houses accommodate more than one family, which is common in Munich. The Siemens factory buildings cover an extensive area of Obersendling but most are screened by trees.

Giesing is divided by a steep hill into Ober- and Unter-Giesing. Before the construction of Olympiapark in the early 1970s, the football teams of FC Bayern Munich and TSV München 1860 were based here. Sports are still catered for, with more facilities than are usually the norm in such a small built-up area. Bordering Giesing in the west are meadows, the River Isar and the Flaucher, a pretty riverside area. The zoo nestles beside the river but is also easily accessible from west of the river, from more up-market Thalkirchen. Here, the green water meadows widen, and you could well believe you're in the open country rather than surrounded by a large conurbation.

Harlaching, Neu Harlaching and Menterschwaige are quiet residential areas for the rich and famous. Bordered to the east by the Perlacher Forst, the only modes of public transport in this part of southern Munich seem to be the quaint little tram and the bus.

The pleasant old residential town of Solln has well-spaced houses and several private shops. A local street sign points to Innsbruck, a famous Austrian ski resort, rather than the next suburb. Maybe everyone heads there at the first opportunity. Sadly, adjacent Stadt Solln was some planner's answer to the housing needs about 30 years ago. The eight-storey blocks of flats are dwarfed by the 13-storey blocks, which in turn appear insignificant next to the central 20-storey block. No amount of tree planting can disguise these.

Forstenried, east of the dividing motorway 95, has a mix of different types of homes, including farms and plenty of open spaces. To the west is Neu Forstenried, where the town planners crammed in more occupants with four and nine-storey apartment blocks. Trees do soften the landscape here, though not the ugly shopping centre.

Right next to this, Maxhof is a quiet residential area where tiny old bungalows with huge meadow-like gardens can still be spotted between the newer developments of detached homes. Neuried is still almost a separate country village as either open country or forest surrounds it on three sides.

Fürstenreid is a leafy suburb where the trees hide cuboid blocks of apartments. Some parts of the suburb boast charming houses but not the busy modern centre. It is separated from its neighbours to the north-west by a sprawling wooded cemetery. At the other side of the cemetery is Hadern, a suburb of larger terrace houses and detached residences, and Grosshadern, an area of denser housing, with a large hospital.

Gräfelfing is the shoulder of a pleasant residential arm that stretches south-west into the countryside. Although the town hall is a concrete monstrosity, the main street is lined with young trees and grass verges and parking spaces front the individual little shops. It is a clean, well-kept district with lots of detached homes. The gardens are much larger than in the towns closer to the city.

Planegg straddles the River Würm, and its main street is so similar to Gräfelfing, it could have been conceived by the same team of planners. The little old saw mill next to the river sets the sleepy pace for residential Krailling. In contrast, Stockdorf has stark modern garage showrooms and industries lining the main road.

To the West

In days of old, the kings and their court had to traverse Neuhausen as they journeyed between the two main palaces in Munich. Neuhausen was then a working class area of breweries. In 1930, a new, modern housing estate for the middle class was developed, incorporating green areas. It was said that, architecturally, the district was ruined as much by the 1960s buildings as the bombs of World War II. Though dissected by the ring road, friends living there love it and say it is like a village, with the Rotkreuzplatz as its centre.

Towards Nymphenburg, home of the Wittlesbach beautiful summer palace, Gern is a select district of grand, detached houses and apartments, where local shoppers bustle along from Notburgstrasse to Romanplatz looking elegant and relaxed.

Over the railway lines south of Neuhausen, the poor areas of Westend and Schwanthaler Hohe are besieged by visitors for two weeks of the year as people head for the Oktoberfest in Theresienwiese. Behind its statue of Bavaria, an old exhibition park has been demolished to make way for more apartment blocks. The huge industrial brick buildings of the Augustiner brewery edge Landsberger Strasse, while Hacker-Pschorr beer is brewed on Bayerstrasse.

Laim has several types of transport links to the city but remains a pleasant suburb with a garden feel. It is bordered in the west by Kleingärten, small allotments for the local flat dwellers, and has a large area devoted to growing saplings, which, when tall enough, are transplanted to the streets and parks. Only an environmentally-aware city would keep such a large area for trees rather than develop it. Kleinhadern also has well-spaced streets and an amiable environment.

Pasing, just to the west of the parks surrounding the Nymphenburg Palace, has the feel of an old town that has been swallowed up by Munich. The old station building, small Viktualienmarkt and huge town hall are a testament to its heritage. Many parts of the town contain beautiful detached houses, and there is a long area of parkland through which the tiny River Würm flows.

Alt-Aubing must have started out as a sleepy farming hamlet but about 100 years ago, houses and shops started to occupy the spaces between the farms. To the south of the railway line, Aubing-Süd is dominated by 11-storey apartment blocks that dwarf the many four-storey blocks. Unlike the areas near the city centre, there is plenty of land for the kids to play on. Across a sweep of fields and two motorways, the suburban village of Lochhausen is divided into three sections by the railway and the busy main road.

The Gs of the west are separate little towns with their own very different identities. Gröbenzell has some industry and a couple of grubby-looking high-rise blocks. But it also has a leafy, spacious cobbled centre dominated by a sparkling white church and modern shops. A little stream and the railway dissect the town. Adjacent in the south is Puchheim-Bahnhof, a grim area of mainly four, seven and 13-storey blocks. It is obvious that town planners are trying hard to improve the area with newer rows of shops and trees lining the streets but in some cases I think only the bulldozers would succeed in improving the place. Puchheim-Ort by contrast is a tiny, rundown farming village into which developers have inserted shiny, new detached houses with pretty gardens. Germering has a big equestrian centre to the north with lots of paddocks and several farms, contrasting madly with its futuristic glass and metal centre. Though there are modern high-rise apartments, they are well-spaced and there is also a preponderance of terrace and semi-detached houses. Gauting is isolated from its neighbours by heaths and forests, a wonderful place for dogs to romp. Its quaint little station is at the top of a hill, while at the base, the old palace, now a museum, is picturesquely sited on a bend of the river. Small shops are situated on the hill and on the road west that leads to a large hospital. An international school is just down the road.

CHAPTER 3

PEOPLE OF MUNICH

'Dümm deaf ma scho sei, bloß zhäifa muaß ma se wissn.'
'You are allowed to be stupid,
if you know how to help yourself.'
According to some Bavarians, one of the greatest
attributes of a person is cunning, regardless of whether
there may be cheating or lying.
—A popular German saying

COMMON PERCEPTIONS

The image of the average Bavarian is that of a happy, carefree man in leather trousers being served tankards of foaming beer by busty, flirty females. While that may be true of some of the local people at Oktoberfest, it is not so for the rest of the year.

Contrary to this pre-conceived notion, Bavarians are not a tall, blond race. The average Bavarian male is of small to medium height, dark-haired and quite bulky. The women tend to have an ample bust, not a very noticeable waist, hardly any bottom and quite slim legs, and they too become broader as they age.

Bavarians are in the main orderly, tidy, law-abiding, honest and reserved with people they don't know. Once you get to know individual Bavarians they can be charming, but getting to know them can be a problem. Bavarians themselves admit that they may often appear grumpy (although they may also point out that Bavaria is renowned for being one of the friendliest regions in Germany). It is disconcerting to walk down a suburban street and no one makes eye contact with you, much less smiles at you. Neighbours rarely pop round to visit without having first gone through a formal introduction, usually by a mutual friend. I am told that until just a few years ago, it was up to the new people in the area to knock on the door of their neighbours and introduce themselves, though this could pose real problems if the new residents were unable to speak fluent German. Nowadays, people doing this in the city would be thought quite peculiar.

Home and family are of supreme importance to Bavarians. A lot of time is spent with relatives and close friends, and there appears to be no need for outsiders. But once you are accepted as part of their 'family', there is no looking back. In fact, the attention can sometimes be almost overwhelming. Recognition, then familiarity, may lead to a nod of the head, then a *"Grüss Gott"* or *"Morgen"* after a few weeks or months.

After two years of living in the same street, a cheery man who I saw several times a week started saying, *"Grüss Dich"*, rather than *"Grüss Gott"*. I felt then that we must finally be on friendly terms.

Bavarians are free with their advice if they see something being done incorrectly. I once parked the car by the curb but facing towards oncoming traffic when a lady started shouting from a garden across the road, warning me that if the police saw the car I would be in trouble. It was good of her to warn me, though her manner was more brusque than that to which I was accustomed.

It is the duty of the people to keep the pavement outside their own house clean and clear of snow. In the autumn,

people sweep the path outside their own home to keep it free from leaves. Several times I have seen people pick up rubbish and put it in the nearest bin. Forbidding-looking punks can sometimes be seen walking out of their way to deposit cigarette cartons in litter bins. Many people are not as conscientious about their cigarette stubs, however, which are often thrown on the ground before they enter a station, or tossed from their car windows leaving trails of sparks. People are increasingly conscientious about the deposits left by their dogs and there are many 'dog stations' close to paths with plastic bags available next to the bins.

FASHION

Until I came to Munich, I had never believed that people would be seen wearing their national costumes as everyday wear but it happens. Many middle-aged and older ladies can be seen wearing the *Trachten* (traditional German costume) while shopping. Especially prevalent on feast days and festivals, one can see the *Trachten* everywhere in Munich. In fact, you may feel like a real outsider if you are not wearing it.

The men wear *Lederhosen*—usually beige or light brown suede trousers that end just below the knee, or suede shorts. Either of these may be held up by embroidered suede braces and straps. To keep their legs warm, thick woollen socks are worn with stout shoes. Shirts are often collarless with full sleeves and may be embroidered with leaves or hunting motifs, and square cotton scarves are sometimes knotted around the neck. Embroidered suede waistcoats are worn over the shirts if it is a little bit chilly. Woollen jackets are usually grey, brown or beige with either horn or silver buttons and are sometimes embroidered too. Hats are worn by most middle-aged and older men and are often adorned with badges, feathers or tufts of fur. The larger the cockade, the more expensive and prestigious it is. I have seen some that cost € 1500, and that's without the hat!

Whatever the ladies' ages or shapes, they all look good in their folk costumes. The women wear full-sleeved, lace-trimmed blouses and full skirts or the *Dirndl*, usually with lace-trimmed petticoats peeping below the hems. The *Dirndl* is worn with an apron, the colour complementing the dress. The *Trachten* can be worn for any occasion. Cotton or linen *Trachten* are used for everyday wear, and wool, taffeta, brocade or velvet are reserved for the evening. To comply with tradition, the skirt should be at least 2.7-m (three-yards) wide and all the pleats must be of the same depth. Buttons are often made of wood or horn but pearl or silver buttons are used in the *Trachten* worn for the evening. Jewellery is silver and chunky, often displaying hearts or flowers. Silk-fringed shawls are sometimes worn around the shoulders. A modern version of the *Trachten* is a low-cut mini pinafore dress made of beige suede or linen, with thick cotton lace showing beneath the hem and a full-sleeved, crisp white blouse. They certainly turn a few heads at the Oktoberfest!

To some extent, fashion is dictated by the weather. When it is cold, heavy woollen jumpers are worn as well as a topcoat, usually green, black or grey. The traditional coat is a *Loden,* which is made of wool. The coat is styled with a deep centre pleat falling from the shoulders on the back. Horn or silver buttons are used, and the coat may be trimmed with another colour. The traditional colours worn by the men are the colours of camouflage to blend with the countryside when they go hunting. Not everyone owns *Tracht* although the longer one stays in Munich, the more likely it is you will end up with at least one item.

From day-to-day, both men and women usually wear trousers and flat shoes. The look, even in the city, is smart casual. I'm told that people in Munich are smarter dressers than elsewhere in Germany. Really sophisticated attire can be seen in Maximilian Strasse, Brenner Strasse and the area just northwest of Stachus, where the law courts and the stock exchange are located. The elegant, glamorous and chic can always be seen at the theatre or the opera.

Teenage fashion is now pretty much universal and the youths of Munich are no exceptions, their 'look' mostly gleaned from the pages of international publications such as *Marie Claire, Glamour* and *Vogue,* and from current films and pop idols.

BAVARIAN SOCIETY

Bavaria is still very much a male-dominated state. Historically, women did not go to work but stayed at home to take care of their children and attend to the needs of their men. Moreover, the German state education system does not make it easy for working mothers, as the times the kids finish school (11:30 am for the younger children and 1:00 pm for the older ones), make childcare a necessity. Unfortunately, because childcare is so expensive, it often becomes uneconomical for a mum to continue to work, especially with more than one child. Children also have a lot of homework and I have been told that the children's studies suffer if mum isn't there to encourage and help them. This perpetuates the role of the man as the breadwinner with his *Hausfrau* at home, her interests centering on the '3 Ks' of *Kinder, Kirche* and *Küche,* or 'children, church and kitchen' in that order. For those who are more fortunate, grandparents take the role of carers while the parents work, but for the many people that are born in other regions of Germany or abroad, this is not a possibility.

Taking care of children used to be a woman's job. But present-day German men are not ashamed of being seen carrying their children, even in a beer garden.

SOCIALISING WITH LOCALS

CHAPTER 4

'Hock di hera, dann samma mehra.'
'Sit down, together we are more.'
—A Bavarian rhyme encouraging gregariousness

MAKING FRIENDS

Living in any foreign land can be an isolating, even lonely experience, especially if you do not go out to work and meet colleagues there. Many of my friends have experienced this once the chaos of arranging the various services and the furniture in their new homes is over. Then loneliness and homesickness often sets in. This settling-in period can last for three to six months, for children as well as adults, but I have known of some wives who have never adjusted and have taken the children with them back to their own country, leaving their husbands in Munich to complete work contracts. It appears easier to adjust if a contract is three years or fewer, as the return home is on the distant horizon.

Usually after about six months, a routine of some sort has been established and everyone in the family begins to enjoy their time in their newly adopted city, often visiting other locations during the weekends. In the early days, once my husband John had left for work and our youngest daughter Amanda had gone off to catch the school bus, I would often look at the clock and work out the number of hours and minutes before I would see either of them again. A few times, I simply sat and had a quiet weep. Our older children were working in London and so did not come with us. Twice, I felt I could not bear the new life any longer and told my husband, "I want to go home!" It seemed that many of my friends had done just the same.

The key to settling down is to create a routine and to stick to it. It helps as well if you have something to look forward to in the not-too-distant future. But to get the rewards out of life, we need to put in some effort ourselves. At first, my lifeline was to write to my friends and family back home. Emails flew backwards and forwards. The phone bills were also pretty high. Each day I would dash down to the post box attached to the outside wall of the flats to see if there was a letter for me. Many months later, I realised I had settled down nicely when I opened the post box and was relieved to find it empty—there were no bills!

After a few weeks, I volunteered my services as an unpaid helper at the international school Amanda attended, and as I had been a teacher, I was soon in the classroom two mornings a week. The contact with children, teachers and other parents in the cafeteria helped tremendously. There were several clubs organised by various parents at the school, as well as a Parent Teachers' Association. The clubs organised

Do's and Don'ts

- Bavarian behaviour is often very formal, especially in the workplace. Almost everyone is addressed as *Herr* or *Frau* followed by their family name, though this is not so in the media world, nor amongst the informal teens and twenty-somethings. Until close friendships develop, adults talk to each other using the formal *Sie* for 'you' rather than the more familiar *Du*, which is usually used with children, family members and close friends. Asking others to address you as *Du* implies a closeness not everyone is prepared for. I actually find it easier to use *Sie* as the verb endings are easier, which I explain to Bavarian friends when they ask me to use *Du*. I am not a formal female, just one who is not very good at German!
- When seeing someone, even if you have met them before, it is common to shake hands. Teenage boys greet their friends by shaking hands, even if they are

activities such as cookery, crafts, running and film visits. There was also a Kultur Klub which visited places of interest in and around Munich with an experienced bilingual guide. Initially, I went to as many of the clubs' activities as I could in order to get to know people who spoke my own language. I also took German lessons.

WOMEN'S CLUBS

I had only been in Munich for a few weeks when I was taken to an English-speaking women's club by another mum from my daughter's school. Although the talks were in English, people of all nationalities met there.

There are two clubs in Munich, one near Wienerplatz and one in Planegg, and the meetings are in the mornings when the children are in school. Children, including babies and toddlers, are not welcome when there are speakers as they could disturb the meetings, but there is a crèche and an offshoot group of young mothers that meets socially

just passing by and hardly have time to exchange a word. Male friends often clasp each other on the shoulder while shaking hands, especially if they are feeling relaxed and happy at the beer garden. Girls and women may shake hands, but when they know each other quite well they usually kiss each other on each cheek when meeting. In a more formal setting, a man will stand to shake hands but the lady extends her hand first.

- If you are invited to a German home for dinner, it is usual for those invited to give flowers to the hostess as a sign of appreciation. It is also usual to take a bottle of wine, which the host may serve or keep for another time. Some guests and those who do not drink alcohol may take chocolates instead of wine, but in my time in Munich, I have only met one person who did not drink any alcohol, and he was an Italian!

from one of the clubs. Both clubs hold monthly meetings, but there are many other functions associated with the clubs throughout each month. I know of several mums who have child-minders caring for their little ones just so they can attend and meet people with common interests. A few women I know attend both and therefore lead quite busy lives. The current phone numbers can be found in the magazine *Munich Found* under the sections, 'International Women's Club of Munich' and the 'Ladies International Association'. Or contact them via a search engine on the Internet.

Supporting a Frauenhaus

The two international clubs for women support different *Frauenhäuse*, and contact can be made via them or the police if need be. Their locations are kept secret from the general populace as the homes cater for abused women and their children. German police statistics have shown that in some cities, as many as a third of women are abused either physically or mentally. The safe houses contain a complete cross-section of society and all the different cultures you can find in Munich. Often the women leave their own homes with just the clothes they are wearing and their children if they have any. Usually they are too afraid to go back to their homes for their belongings.

The lease of their buildings, first instituted in 1977, and the wages of the permanent staff are paid by the city of Munich, with a small contribution from the Bavarian State. The houses can only accommodate between 17 and 20 women, who usually stay between six months and a year. There is a lot people can do to help, such as holding sales for funds, supplying toys, clothes and household effects as the aim of the houses is to keep the women and their children safe and empower them to manage life on their own. It keeps the helpers busy and fulfilled too.

BE A VOLUNTEER

Many people who have time on their hands, or who choose to make time, do some form of voluntary work. The Tatendrang

München helps fit volunteers to suitable work; Thiersch Strasse 17; tel: (089) 290-4465; email: Tatendrang@freiwil lingenagentur.de.

Munich also has a scheme called Bürgerschaftliches Engagement, or citizens involvement, which can be contacted through its website: http://www.muenchen.de/ehrenamt. Although both the websites are in German, English speakers are welcomed as volunteers.

The Missionaries of Charity

Mother Teresa first instituted this charity, which now functions world-wide. The sisters in Munich never ask for help but feed around 40 people every day and up to 70 during the weekend. They also provide accommodation for over 25 homeless people and welcome assistance, especially with cleaning and preparing food. You can volunteer at Kidlerstrasse 34; tel: (089) 776-281.

Reim Refugee Support Group

The refugee camp is home to around 400 people, including about 100 children who are waiting to be given asylum. Anyone who can speak a little German, a new language for most refugees, can help the children in various ways and act as chaperones for outings. Even if you do not speak German, you can help by raising funds and donating toys, clothes and school supplies and taking them to the English-speaking Mission at Kreuzstrasse 10, 80331, Munich, near Sendlinger Tor.

Rotes Kreuz

There are several jobs that volunteers can do for the Rotes Kreuz (Red Cross), including social care, helping with refugees or being lifeguards at the local lakes. There are offices in most areas of Munich, so check the phone book for a group in your area.

Tierschutzverein München e.V.

The Society for the Protection of Animals is always on the lookout for people to help them look after the animals under the society's care. Contact their centre at Riemer Strasse 270, Munich; tel: (089) 921-0000.

The English-Speaking Prisoners Support Group

It can be lonely in a foreign country but it must be terrible to find oneself in prison and friendless. If you cannot travel to a prison in person, letters are always welcome, with the officiating church acting as post box. The support group is run from the Peace Church at Frauenlobstrasse 5, 80337, Munich; website: http://www.peacechurch.de.

Help for AIDS Sufferers

The Münchner AIDS-Hilfe e.V. welcomes commitment from volunteers and gives informative talks in the evenings for them. The talks take place at 7:00 pm on the last Friday of each month. The office is at Lindwurmstrasse 71; tel: (089) 5446-4725; website: http://www.muenchner-aidshilfe.de. Subsequently, there are four-day training sessions for people who want to be involved. If you cannot spare much time, even one odd day is welcomed.

Amnesty International

There are over a dozen groups in Munich, each assigned to an individual case. Volunteers are paired up, then together they write letters on human rights abuse to the governments concerned. The organisation especially welcomes English speakers and has an English-speaking group in Munich. Go to Leonrod Strasse 19, Munich; tel: (089) 165-412.

HELP LINES

If someone does not know where to turn to in times of trouble, there is a wonderful place under Marienplatz called Münchner Insel. It is an information centre for people with problems of any sort. No appointments are needed. One is met with a welcoming smile and can be assured of total anonymity. The people manning the offices are German but can also give advice in English. Or if they feel that their English is inadequate, they will give addresses and phone numbers of others who can help.

The aim of the help centre is to provide psychological, legal, social and spiritual support. The office is in the underground area, Untergeschoss Marienplatz, close to the exit for the Viktualienmarkt. It is open Monday to Friday from 9:00 am to 6:00 pm, except on Thursday when it opens two hours later at 11:00 am; tel: (089) 220-041; fax: (089) 223-130.

BEER GARDENS—THE SOCIAL EQUALISERS

This is a great place to make friends! It is in the beer gardens that all formality melts away. People mix freely and are friendly, even to strangers. There is no rigid class structure here and people from all walks of life socialise together. The long wooden tables are shared by whoever comes along, but ask if the places are free first, as they may be reserved for their friends. Conversations are often exchanged and many people love to practise their English.

I once asked a Bavarian friend if an accent denoted the social class of the speaker and received a very strange look in response. One's accent, I was duly informed, depended on the region from which one hailed. The British are the peculiar ones in that regard.

FOREIGN COMMUNITIES
The Turkish Community

Few women from the Turkish community, the second largest ethnic group in Munich, go out to work. Those who do work are often engaged in early morning office cleaning. The first *Gastarbeiter* or 'guest workers' were invited from Turkey in 1961 mainly to do construction work. While many Turks still hold labouring jobs today, others have managed to set up their own businesses and are investing in their children's education. Of course, though many Turks have succeeded in their adopted land, there are many who have not and some Turkish families are among the poorest in the area. Many second-generation Turks still feel like outsiders or *Auslanders,* and think of themselves as targets for discrimination. Most, however, believe that the next generation will feel truly German and their mastery of the

German language will be better than that of their parents and grandparents.

The Asian Community

There are Asian-based companies around the Munich area though their total number here comes to less than 3 per cent of the population. Many of the employees are single men in their twenties and early thirties but a few come to Munich with their families. Most of the women cannot work outside the home as they do not have working visas. A close-knit community, their activities outside work centre around family, friends and their national associations.

Others

Over 8 per cent of Munich's population comes from differing parts of the European Union, whereas America and Africa each contribute less than 1 per cent. Munich prides itself on being the most cosmopolitan city in Germany.

A 'rainbow' man takes part in the Christopher Street (Gay) Parade.

GAY AND PROUD

A law which came into effect on 1 August 2001 made it possible to register a same-sex partner in Germany, giving them some legal status. The new ruling also made it possible for a partner who is not a German citizen to be allowed to live with their partner in Germany and to inherit from them. While they will not have the same status as a married person, as they are not be eligible for tax or welfare benefits, it is still an important step towards parity with heterosexual couples.

Munich is becoming one of the most open-minded cities in Europe regarding its gay population, with the mayor and town council supporting locally organised events. The highlight of the year for the gay community is the Christopher Street Parade in July. A magazine published for the gay community in Munich is called *Our Munich*. Although rainbows have been a recognised symbol for gays for many years, a pink triangle is also being adopted as a sign of gay visibility and resistance. The pink triangle was first used to identify homosexuals in the concentration camps of the Third Reich, many of whom never returned home.

CYCLE OF LIFE
Geburt

It is a tradition in Bavaria that whenever a child is born *(Geburt)* to decorate a tree or a pole in the garden. A pole on which there is a large red heart may have been erected for the parents' wedding, with their names and the date of the wedding painted on and would still be in place if the birth of the child happened within the year. Baby clothes, blue or pink, are the main items of decoration, and sometimes even a pram is hoisted aloft. The pole also has a wooden sign nailed to it giving the name of the baby and the date of the birth, so the neighbourhood is informed of the event, and friends can come and have a beer to celebrate. Some of the items remain on the pole for as long as a year. I have also seen giant storks fixed to balconies announcing an arrival. So if you have a Bavarian baby, be sure to let the neighbours know.

Taufe

Christenings or *Taufe* are similar throughout the world, with holy water being poured on the child's head and a candle being lit from the flame of the altar candle and presented to the parents. God-parents for the child are chosen by the parents and after the church service, a celebration is held.

Geburtstag

Children's birthdays or *Geburstag* especially are a time of excitement, opening cards and presents and having parties. Much is made of the sixth birthday in Bavaria, as it is the last one before the child starts school. Often there is a large family party.

Starting School

A major landmark in a child's life is when he or she starts Grade One at school, a serious step after the more relaxed atmosphere of *Kindergarten* (nursery school). Children usually wear quite smart clothes and are accompanied to school by their parents. Each child is given a *Schultüte*—a colourful cardboard cone about 0.6 m (24 inches) tall—in which they will find all their needs for a day at school: pencils, crayons, rulers, erasers and some exercise books. The state schools issue a list of the necessities beforehand. Also included are small presents and lots of sweets to ease the children's way into school. For children attending German schools, the first day lasts for only an hour, after which they may all go home or to a restaurant for a celebratory brunch with family members.

First Communion

When a Roman Catholic child is nine years old, he or she takes a course of lessons with a priest to prepare for his or her first communion. The day is very much looked forward to as it signifies the child's entry into the church community. New clothes are bought—usually long white dresses for the girls and white shirts with smart trousers or suits for the boys, though some children prefer to wear pale robes, similar to those worn by monks. Many areas have sales of second-hand first communion clothes as they tend to be expensive and are only worn once. After the church service, family and close friends give the children gifts, which will include a Bible. The family then goes home or to a restaurant for a celebratory meal, or they go out for a day of enjoyment.

Celebrating the End of Military Service

In Germany, every boy must do *Wehrdienst* (military service) for 10 months after receiving their call up papers at the age of 18. Conscientious objectors must attend a hearing to present their case and may be allowed to do *Zivildienst* (social service) instead. An increasing number choose the latter option. The young men cannot choose where to do their social service but it is often in a hospital, an old people's home or a children's home. Some monetary incentive is given but not a substantial wage. The girls are not enlisted for military or social service, as historically they were not allowed in the army. On the weekend that the boys are released from their military service, they often party wholeheartedly! People in Munich tend to look on with understanding at the loud celebrations of these young men.

Hochzeit

The night before the *Hochzeit* (wedding), right up to midnight, friends of the bridegroom may turn up at his house and smash crockery outside, as a way of ushering luck in to married life. It is the job of the bridegroom to sweep up all the broken pieces to prove that he will be a good husband. Another tradition is the kidnapping of the bride the night before the wedding by friends of the bridegroom. He is then contacted and the bride's whereabouts disclosed. The groom is then expected to go to the bride's rescue and pay a ransom, which is usually the cost of beer for all her kidnappers.

As in many Western countries, a *Zechabend* (stag night) is organised for the groom by his friends, as they celebrate his last night of freedom, though these days it often takes place about a month before, so that the groom doesn't suffer the after effects on his wedding day. The stag night is usually held in a bar or night club, and the beer flows freely.

Some Bavarian friends may erect a wedding pole outside the couple's new home, a major feat as a deep hole must be dug to ensure the tall pole is secure. This is then decorated by the friends and remains in place until the first child is born or until a year has elapsed, whichever comes first. A party is usually held when the pole is cut into firewood. Occasionally the pole is left and painted in blue and white, becoming the couple's Maypole, a traditional symbol in Bavaria.

All German couples getting married must first have a civil ceremony at the town hall. Sometimes the couple chooses to have only a civil ceremony. Many Bavarians choose to have a church service as well, usually a day or two later, where the bride may wear a long white wedding dress or the *Tracht*. The *Tracht* can be any colour but for such occasions, it is usually made of brocade, velvet, silk or wool. Wedding rings are exchanged, with all Germans wearing the rings on their right hand. After the ceremony, guests who have attended the wedding join the couple for a wedding feast, which may be in the afternoon and is often accompanied with dancing that goes on throughout the evening. It is the custom that the wedding guests pay for their own meals.

Beerdigung

The majority of people in Munich wear black for *Beerdigung* (funerals). Family and friends gather at the church for a service of thanksgiving for the life of the departed, though the coffin is not always placed in the church. A large photograph of the deceased may be displayed at the front of the church instead, as the coffin could be in a chapel at the cemetery. After the service, in which there is usually some singing or music, as well as prayers and tributes to the deceased, the attendees walk or drive to the cemetery for the burial.

Cemeteries and graves are well-tended, many being visited every day. In the evenings, little candles are often lit in red glass containers, which flicker prettily through the early hours of darkness. In Munich, visiting and caring for their relatives' graves has become an integral part of some people's lives.

SETTLING IN

CHAPTER 5

'*Dahoam ist Dahoam.*'
'The best place is at home.'
—A popular German saying

MUNICH, AN INTERNATIONAL CITY

Munich is a truly international city. At present it has a population of around 1.3 million with another million people living in neighbouring areas. Over 20 per cent of the residents of Munich come from countries outside Germany and about 75 per cent of the population are not native to Munich.

Approximately 9,000 foreign students come to study every year and are enrolled at the three universities, staying for between six months to four years. They often take some form of paid employment to help subsidise their living costs. Foreign workers are often here for a set period, having contracts with companies based in Munich, usually for between one and five years.

As everyone is required to register in the district where they live, it is easy for the government to track the areas that are preferred by the various nationalities. Many English-speaking families who move to the Munich area choose to live in the outlying districts, which are closer to one of the international schools, or just to be away from the hustle of city life. They are therefore not registered as living in Munich but in towns such as Starnberg, Dachau or Freising.

A SAFE CITY

Munich is the safest city I have ever been to. When we first arrived, we were worried about our daughter Amanda—16 years old, blond and pretty—going into the city alone at weekends, so we arranged to collect her from the centre to escort her home. On the third occasion, no parking places could be found, so we were late arriving at Marienplatz. She had been there alone for around 20 minutes and it was approaching midnight. In that time, only one man had tried to talk to her, but he went away as soon as she told him to.

Every Man for Himself

Though people in general are orderly and do queue for buses, this is not true for trains or planes. On one occasion, I was at the Munich airport when the passengers had to walk from a bus to the plane in the pouring rain. I was quite horrified to see chunky men, some wielding umbrellas, dash from the back of the bus and push their way to the front of the queue to be among the first to get onto the plane. The last bedraggled travellers to get on the plane were the women and children.

On getting to know more people, we were assured that she would be safe even on late night trains, and it proved to be true. During her stay here and later her visits, she would occasionally come home from clubs between 1:00 am and 5:30 am. She sat in the carriage behind the driver as a precaution and never had any real hassle. Where else would that be the case? Ladies and men of all ages I have talked to say how safe they feel in the centre of town, in Munchener Freiheit or around Rosenheimer Strasse, on their own late at night. It is, however, wise to avoid isolated areas such as the riverbanks at night and also some areas around Hauptbahnhof.

HONESTY IS THE BEST POLICY

We had lived on the outskirts of Munich for a year when we forgot to lock our bikes one night after a visit to the local beer garden. The next morning, we were surprised to find them missing from outside our flat. The police were also taken aback as having two bikes stolen was almost unheard of in our area. They said that occasionally someone who had overindulged at the beer garden might borrow a bike to get home, but it would usually turn up again a day or two later. Unfortunately our bikes never did.

A happier occurrence took place after my husband's arrival in Munich from a business trip to the United States. He got a train straight from the airport to work and fell asleep along the way, only to wake up just as he arrived at his station. He quickly grabbed the bag containing his computer and jumped off, only to realise that his new leather suitcase was still on the train. It contained no ID and included a brand new suit. He thought that he had seen the last of both suitcase and suit! On arriving at work, his German colleagues reassured him that it would be handed in. He reported the loss to the Deutsches Bahn lost property office but had to wait until the next day to see if his suitcase had been handed in. It had been—with everything intact!

In Germany, the trains operate on a trust system for payment. A French guy once remarked to his German colleague that a large amount of income must be lost by not having barriers or inspectors stationed at the entrance to every station. "No," replied the German, "Your country has a problem because it needs to have barriers!" There are of course occasional inspections but very few are caught without tickets.

TEMPORARY ACCOMMODATION

As most of the foreigners in Munich usually know some time in advance whether they will be staying in the city for just a few days, or whether it will be a longer stay, there is usually time to arrange for a place to stay at least for a short period; unless, that is, you arrive during Oktoberfest or during a big event such as an exhibition, when almost everything in Munich will be booked. If you carry little luggage and want very cheap accommodation for a short stay, a campsite is your best choice.

Campsites

The Tent offers the cheapest accommodation for young people. It is open 24 hours a day from June until early September. Everyone sleeps in a big tent; breakfast is provided; and there are hot showers available. There is also an area for pitching your own tent. A tent for groups of over

15 people is available but you must book in advance. There is a beer garden, a café and Internet access on site, as well as a volleyball and table tennis court. Washing machines and lockers are available for a small fee. The Tent is a 13-minute tram ride from Hauptbahnhof. To get to the Tent, take tram 17 towards Amalienburgstrasse, to the Botanischer Garten, Franz-Schrank-Strasse stop.

- The Tent
  In den Kirschen 30, 80992 Munich
  Tel: (089) 141-4300
  Fax: (089) 175-090
  Email: see-you@the–tent.de

Other campsites are located around Munich. Thalkirchen campsite is the closest to the centre of Munich, located in the south of the city and close to the River Isar, open from mid-March to the end of October. The zoo is located on the far bank of the river and it is set in beautifully landscaped grounds. Obersending U-Bahn station is about 1 km (about two-thirds of a mile) from the campsite. If you are camping in the area, you can drop by for a visit at Zentralländ 49, 81379 Munich; tel: (089) 723-1707; fax: (089) 724-3177.

Youth Hostels and Youth Hotels

These provide a little more comfort, especially if it is cool or raining.

The Euro Youth Hotel is a backpacker hostel that has no age limit, is open 24 hours a day and is conveniently situated near the main station, Hauptbahnhof. Rates vary from € 12.50 to € 32.50 according to how many share a room. Find it at Senefeldstrasse 5, 80336 Munich; tel: (089) 5990-8811; fax: (089) 5990-8877.

To stay in some of the other hostels you must be a member of the Youth Hostel Association in your own country in order to use the German hostels. It is possible for foreign visitors to buy an International Guest Card, which is valid for 12 months. You must be 26 years old or younger to stay in the Bavarian Youth Hostels, although group leaders and families with at least one child under 18 are allowed to stay. It is best to reserve a place beforehand. Prices vary according to the

number of people sharing a room and the facilities available, from € 15 for sharing to € 40 for an individual room. The current rates can be found in the brochure, *Infopool-A Young People's Guide,* which is available from the tourist offices. The largest hostels are most likely to have rooms available at short notice; a list of them as follows:

- Jugendgästehaus haus international (hi)
  Elisabethstrasse 87, 80797 Munich
  Tel: (089) 120-060
  Fax: (089)1200-6790
  Open 24 hours, it is located north of the city centre but close to Hohenzollernplatz U-Bahn station, four stops up the U2 from Hauptbahnhof. It is also accessible by tram 27 and bus 53 to Nordbad, or tram 12 and bus 33 to Barbarastrasse. Located within walking distance of the university, Leopoldstrasse, and Schwabing, where there are lots of activities especially on Friday and Saturday nights. Breakfast is included, and facilities for the disabled are available. Groups can be accommodated if pre-arranged. Conference and seminar facilities are also available. Book Monday to Thursday 8:00 am to 4:00 pm, Fridays 8:00 am to 3:00 pm.

- DJH Jugendherberge
  Wendl-Dietrich-Strasse 20, 80634 Munich
  Tel: (089) 311-56
  Fax: (089) 167-8745
  Open 24 hours. Three stops on the U1 from Hauptbahnhof, in the direction of Westfriedhof brings you to Rotkreuzplatz station. A bistro and TV room are available, as are washing and drying facilities.
- DJH Jugendgästehaus
  Miesingstrasse 4, 81379 Munich
  Tel: (089) 723-6550/60
  Fax: (089) 724-2567
  Open 24 hours. Just a five-minute walk from the U3 at Thalkirchen, it is close to the green banks of the Isar and the delightful zoo. Room sizes vary (reflected in the charges) from rooms that sleep three or four to rooms for 15 people. The basic charge includes bed linen and breakfast, but lunch and dinner are available on request.
- CVJM–Jugendgästehaus (YMCA)
  Landwehrstrasse 13, 80336 Munich
  Tel: (089) 552-1410
  Fax: (089) 550-4282
  Open from 7:00 am to 12:30 am. It is situated just a short walk from Hauptbahnhof, U1, U2, U3, and U6 to Karlplatz, trams 17, 18, 19 and 20 or buses 31 and 56 to Karlsplatz/Stachus; or trams 17, 18, 20, 21 and 27 to Sendlinger Tor. Breakfast is included and dinner can be ordered in advance by groups. Discounts are available for people who stay more than three nights, as well as for groups of over 20 people.
- München-ökologisches Jugendgästehaus u
  Hirten Strasse 18, 80335 Munich
  Tel: (089) 552-1660
  Fax: (089) 5521-6666
  Email: info@the4you.de
  Website: http://www.the4you.de
  Open 24 hours, it has a restaurant and a bar, offers a buffet breakfast and is suitable for people with disabilities.

- Kolpinghaus St Theresia
  Hanebergstrasse 8, 80637 Munich
  Tel: (089) 126-050
  Fax: (089) 1260-5212
  Just a short walk from Olympiapark, west of the Munich
  ring road, then off Landshuter Allee, U1 to Gern, or
  trams 20 or 21. An overnight stay includes breakfast.
  Dinner or lunch can also be provided for groups not
  staying in the Klopinghaus if pre-arranged.
- Jugendhotel Marienherberge
  Goethestrasse 9, 80336 Munich
  Tel: (089) 555-891
  A small hostel for females under the age of 25 only. It
  closes its doors at midnight. Breakfast is provided. The
  hostel can be reached on foot from Hauptbahnhof, by
  U1, U2, U4, and U5 or on tram routes 18, 19, 21.

More information about the various campsites and youth
hostels can be obtained from Jugend Informations-Zentrum,
open Monday to Friday between midday and 6:00 pm. It stays
open till 8:00 pm on Thursdays; tel: (089) 5141-0660.

Hotels

Munich hotels range from very cheap to very expensive.
The *Gelbe Seiten* or *Yellow Pages* phone book is a good place
to start your search. The selection is conveniently divided
into areas, so you can choose one close to work, friends,
or entertainment venues. Bookings can be made through
the Tourist Information Office, either at the main station—
Hauptbahnhof from Monday to Saturday, 9:00 am–10:00
pm; Sundays, 10:00 am–6:00 pm; tel: (089) 2339-6500
or in Marienplatz open Monday–Friday, 10:00 am–8:00
pm; Saturdays, 10:00 am–4:00 pm; tel: (089) 2333-0233.
Alternatively you can send a fax to (089) 2333-0233. The
website is at http://www.muenchen-tourist.de. There is also
a listing of all Munich hotels in the monthly programme,
Monatsprogramm, available from the tourist office.

The exclusive and traditional Kempinski Hotel Vier
Jahreszeiten is situated on Maximilianstrasse, the most
prestigious street in town. A sister hotel, the modern and

spacious Kempinski, is conveniently situated by the airport. Another elite and sophisticated hotel with quiet lounges and sparkling chandeliers is the Mandarin Oriental, right in the heart of Munich, next to the historical Hofbrauhaus. The luxurious Hotel Bayerischer Hof is one of the best known in Bavaria. It still plays host to several gala events and has been the place to see and be seen since 1841. All are wonderful places to visit for a special occasion meal too.

International hotel chains are also represented in Munich. The Hilton group has two hotels in central Munich, München City, in Rosenheimer Strasse and München Park, just east of the Englischer Garten. There are five Holiday Inns around Munich and one Marriott, in Berliner Strasse, Schwabing. The Blattl hotels have four to choose from. Best Western is another group that is represented in Munich. A little cheaper but still very comfortable are the Mercure and the Ibis chain of hotels. Several hotels, both privately-owned and those within larger groups but in the mid-price bracket range, have apartments attached. These make convenient temporary abodes when families are house hunting.

- Kempinski Hotel Vier Jahreszeiten
  Maximilian Strasse 17, 80539 Munich
  Tel: (089) 2125-2650
  Fax: (089) 2125-2000
  Email: reservation.vierjahreszeiten@kempinski.com
- Kempinski Airport Hotel
  Terminalstrasse Mitte 20, 85356 Munich
  Tel: (089) 9782-0
  Fax: (089) 9782-2610
  Website: http://www.kempinski-airport.de
- Mandarin Oriental
  Neuturmstrasse 1, 80331 Munich
  Tel: (089) 290-980
  Fax: (089) 222-539
  Website: http://www.mandarinoriental.com/munich
- Hotel Bayerischer Hof
  Promenadeplatz 2-6, 80333 Munich
  Tel: (089) 2120-0
  Fax: (089) 2120-906

Email: info@bayerischerhof.de
Website: http://www.bayerischerhof.de
- Hilton International-Munich City
  Rosenheimer Strasse 15, 81667 Munich
  Tel: (089) 4804-0
  Fax: (089) 4804-4804
  Email: mucchtwfom@hilton.com
  Website: http://www.hilton.co.uk/munichcity
- Hilton Munich Park
  Am Tucherpark 7, 80538 Munich
  Tel: (089) 3845-0
  Fax: (089) 3845-2588
  Email: info.munich@hilton.com
  Website: http://www.hilton.co.uk
- Holiday Inn Munich City North
  Leopoldstrasse 194, 80804 Munich
  Tel: (089) 381-790
  Fax: (089) 3817-9888
  Website: http://muenchen-citynord-holiday-inn.de
- Holiday Inn South
  Kistlerhofstrasse 142, 81379 Munich
  Tel: (089) 780-020
  Fax: (089) 7800-2672
- Holiday Inn München-Unterhaching
  Inselkammerstrasse 7-9, 82008 Unterhaching
  Tel: (089) 666-910
  Fax: (089) 6669-1600
  Email: info@holiday-inn-muenchen.de
- Marriott Hotel
  Berliner Strasse 93, 80805 Munich
- Best Western Atrium Hotel
  Landwehrstrasse 59, 80336 Munich
  Tel: (089) 514-190
  Fax: (089) 535-066
- Mercure Munchen
  Konigin Elisabeth, Leonrodstrasse 79, 80636 Munich
  Tel: (089) 126-860
  Fax: (089) 1268-6459
  Email: H1702@accor–hotels.de

- Mercure Schwabing
  Leopoldstrasse 120-122, 80802 Munich
  Tel: (089) 389-9930
  Fax: (089) 349-344
  Email: H1104@accor.com
- Mercure Muenchen City
  Senefelderstrasse 9, 80336 Munich
  Tel: (089) 551-320
  Fax: (089) 596-444
  Email: H0878@accor.com
- Mercure Orbis
  Karl-Marx-Ring 87, 81735 Munich Perlach
  Tel: (089) 6327-0
  Fax: (089) 632-7407
  Email: H1374@accor–hotels.com
- Mercure Muenchen Nord
  Rathausplatz 8, 85716 Unterscheissheim
  Tel: (089) 317-8570
  Fax: (089) 317-3596
  Email: H0936@accor.com
- Ibis Hotel-Munich City
  Dachauer Strasse 21, 80335 Munich
  Tel: (089) 551-930
  Fax: (089) 5519-3102
- Ibis Hotel-Munich
  Ungererstrasse 139, 80805 Munich
  Tel: (089) 360-830

ADVANTAGES OF RENTING

It is more common to rent a place in Munich than it is to buy, as rent is cheaper in comparison to the high real estate prices.

A few years ago, a friend of mine had a long list of over 100 apartments; either she or her husband visited 46 of them before deciding on a place to rent in Gern. That was in 1998 when there was no shortage of rental places. As it was just for the two of them, they could afford to pay a high rent but preferred somewhere close to the centre of Munich. The apartment they decided on was on the first floor of an elegant villa. It had two large bedrooms and two even larger reception rooms connected by sliding doors, but it had neither a balcony nor a garage.

For the same rent as the apartment in Gern, another friend rented a lovely, modern double-garage detached house with three bedrooms in Pliening, north of Poing. This little village in the countryside east of Munich is not along any train line. The disadvantage of being farther from the city, however, was compensated by the advantages of a cheap rent and a peaceful lawned garden. The hall and stairs were covered in marble and the banisters and the decorative grill beside the stairs were of wrought iron, a typically Bavarian feature. The bedrooms were spacious and the bathroom was huge with a corner bath, a separate shower cubicle, a toilet and two basins. On the ground floor were three separate reception rooms, two of which had access to the garden, a kitchen and a cloakroom. The cellar was of another world, with four rooms, one of which housed the heating apparatus and another, the laundry, leaving two for sports equipment or junk!

Rent starts at around € 12 per sq m per month in Munich but costs vary according to the area. For around a quarter of the price of the Gern and Pliening properties, a single colleague of my husband's secured a 30-sq-m flat near Ostbahnhof. Within this space, she has a kitchen, bathroom and a studio and is delighted with it. Though tiny, the flat is near the centre of nightlife activity and within easy access of shops and museums. From the time she arrived, she scoured the newspapers (the papers on Wednesday and Saturday contain the most useful information), asked colleagues if they knew of anywhere to rent and called on estate agents. Word of mouth is the best way of learning if people are considering moving. Frequent the bars in the areas you hope to move into and get to know the locals, especially the well-informed bar staff.

The Roman Catholic Church owns a lot of property in Bavaria, so if you are Roman Catholic, it is worth asking if they have any accommodation available. I know one English lady who has lived in a church flat in central Munich for 26 years.

A few people have success advertising for a home. A young married couple from Leipzig with a baby boy had no success searching for a new home to rent on their own, and so decided to advertise in the *Suddeütsche Zeitung* newspaper specifying what they were looking for and the general area they were interested in. They also mentioned their professions. They received six replies and though the first two they visited were less than ideal, the third apartment proved to be suitable.

Yet another couple we know had to sign a declaration that they would not have a baby while occupying a certain flat as the landlady did not want to be disturbed. They were happy to comply as the flat was too small to house a baby anyway, and they had no plans for a child yet. In actual fact, it is quite difficult to find a flat to rent if you have children and the more children you have, the more difficult it becomes to find your ideal home.

If families moving to Munich have school age children, it is worth enquiring with school staff. They may just know of families that are moving away and leaving a potential property vacant. Some parent-teacher associations maintain notice boards that occasionally display available properties. School secretaries are also full of interesting, relevant information.

Many new properties are being built in and around Munich at present, but the fact that most people between the ages of 20 and 40 rent means that rental properties are scarce, which drives prices up. One girl saw an advertisement in the newspaper that requested applicants to apply in writing. She complied and found out subsequently that there were over 100 applications. The landlady then invited 26 applicants to view the flat. Of these, she selected three couples to interview and chose the most suitable as her tenants.

HOUSE RULES

There are lots of house rules attached to all flats here and tenants in detached houses are expected to abide by them too. They are based on consideration for other people, though some of the rules may sound strange to people from other cultures. For instance, you are allowed to feed birds but not

pigeons as they are regarded as vermin. I would think it impossible to dissuade the pigeons from eating food put out for other birds.

Yet another practice is the strict observance of certain quiet times during the day, from 1:00 pm to 3:00 pm and between 10:00 pm and 7:00 am the next day. During these times, one should refrain from making excessive noise, which includes vacuuming the house, using a drill, mowing the lawn or allowing the children to play noisy games. If you play a musical instrument, you are limited to 90 minutes of practice a day, and you must not disturb your neighbours. If you are going to hold a party, your neighbours should be informed, particularly if you live in a rented apartment. People are allowed to have a barbecue on a terrace or balcony, but again the neighbours must not be disturbed by the noise or smoke. I was also told that political posters should not be displayed on an apartment's outer walls or windows, as they may offend the other tenants.

Tenants should always check with their landlords first if they are thinking of running a business from the rented property, erecting an antenna or a satellite dish, or keeping a pet. A landlord, however, cannot forbid a tenant's partner from moving in. Of course, the denser the populated area, the more likelihood there is for disagreements. But on the whole, people are tolerant.

When looking for a property in the newspapers, one is confronted by tables of abbreviations, most of which are not immediately recognisable. So here is a list to help.

+ (Pr)	*mit Provision*	With commission
O (Pr)	*Ohne Provision*	Without commission
AB	*Altbau*	Old building
Abl.	*Ablöse*	Payment for 'left-over' items—kitchen, blinds etc.
App.	*Appartement*	Apartment/flat
Ausst.	*Ausstatung*	Furnishings/equipment
Bd.	*Bad/Bäder*	Bath
Bek.	*Betriebskosten*	Running costs—overheads, excluding electricity
Blk.	*Balkon*	Balcony
DG	*Dachgeschloss*	Attic storey
DHH	*Doppelhaushälfte*	Half a semi-detached house
Dl	*Diele*	Hall
Dn.	*Dielen*	Halls
DU	*Dusche*	Shower
EBK	*Einbauküche*	Built-in kitchen
EbN	*Erstbezug Neubau*	First purchase of a new property
EFH	*Einfamilienhaus*	Detached house

EG	*Erdgeschoss*	Ground floor
FbH	*Fussbodenheizung*	Under-floor heating
FH	*Familienhaus*	Family house
G-WC	*Gäste-WC*	Guest's toilet
Ga	*Garten*	Garden
Gge.	*Garage*	Garage
Gfl.	*gefliest*	Tiled
GH	*Gasetagenheizung*	Gas heating, daytime
h	*Uhr*	Time
HH	*Hinterhaus*	House set behind another
Hob.	*Hobbyraum*	Hobby room
HP	*Hochparterre*	Ground floor
Imm.	*Immobilien*	Estate agent
Ka.	*Kamin*	Fireplace
Kf.	*Komfort*	Extras
Kl.	*Keller*	Cellar
KT	*Kaution*	Deposit
Lg.	*Loggia*	Open-sided arcade
LuxA	*Luxus-Ausstatung*	Luxury furnishings
MFH	*Mehrfamilienhaus*	Property for several families/several apartments in one house
MMK	*Monatsmiete(n) Kaution*	Deposit of monthly rent

Mn.	*Maisonette*	Small house, or part of a house, usually not on one floor
NB	*Neubau*	Newly built
NK	*Nebenkosten*	Additional costs
NM	*Nachmieter*	The tenant taking over
OG	*Obergeschoss*	Top floor
OH	*Ofenheizung*	Stove heating
Öl.	*Ölheizung*	Oil heating
Pk.	*Parkettboden*	Parquet flooring
ren.	*Renoviert*	Renovated
renbed.	*Renovierungsbedürftig*	In need of renovation
RH	*Reihenhaus*	Terrace house
Sou.	*Souterrain*	Basement
tgw.	*Teilgewerblich nutzbar*	Part available for commercial use
t-möb	*teilmöbliert*	Partly furnished
Tep.	*Teppichboden*	Carpeted
Terr.	*Terrasse*	Terrace
TG	*Tiefgaragenplatz*	Underground car parking space
UM	*Untermieter*	Sub-tenant
VH	*Vorderhaus*	Front house
v-möb	*Voll möbliert*	Fully furnished
Wg.	*Wintergarten*	Conservatory
Whg.	*Wohnung*	Flat
WG	*Wohngemeinschaft*	Group of people sharing
Wt.	*werktags*	Workdays
ZH	*Zentralheizung*	Central heating
Z	*Zimmer*	Room

Some supermarkets have boards on which you can display cards to notify others that you are searching for a home, the amount of space you need and how much rent you can afford. Occasionally, places can be found advertised on these boards.

House hunting can occupy a huge amount of time in Munich. People can sometimes be seen waiting for the latest newspaper to arrive in the shops in desperate attempts to be the first to phone available places.

LEGAL REQUIREMENTS

Foreigners can usually stay in Munich for 90 days on a tourist visa. Citizens of the United States, Australia, Canada, Israel, Japan, New Zealand and the EU can apply for residence and work permits after entering Germany without a visa. Citizens from other countries must obtain a visa prior to entry, even if they have a German spouse.

If your intention is to stay more than 90 days, as soon as you have found a home, you must apply for an *Anmeldung* (police registration) through the nearest registry office. Outside Munich, it is usually the *Rathaus* (town hall) but within Munich it may be at any of 10 locations. These *Meldestellen des Einwohnermeldeamtes* are listed in the phone book, but the main one is at Ruppertstrasse 19; tel: (089) 2330-0. It is open Monday to Friday, 8:00 am–noon; and Tuesdays, 2:00 pm–5:30 pm.

Everyone planning to stay for over three months must also have a *Aufenhaltserlaubnis* or residence permit. Application forms are available from the offices listed below. It is not easy to negotiate the process if you do not speak German, so do bring along a translator if possible. People living in the city have to go to the *Kreisverwaltungsreferat* (an office that deals with citizen registrations) located at Ruppertstrasse 19, near Poccistrasse U3/U6, while those living in Munich's outer areas or *Kreis München,* as indicated on the yellow road signs to the suburbs, must go to the Landratsamt, Mariahilfplatz 17 (tram 27 or bus 52). The offices operate Monday to Friday, between 8:00 am and noon, but try to be there at opening time or before; otherwise the wait may take you all day!

On arrival, you are issued a number and you must wait for that number to be called. This will be followed by a loudspeaker announcement, in German of course, informing you which room to enter. You should bring your passport, as residence may be granted only until the expiry date of the passport or for a maximum of five years for EU citizens, whichever date is earlier. You must also have an official letter from your place of employment or study, in addition to two passport-sized photographs and the police registration. Permits cost about € 60, but the price is reduced for permit extensions and for children. Never allow your residence permit to expire, as this may lead to a large fine; so be sure to go early to renew it.

Non-EU citizens must have passed a medical examination, hold a correctly completed recent medical form from the examining doctor, available from a *Gesundheitsamt* (health centre), have a urine test and a chest X-ray.

Everyone in Germany should carry some official form of identification at all times. It could be a passport, resident's permit, or an official card issued by a school or university. Many people carry a photocopy of their passport, though the new EU driver's licence with a photograph would be considered sufficient. If a passport is nearing its expiry date, you can apply for a new one through the passport section of your consulate in Germany.

RELOCATING PETS

In most households, a pet occupies a special place in the family, so when the family moves, so does their pet. Several people attribute the number of friends they have made to walking their dog. Somehow, dogs seem to break through most people's reserve, especially if they are friendly and well-behaved.

Whether the pet is allowed in Germany depends on a number of factors, such as the type of pet, the country it is originally from and the necessary vaccinations it has taken to ensure that it is not carrying any diseases. Depending upon where a person is moving from, special transportation and accommodation arrangements for the pet in Bavaria will need to be made. Some animals, regarded as endangered or dangerous, may not be allowed to live here.

There are strict rules for dogs regarded as dangerous, and under Bavarian law, licences are rarely granted to five specific breeds. Category 1 dogs include Staffordshire Terriers, American Staffordshire Terriers and American Pit Bulls. There are breeds in category 2 that are regarded as dangerous, so each dog needs to be individually checked. There are nine types of dog in this category, which includes Bull Mastiffs, but any dog may be tested to check whether it poses a danger to others—a friendliness check!

All dogs coming to live in Munich or bought here must be registered within two weeks; there is also an annual tax imposed. This *Hundeseuer* is paid via Steueramt, Herzog-Wilhelm-Strasse 11, 80331 Munich (tel: (089) 2332-6297) or at your local *Rathaus* if you live outside the city boundaries. It is also sensible to have liability insurance for your pet, called *Tierhalterhaftpflicht*, in case of accident to other people or their property. Cats are covered by the owner's individual policy, but for a dog, the cost of a policy could be approximately € 80 a year. There are also pet health insurance policies to protect against unexpectedly high bills for veterinary care.

A dog should be kept on a lead at all times in the city and also in the countryside unless it has had the necessary vaccinations. If you take your animal to the countryside, be aware of ticks. These may attach themselves to your pet and cause a nasty illness, so give your pet a thorough check after a walk in the country. Any mess left by dogs must be picked up and disposed of by the owner, as a fine can ensue if an offence is spotted. Many areas have bins available for this.

In Bavaria, all dogs must wear an identification tag to indicate ownership and place of residence as well as confirmation that payment of the tax has been made. Most dogs in Munich are amazingly well-behaved and are rarely heard disturbing the neighbourhood with their yapping or barking. One reason may be that Bavarians usually take their dogs to obedience training classes.

Should you be heading for a holiday, do arrange for your pet to be taken care of while you are away. Do make arrangements early if you intend to lodge your pet at the *Tierheime* or *Hundepensionen*. Or better still, have a caring friend take care of your pet!

SETTING PRIORITIES

We were very fortunate. My husband's company found our first flat for us, so we used it as a base from which to look for a more permanent home. We had already prioritised our needs. The first was that our new place should not be too far from John's work so that he could cycle to work most days, obviating the need for two cars. Second, we did not want to be too far from Amanda's chosen school as more travelling time meant less study time (at least that's the parents' view) and greater distances would mean higher bus fares. Thirdly, we also wanted to be in a town with easy access to an S-Bahn so we could get into the centre of Munich easily. A bonus would be to live close to the S8, as that would mean easy access to the airport—my escape route home, if need be!

As I refused to sell our home in England, it meant we were going to rent at first, which worked out to be much more expensive than our 22-year-old mortgage repayments. So running just one car was sensible. We later realised that to buy a house comparable with ours in England, and one that was not too far from Munich city would have cost half as much again as in the English Home Counties, with a much smaller garden. We decided that we did not need a big garden but a south facing little plot or balcony would be lovely.

Our Relocation Agency

The most wonderful thing about our search was the relocation agency John's company introduced us to. Cathy and Ellie of Swift Relocation Service were kind, sympathetic and hard working. We told them what we wanted and they went to work, searching the newspapers and trawling the *Makler* (estate agents). Several banks also display leaflets of properties for sale in their windows.

We wanted at least 100 sq m (1,076 sq ft) of living space, and while this is usual for a house, many flats for rent close to Munich are only about 80 sq m (861 sq ft) at most. And we did not want to pay a fortune (who does?). Little did we realise what a task we had set Swift.

In England, houses are described by the number of reception rooms and bedrooms, but in Munich, a typical description of a property would give the total number of rooms and the overall area. *Drei Zimmer* means three rooms, excluding the kitchen and bathroom.

We were first taken to look at a couple of lovely houses in Eching, a small town about 35 minutes' drive north of Munich, that is, if there are no traffic jams up the A9. Two out of three of our criteria were fulfilled as Eching is on the S1 train line to the airport and town and quite close to school. The town looked just right on the map—an almost square town plan—with the shops and two churches in the centre and a small lake to the south. The first houses we saw were a *Doppelhaus* (semi-detached) and a *Reihenhaus* (terrace house). Both had a good-sized kitchen and a garden for me to tend, but we decided that both houses were just too far for John to cycle to work. Our decision proved to be right. We met a girl of about 17 who was serving in the fruit and vegetable department of the local supermarket, so we asked her what life was like for a teenage girl in Eching. Luckily for us, she spoke excellent English. Her advice was that it would be better to live nearer to Munich as most of the teenagers went there for entertainment, so the train ride back at night was too long.

The more we saw of the small towns, the more we realised how open the Bavarian houses are to their neighbours' view. Many of the gardens have fences rather than hedges, and as the gardens are quite small, there is often no privacy. In fact, few have gardens as the English know them. Most gardens have some grass (not a manicured lawn) and are adorned with a few shrubs and a couple of trees. Flowerbeds are scarce. In the summer though, houses and flats are festooned with tubs of geraniums and petunias, begonias and fuchsias, which also hang in profusion from the window boxes.

Next we were taken to Garching, which has older buildings on the main north/south road. Hidden away behind these buildings is a new centre with the *Rathaus* and a spacious community hall, shops and flats. As with many suburbs of Munich, there are older detached houses with their own

gardens in some areas and newer developments towards the fringes of town. We were taken to one of the newer buildings to see a huge second floor flat, which had a lovely view over fields but no garden or balcony. We could almost have lived with all the wonderful space, but the washing facilities were in the *Keller* (cellar), and there was no lift. I really could not imagine hauling baskets of washing up three flights of stairs several times a week even if I had a strong back, which sadly I haven't.

That evening we were taken to see a detached cottage in Aschheim. It was a dear little place that was being refurbished, but the improvements had not yet been completed. We could see from the upper rooms the state of disrepair the place had been in as the rafters still looked as if birds roosted there. Though we liked the place, there was no S-Bahn and we did not like it enough to overrule that point. There is talk now about extending the U-Bahn to Aschheim.

The next day we saw two flats in Ismaning. We had walked around Ismaning the previous evening and liked what we saw. It is bordered by the River Isar, the large river that flows through Munich. A couple of streams snake through the town providing some pretty areas for leisurely walks. The *Rathaus* had formerly been a *Schloss* (a palace) and was still surrounded by parkland, complete with a small orangery. Though the shopping facilities were a bit scattered, there were trains on the S8 every 20 minutes to both the airport and central Munich.

THE SEARCH ENDS

The only other flat for rent that fulfilled our criteria at the time was in what looked like a large detached house. Many houses in the suburbs that look as if they housed only one family actually accommodate several families. You can always tell how many people live in a building by the number of doorbells or post boxes outside the home.

The flat for rent was on the first floor. The landlord lived on the ground floor, and there was another smaller flat under the sloping roof. There were two bedrooms and an office, all quite small. In contrast, the lounge was a generous 32 sq m, and there was a separate dining room, as well as a pantry, attached to a 10-sq-m kitchen—a good size kitchen for a flat in Munich. Right along the back of the flat was a south-west facing balcony, while a 45-sq-m roof garden could be accessed from the lounge. We decided that was it.

One thing that really amazed me about the flat was that it did not have a built-in kitchen. In fact, the kitchen was just an empty space with a tiled floor, tiles above non-existent worktops and three pipes protruding from the wall! We soon learnt that it was normal in Germany to take along the kitchen with the rest of the furniture when moving out. If you want the previous tenants to leave the kitchen, you must negotiate privately for it. The kitchen was one expense we had not bargained for. The previous tenants obviously never cooked as there were no facilities, and the only water was to be found in the bathroom.

The bathroom was like a black hole. The tiles were dark brown and tan, and there was no mirror or window, just a fan to rid the room of condensation. We subsequently learnt that few flats have bathrooms with natural light and that if they have a window, it is a bonus that estate agents usually mention. We decided we could learn to live with the colour scheme once we added mirrors and spotlights. The landlord told us that he did not like white paint everywhere as it attracted spiders. Well, I thought spiders would be more easily spotted on white walls rather than on a dark background!

Another difference that we noticed was that few rooms had built-in furniture. One reason for this is that as most people rent, they naturally want to take everything with them when they move out. An ancient wardrobe that we bought second hand when we got married was resurrected and came with us to Munich.

Having told the agent that we would like to rent the flat, we were asked to return the next day to finalise arrangements. The landlord's flat had much the same layout but was quite dark as much of the décor was brown or cream. Sitting round their dining table, the landlord and his wife interviewed us, asking about our professions, our family and our lives back in

England, trying to ascertain if we would be suitable tenants. We must have passed the test as forms were taken out for us to sign. We wanted a two-year lease, as we did not know how we would adjust to our new lives. The landlord, having been very affable, became quite angry about our suggestion and started banging on the table with his fist insisting that we could only have a minimum lease period of three years if we were to rent his flat. We agreed.

It is usual for a *Kaution* (deposit) to be paid, usually comprising of three months' rent, and registered at the bank. The landlord is not allowed to spend the deposit money. Rather, it is a safeguard for him against tenants wrecking the flat or not completely repainting and cleaning it before they leave. Any rented place must be left in the same state as when the tenants first moved in, or some, if not all, of the deposit is forfeited. In fact, it is said that there are arguments over nine out of 10 of all *Kaution*! A bottle of champagne was produced, and we drank to the new venture with their little dog snuffling round the bags and their house rabbit hopping over our feet. We were told that we could keep a pet, as long as it was not too big.

If one rents through a letting agency, under *Mitwohnzentralen* in the *Yellow Pages* phone book, they often charge 30 per cent of the monthly rent or one and a half month's rent for a let of one year.

LETTING AGENTS
- City Mitwohnzentrale
  Lämmerstrasse 6, 80335 Munich
  Tel: (089) 1943-0
  Website: http://www.mitwohnzentrale.de
- Mr LodgeGmbH
  Barer Strasse 32, 80333 Munich
  Tel: (089) 340-8230
  Website: http://www.mrlodge.de

RELOCATION AGENCIES
There are several relocation agencies around but get recommendations before appointing one.

- Swift Relocation Service KG
  Hofmarkweg 4, 82008 Unterchaching
  Tel: (089) 6659-9971
  Fax: 089 6659-9972
- Elisabeth Sommer Relocation
  Widenmayerstrasse 17, 80538 Munich
  Tel: (089) 954-7410
  Fax: (089) 9547-4129
  Website: http://www.Elisabeth-Sommer.de
- Accent Relocation
  Matterhornstrasse 32, 81825 Munich
  Tel: (089) 4201-7200
  Fax: (089) 4201-7201
  Email: Accent_Relocation@web.de

Living without a Kitchen?

On my next trip to Munich, we went hunting for a kitchen.
There are many kitchen showrooms around Munich, but we
needed one with an extensive choice and where we could
negotiate in English. Our relocation agent recommended

Segmüller, a huge furniture shop by German standards, at junction 9 of the A94 which heads east from Munich.

The first salesman did not speak fluent English but found us someone who could—a tall willowy blonde named Doris. She showed us around and suggested several features that we had never seen before, such as a triple bin under the sink to sort the rubbish, as required in Munich, and a tap on a hose—invaluable for filling buckets. We liked three kitchens, but then we were told the waiting periods for delivery. It is not unusual for people to move into their homes in Munich and not have a kitchen for between nine and 12 weeks. We were due to move in three! Doris saw the panic on my face and said she would see what she could do.

SETTLING IN

The kitchen was delivered the day before our furniture and was installed in a day! The fitters arrived at 9:00 am and left at 9:15 pm. They did not break for any meals although I had offered them food, and they hardly talked to each other. I was so relieved to be able to unpack straight into cupboards.

We were also able to buy wardrobes and bedside cabinets from Segmüller, which were also installed the day before our furniture and clothes arrived. The tiny spare room was to have a dual role as office and guest room. To facilitate this, we bought a unit from Hess, on the Euro Industrial Estate, that contained a double wardrobe and a large double bed disguised behind three more wardrobe doors. It is wonderfully balanced and only needs a slight pull on the handles to bring the bed down into the room, once the computer has been wheeled out into the dining room.

A few days before we actually moved in, and once the other tenants had moved out, we went round the flat with Ellie, our estate agent, and the landlord. Ellie noted down things that needed to be done before we moved in as well as faults such as a chip in the marble of the stairs, roller blinds that did not shut out all of the light, and a small, dark stain on the carpet. This list had to be officially signed as part of the leasing contract, or we could be accused of causing those faults at a later date. Three years on, it would have been impossible to remember just what was agreed upon if it had not been written down.

We were due to take on the lease on the first of July but hadn't realised that lorries were not allowed to travel through Germany on a Sunday or a bank holiday. So it would be the fourth of July before our furniture could be moved in. We went to look at the flat on the first, to find that nothing on our list of things for the landlord to do had been done, so we stayed in the other flat for the weekend. One more week's rent there, as well as paying for the new flat. The faults were still not rectified by the following Tuesday when we moved in, nor a year later!

Up for Rent

Germans who know the ins and outs of renting would not have put up with our situation for so long, but we just kept on hoping. In the end, we told Swift, and they wrote a letter stating that we would reduce our rental payments if the faults were not corrected. The following week, a man turned up to replace the missing paling on the balcony, reattached the dangling light on the balcony but did not resurface the roof garden which showed flaking concrete and bands of tar where it had been mended before. Covered with tubs of flowers and a winding path of small paving stones that we had bought, we decided it did not look too bad, but we had to remove every stone when we left!

The day the furniture was delivered, the double container truck arrived early. But the men from Munich who were to help the driver unpack did not. He made frantic calls on his mobile phone and started on his own. He was a lovely guy—cheery and helpful—but not so the local men. They were surly and brusque, even with each other. All the boxes were unloaded into the rooms marked on the boxes, but I realised that once unpacked, I would have to reorganise everything again. So I said that I would empty the final 11 boxes myself. The driver was really apologetic and wanted to stay to help, but I was not in a rush so I signed for the boxes and away he went. Later, I realised that I should have counted how many boxes had gone on the lorry. After three months, we found that a large box containing the car tools and my painting equipment was missing. We had thought it was among the items in the cellar.

A big shock was finding that there were no lights in the flat, another occurrence that is not unusual. All that was left were wires hanging out of the ceiling in each room. Fortunately it was summer, so it was light until late. We had several table lamps but could not use them till we got the plugs changed to European standard. We laugh now and say that we should have bought shares in Obi, our nearest DIY shop, as we seemed to spend several days of the week there. As John has a background in electrical engineering, he took a couple of days off from work and connected all the lights once we had bought the fittings.

The day John went to work, I sat there in silence and sobbed. Our daughter was still in England, I knew no one, had no TV or radio that could pick up an English-speaking station and no telephone. The local supermarket felt alien, and I had not come to grips with the value of the money. I wanted to go home badly.

Happily, our eldest daughter Caroline had arranged to come over and help me get organised at the end of the first week. It was wonderful to see Caroline's smiling face at the airport when we drove up to meet her in our hire car. I felt as if I had been on my own for weeks rather than just three days. How pathetic! I thought that I'd cope better than that.

Caroline's help was invaluable although we got few boxes unpacked. She said that I could do that at any other time. Instead, we went out. We walked around the local area and became familiar with it, visited local shops and went to the centre of Munich to get to know the stores. We also saw a film at a little cinema that screened films in English.

She also prodded me to invite Doris, our kitchen designer, for a meal cooked in our new kitchen. I was a bit reticent, but we had to go to Segmüller for some bits and pieces, so we called on Doris, had a chat and invited her for the following week. She was delighted. She had been designing kitchens for almost 15 years, and it was only the third time that she had been invited to see the kitchen being used. After four days, Caroline left, but I did not feel quite so lost any more. Doris came round for another meal the following week and has since become my closest German friend. The flat was now beginning to hold memories of happy times in Munich.

WASTE RECYCLING

A couple of weeks after I'd arrived in Germany I found that I was drowning under a sea of packing paper. I had no idea what to do with it and so got out the welcome pack supplied by Amanda's school. I phoned the organiser for our area, who told me to cut up all the boxes and post them into one of the big bins located around the corner.

There are recycling bins within walking distance of every home in Munich and its surrounding area into which you separate glass (clear, green or brown), paper and cans. Some places also have bins for old clothes. There are specific times you can use the bins, between 7:00 am and 7:00 pm but not between noon and 3:00 pm as this is the quiet time.

Bin Etiquette

Remember you should never use the bins on Sundays as that may disturb the neighbours. The rules for each location are usually printed on the side of one of the bins. To avoid a possible fine, it is best to adhere to the rules.

Our area organiser also explained the rubbish sorting system in our area and arranged to come round and take me to the town hall to ask for *der Gelbe Sack,* or yellow sacks. All packaging waste, except for paper and glass, is put into these yellow sacks, and they are collected by the garbage authorities once a fortnight. The types of rubbish acceptable are printed on the different types of sacks, and they include things such as milk and juice cartons, wrappings from food or drinks, cans, bottle tops, foil, polystyrene and plastic tubs,

which must be thoroughly washed. A friend forgot one time and put her waste paper in too. She was traced by her address on an envelope and fined for her misdemeanour!

Where we live, there is a dual rubbish system, with biodegradable household rubbish—*Biotonne*—collected one week and general rubbish—*Restmülltonne*—the next. The bags are collected from separate, deep wheelie bins. Do not put your bio-rubbish in plastic bags (which are not biodegradable) as the collector will not take the bags and they may be left for weeks. You will be charged for each bin by the city, so don't ask for more than you need.

There are several things that you should not put in the general rubbish bin, which is called *Problemmüll* or 'problem rubbish'. The 'problem rubbish' goes to the Giftmobil, but the collection times can be really inconvenient, such as one day in a month between 3:30 pm and 4:00 pm in outlying areas. The *Problemmüll* include batteries, oil filters, pesticides, fertilisers, acid and alkaline solutions, paint, lacquer, adhesive, disinfectant, household cleaners, fat, oil, wax, lead, light bulbs, tubes, and aerosols with CFCs.

There are also depots around town to dispose of large amounts of rubbish such as garden refuse, shoes, textiles, wood and electrical appliances. We took a broken plastic suitcase to one of the depots, but it was rejected. The only option we had was to cut it up and feed some of it into the general bin each fortnight. Most tips have scales where they weigh uncategorised non-hazardous rubbish and charge by the kilogramme for disposal.

There are a few centres where you can take large items for disposal, such as beds, settees, light fittings and broken plastic bins, free of charge. Proof of residency within the area is usually necessary. These centres are located at:

Munich North
- Duisburger Strasse 10
  Tel: (089) 361-1516
- Lerchenauer-/Faganastrasse
  Tel: (089) 1506-129

Munich South
- Thalkirchner Strasse
  Tel: (089) 7429-9094

Munich East
- Truderinger Strasse 2a
  Tel: (089) 477-305
- Schwablhoferstrasse 2
  Tel: (089) 439-1422
- Bayerwaldstrasse 33
  Tel: (089) 630-1954

Munich West
- Lochhausener Strasse 32
  Tel: (089) 811-0721
- Arnulfstrasse 290
  Tel: (089) 1780-9215
- Am Neubruch 23
  Tel: (089) 1407-9242
- Tübinger Strasse 13
  Tel: (089) 547-0170

Information regarding what must be taken to the Giftmobil, the timing and the venue can be found at the information office, next to the tourist office in Marienplatz and in your local *Rathaus*. Our area has an A4-sized card delivered twice a year itemising costs for rubbish, what goes into each bin and the collection times. Ask at your *Rathaus* for this card—*Abfallkalender*. All the rubbish that the city is unable to recycle is taken to be incinerated at one of the huge power works, and the heat given off by the incineration is used in the local homes.

After a few weeks, sorting rubbish becomes second nature. I was surprised how little actually ends up in the general waste bin—about one medium-sized bucket a week for three people.

SERVICES
The main provider of electricity, gas heating and water in Munich, Stadtwerke München GmbH, known as SW/M, has its main offices at Emmy-Noether-Strasse 2, 80287 Munich; tel: (0180) 279-6796 (for private customers); email: privatkunden@swm.de.

Electricity
All homes in Munich have electricity already installed. Make sure that the meter is read and witnessed as you move in so that you are not charged for what has been consumed by the previous resident. There are now several private companies from which one can apply for *Strom* (electricity) but it is easier as a newcomer to continue using the company used by the previous occupant.

Electricity and Wattage

The electricity is at 230V AC 50 cycles, single-phase, apart from appliances using over three kilowatts. The sockets are for two-pin Schucko plugs, and light sockets are for screw-in bulbs of varying sizes. Many modern light fittings use small halogen bulbs.

If you wish to check out the different companies, they are listed under *Stromversorgung* in the *Yellow Pages*. To reach the city electricity department, call tel: (089) 381-0101.

Gas

Be sure to check whether the accommodation you are moving into already has gas connected, as not all homes in and around Munich do. Some private companies now supply packages including both gas and electricity at a slightly lower price than if you were to buy them separately. The city's gas department can be contacted at tel: (089) 153-016/17.

Water

Some homes have water meters, while others pay a fixed amount each month. For more information, tel: (089) 182-052 or tel: (089) 2361-3378.

Telephone

Deutsche Telekom is the main supplier of telephone landlines in Germany. Trying to get organised with them is not easy. I tried the customer service number listed in the book, then was told to try another for new customers, tel: (089) 0800-3302-000. There was an answering service (in German, of course) which did not give the advice I wanted. It did however lead me to the website: http://www.telekom.de, which gave lots of information about rates for phone calls (half the price in the city or within Germany if calling between 6:00 pm and 9:00 am) and Internet prices, but it did not provide information on how to get a new line.

There are several T. Punkt shops around town, but I could not find their listing in a phone book, so I started a search on foot. I went in to the large Deutsche Post in Orleansplatz, which luckily had a Deutsche Telekom stand manned by a lovely lady who spoke some English. At last! I was told that to get a new line, two to three weeks' notice was needed. But the process could be quicker if you knew the address where the phone would be needed, then the connection could be established with a few keystrokes on the computer. To have two lines installed, check for information on offers at website: http://www.t-online.de.

I also came across a T-Punkt shop in Orleansplatz, with opening hours from 9:00 am to 7:00 pm, Monday to Friday and between 9:00 am and 2:00 pm on Saturday. Their main office is at Sonnenstrasse 24-26, 80331 Munich. I subsequently found that there are 11 T-Punkt shops in all, listed in the front of the phone book. But if you do not yet have a phone line, you are unlikely to own a phone book!

Deutsche Telekom no longer has a monopoly on German telephones and now has to compete with other companies. Hopefully, this will translate to more options for consumers and better service. One friend who arrived in Bavaria in 1998 had his phone service connected after 12 weeks of numerous calls. In the end, the company did try and make some amends by not charging for the installation. Our second home in Munich had the old number transferred to the new address, and we were connected on our second day. To check out the cheapest services for making overseas telephone calls try website://www.teltarif.de or http://www.verivox.de for the prefix numbers. Using prefixes, we were able to call Australia for 2.5 cents a minute, sometimes even 1.9, when Deutsches Telecom was charging 73 cents.

Telephone Directories
When you subscribe to a fixed line service or Internet connection with Deutsche Telecom, you will be supplied the two telephone directories, *A-K* and *L-Z*, and a *Yellow Pages*. Each year when these are due to be renewed, the subscriber will receive a postcard through the post informing them

that they can pick up the new books from the post office, Aral petrol stations or from Media Märkte (a large retailer of consumer electronics). There is a three-week period allowed for this, and though the first batch may disappear quickly, they are replenished just as quickly. Big bins are provided in which to throw the old books so that they can be recycled.

Try to familiarise yourself with the telephone books. You will find it worth your effort. If there is an umlaut over a letter, it is listed as if the letter had an *e* after it. I once tried to find the contact number of a certain bar, so I looked it up in the telephone directory under its name but to no avail. A German friend found it for me in a section headed *Gaststätten* (I had no idea what that meant) under the sub-heading, 'Bar'. Under the same section, there are listings of cafés, followed by restaurants. Hotels are not listed by name but under the heading 'hotels', and all hospitals are listed under *Krankenhäuser*.

Always check the *Ihre Rechnung*—phone bill—and keep records of payment, which includes the 16 per cent tax. Several times, we had faxed the bill to the bank, and some time later would receive another bill but for a different, smaller amount. It is confusing as Telecom only chases up their own account. For most of the overseas calls made through cheaper-rate organisations, Telecom itemises them on the back of the original bill; however, they do not list them on reminder notes. As the competition for customers is so great, tariffs for the different phone companies vary greatly, so you need to constantly check prices.

If you use direct debit, the bank will record it on the bank statement. Sometimes, Telekom was unable to find any record of the payment and we had to supply photocopies of the payment slip or bank statement to show that payment had been made. Be sure to act promptly, or your phone line may be disconnected.

PUBLIC PHONE BOOTHS
There are Telekom phone boxes with bright pink tops around Munich where phone cards, credit cards and coins are accepted. Several train stations have bright yellow

telephone stands, with *Taxiruf* printed on the side, from which you call taxis.

Mobile Phones

To have same day access to communications, buy a mobile phone or a handy as the locals call them. There are several D2 Vodafone shops around Munich, owned by Mannesmann Mobilfunk of Düsseldorf. We used the one just round the corner from Marienplatz, in Rosenstrasse. The salesman spoke English, and we were able to choose a plan that suited the family, so calls to the home phone number were very cheap. Payments are usually made by direct debit by the phone companies, though some do have pre-paid cards. Others have a special number which you can call to 'top-up' the account. Deutsche Telekom's mobile phone centre is at Hansastrasse 28; tel: (089) 547-510 or try the toll-free number, tel: (0800) 330-1000. Other mobile phone shops in Munich include O2 and Orange (which offer differing contracts), ABC Phone Station, E-Plus, Krebber Communication at the Nokia Shop (website: http://www.krebber.com) and Viag Interkom Shop. The contracts do vary, and it is not always easy to discontinue use. Be aware that sometimes you must give three months' written notice before the renewal date to terminate a contract, otherwise you are bound to pay all the fees for the following year.

DEALINGS WITH LANDLORDS

Ask any tenant in Munich what their landlord is like and there are moans and groans nine times out of 10. The stories of their exploits could fill volumes. Local landlords have been known to let themselves in without permission to check the place out when their tenants are away. Some have left notes, saying that the curtains were not hung straight when seen from outside; others had the chimney swept and left the bill; and there were those who shifted the position of the fence to give themselves more space for their adjacent garden at the expense of the tenants. People have also been asked to clean their windows more often or leave their car in a different place on the public highway.

Protect the Wasps

There are some problems, however, that do not involve landlords. One such incident took place a couple of years after moving in. We discovered that some wasps had made their home in the roller blind cavity over the dining room window. We thought we should call in the pest exterminator, so consulted Ellie, one of our former relocation agents, now a good friend. Imagine our amazement when we were told that we were not allowed to destroy the nest as wasps, like bats, are protected under German law.

But there are also appreciative tenants with comments on how wonderful their landlords are. Those are the landlords who left vegetables on their tenants' doorsteps; those who returned money as the new tenants did not use as much electricity or water as the previous ones; and those who offer to baby-sit.

An Official Notification

It was shortly after the wasp incident that I received an official letter one Saturday morning. The girl who delivered the letter needed to record the precise minute the letter was handed over to me and would not accept my approximation of the time (it was about 9:00 am). Immediately, I started to worry. The letter was not addressed to anyone in particular, just to Herr/Frau/Firma Smith. The envelope had the name of the organisation, Zentralfinanzamt München—the Central Finance Office—which was yet another mystery, as we had no dealings with that office.

I headed for the bookshelves and took down our largest German dictionary to help me make some sense of the enclosed missive. The first three words, *Pfändungs und Einziehungsverfügung* translated as 'seizure and requisitioning order'. Certainly it was not the most pleasant way to start the weekend! My immediate thoughts were that we were going to lose everything. And I did not have any idea why. With rising panic, I tried translating the words I did not recognise, which was far from simple. After 20 minutes or so of feverishly flipping through the dictionary, I concluded that a debt had been incurred by our landlady, and that the Central Finance Office was going to recover it by commandeering our lease until the debt was paid. We would have to pay them directly, bypassing the landlord's bank account.

To be sure of what we needed to do, I phoned Ellie again (bless her, she's always available in our emergencies), and we arranged to meet the following Monday. As she had never seen a letter like the one we received, she phoned a lawyer. His advice was that the letter was equivalent to a Court Order and that we had no choice but to comply. If we continued to pay our landlord, we would be liable to the Zentralfinanzamt as well. Our next course of action was to make a trip to the bank to change the standing orders. As we had an inclusive rent, in which the landlord is paid for the heating and hot water, we had to arrange to pay the heating separately by monthly cheques.

The official letter also requested that we notify them of the payment arrangements and to inform the landlord of the changes, which created more problems for us. We needed to write two official letters in German! Again, we had to call upon our friends. The next Sunday around lunchtime, we took the letters and rang their doorbell with feelings of trepidation. In my inadequate German, I tried to explain to the landlady about the content of the letters. She said she had no idea what I was talking about and invited us in. She claimed to know nothing about the demand, a copy of which we enclosed and which was in her name. She called her husband, who strolled in, looked briefly at our letter and with a dismissive "All is clear," walked off again. No explosion, no denial. Surely he must have been prepared for our visit. His wife said she would phone the finance company the following day and sort it out. Another crisis was over for us but what a hassle!

BUYING A PLACE OF YOUR OWN

Once a decision to buy is made, finances need to be assessed and if necessary, banks approached to ascertain the possibilities of loans. Banks do not lend 100 per cent of a home's value, wanting at least a 20 per cent deposit. Homes have to be paid for before you move in, and if waiting for a property to be built, each stage of the process has to be paid for as it is completed. This works out to be about 30 per cent when the cellars are completed, 30 per cent when the walls are up and the roof is on, and so forth. Some homes are completed within a year but if it is part of a complex, it can take much longer. Our new apartment took 22 months from the time we saw the plans and agreed to buy. At that time, work had already begun to clear the land. Of course, it meant we would be making double payments during this period, rent to our landlord as well as paying the builder.

Apartments in Munich are sold by the square metre, and the price reflects the location and specifications of the property, prices ranging from € 3000 to € 5000 per sq m.

Homes within the inner ring on the transport system are more expensive, but 40 minutes drive away from the city centre, there is a dramatic price drop and the likelihood of a garden. Even these are still not cheap in comparison to other areas of Germany. One needs to decide whether an inconvenient commute is worth the extra space. Before making the decision, do travel to work at peak hours from the area you hope to live in. What may take 20 minutes by car on a Sunday could take two, three or four times as long at rush hour, but the train system is pretty reliable.

As with rented homes, those for sale are advertised in newspapers, banks, estate agents, and on hoardings where new work is being carried out. When buying from an agent, be aware that it is the buyer here who has to cover the estate agent's fees. There are also hidden fees too, but we'll come to that later.

Many new homes of all types are springing up in and around Munich, but what seems a spacious complex on paper may be being built in stages, and there may be little space between the buildings in the end. By visiting a building site in winter, one can see just how much sunlight reaches the windows, or whether the building opposite casts a shadow all day. Bavarian friends advised us to make sure that the walls of a building are still standing after severe winter weather and that they have not cracked in the cold, before taking possession and making the final payments. It can be difficult to get things put right once everything has been paid for.

Hidden Costs

The standard price of an apartment or house includes the fittings listed in the specifications. Additional costs are added for garages, usually underground in the case of apartments, and for reserved parking places. These come to light immediately after a sale is made.

What are less apparent are the taxes. Houses and ground-floor apartments have a ground tax, which is usually 10–15 per cent, while other flats are liable to a percentage. This is in addition to the tax for owning a property. The *Notar* who draws up the deeds must also be paid, in addition to the payment for registering the deeds. On completion of the transaction, a surveyor's fee is payable. Therefore, several thousand euros need to be added to the stated price of the property. In our case, it amounted to about € 15,000 more.

COUNCIL CHARGES

There are no council charges as such. If renting, any incidental costs will be payable to the owner of the property, but if you own the property, the local authorities will send a bill via the *Rathaus*.

PARKING

Especially in the city, car parking can be a real problem. To save yourself the time of cruising round looking for a space to park, look into renting or buying a parking space when deciding on a home. Many of the newer properties have underground car parks, the spaces of which can be bought or rented. Between € 14,000 and € 20,000 is a normal price to pay for an underground parking space in Munich. Some developments have spaces allocated outside for much less, between € 4000 and € 7000, but sometimes non-tenants avail themselves of these spaces. A way to avoid this is to have a short metal post set into the ground towards the front of the space. These posts can be unlocked, allowing them to lie flat, when the owner returns. Others put their faith in luck and honesty, and stake ownership of the lot by having the car registration number replicated on a post at the back end of the parking space.

Locks

Newcomers to Germany may not be familiar with the doors here. Most have a combination lock that locks the door automatically as soon as it closes, only allowing someone who possesses a key to gain entry. The doors can also be dead-locked from outside by using the key. Many American friends, unused to these locks, have found themselves on the wrong side of a locked door when just popping out to the outside bin or hanging out the washing. Locksmiths can charge a fortune, especially at night and at weekends, and that is if you know of one! Locksmiths are listed under *Schlussel u. sSchlösser, Schlossereien* and *Aufsperrdienste* in the *Yellow Pages*.

Having a small wooden wedge permanently next to the door, which can be pushed with a toe to keep the door ajar, can solve the problem cheaply. It would also be wise to have an extra key cut and kept in a secret place or with a trustworthy neighbour. Mister Minit, who cuts keys as well as repairs shoes, is to be found in several department stores in Munich. When you live in rented premises, you must obtain permission from the landlord to make extra sets of keys.

SHOPS AND SERVICES
Waschsalon
If you are new in the area and desperate for clean clothes but the idea of paying *Wäschereien* (laundry) prices is loathsome, there are three *Schnell und Sauber* shops where you can do your own laundry on the main roads around Munich. Ratzingerplatz, Landsberger Strasse 495, and Alb. Rosshaupter-Strasse 64, all open 24 hours, including holidays. For more information, check the website, http://www.schnellundsauber-waschcenter.de. There are lots of others too: Eco-Express has shops at Kapuziner-strasse 39 and Ohlstadterstrasse 52; tel: (089) 2023-8612.

Wäschereien/Reinigung
I must admit that even after inquiring, I could not find our local *Reinigung* or dry cleaners shop for almost two years. The little shop was not so hidden though, if you knew just where to look. Friends around town have assured me that the further you are away from central Munich, the cheaper the charges. Some of these shops also offer mending services.

Frisseur
My daughter's school friends always had their hair cut in England as they said they preferred the styles back home, plus it was cheaper. I have seen all styles here, so if you know someone with a good cut, ask him or her where it was done. You will find the internationally renowned Toni and Guys in Munich, but hairdressers *(frisseur)* making house calls may be just as good. In 1999, it appeared that one in six of all adult females in Munich used the same burgundy hair dye. Three years later, those same heads took on a more orange tinge, then the uniformity disappeared! I do wonder who sets the trend in hair colour in Munich.

PUBLICATIONS
At the beginning of each month, the question on the lips of each informed English-speaking newcomer is, "Have you got your *Munich Found* yet?" This 50-page magazine is indispensable to the recently-arrived and is informative

A wide variety of reading material can be found in the bookshops of Munich.

and helpful to those who have been residents for a longer period.

Several pages are devoted to news and views, with short articles about events scheduled for the following month, features about places within reach or easily accessible from Munich, Bavarian traditions, and reviews of restaurants, films, books and art exhibitions. There are usually about 12 pages of announcements on what's showing at the theatres, cinemas and museums around Munich throughout the month, so everyone can plan in advance. But especially useful to the recent arrivals is the section, 'Find It: A Guide to Services, Clubs, and Groups'. This section lists telephone numbers for all the emergency services and the English-speaking consulates in Munich, tourist information including lost-and-found offices, the main libraries and their opening times, places of worship with English services, as well as around a hundred clubs and groups. Everyone should be able to find ways of occupying their time and enjoying themselves by referring to the pages of *Munich Found*. The magazine can be purchased from the international press shops at the two main railway stations and at the English cinemas.

A German language publication, *In München*, is a similar but slightly thicker magazine, as it includes the main German-speaking events, theatres, concerts and clubs, listed under 'Party'. Although the classical events are listed, the magazine caters for the young and trendy. There are lots of advertisements for nightclubs, travel agents, job placements, and specialised sports and dance classes of every description. It also has brief listings for the 13 main television channels in Munich.

NEWSPAPERS

Several European and American newspapers are available from the two main stations and airport newsagents, though occasionally the newspapers are a day old. The *American International Herald Tribune, USA Today* and *The Wall Street Journal Europe* are on sale. For the British, the *Financial Times, Guardian, Independent, Daily Telegraph, Daily Mail, Daily Express, Mirror* and *Sun* are available. *Time, Newsweek* and *The Economist* can be purchased each week too. There are also publications in French, Greek, Italian, Spanish and Turkish.

The most widely-read quality newspaper in Munich is *The Süddeutsche Zeitung-Landkreis München*. It has many informative articles but readers need a good knowledge of the German language to understand it, though on Mondays there is a supplement of the *New York Times* in English. Another quality newspaper is the *Frankfurter Allgemeine* which gives German and international news but also has a section for the Munich area. The *Handelsblatt* specialises in economics and finance, but an excellent knowledge of German is needed to assimilate all the nuances in this paper.

The second most popular paper is the *Münchener Merkur*, which is not only informative but is also easier to read and understand than the other publications. It provides plenty of information about future events around the city. So often I have been asked, "How do you know what is going on?" Well, this paper really offers a lot, even if we are unable to understand all that is written!

The 'Rainbow Press' is a term given to the popular press in Germany. The most commonly read newspapers are the *Bild*, the *TZ* and *Abendzeitung*, which have their front pages printed in colour with lots of photographs and large headlines. Their articles are written in a more sensationalistic style but are quite easy for anyone with a basic grasp of German to understand.

What has amazed me time and again in Munich is the trust people have in each other. Most newspapers are deposited in metal containers with transparent lids, which can be found on street corners and thoroughfares. The prices for the weekday and weekend editions of the newspapers are listed. There is a slot for you to drop in the appropriate amount when taking a paper but no one is at hand to check if the correct payment has been made. It is presumed that everyone is honest.

Each area of Munich has at least one free newspaper such as *Münchner Blatt, Hallo, Bogenhausener Anzeiger,* or *Sendlinger Anzeiger.* These papers are usually about 40 pages long and carry articles about events in the local and adjoining districts. Much of the content though is taken up with advertisements to buy or sell private items, cars, houses and flats and for job opportunities. Some stores, such as Conrad, the electrical store on the Tal, sometimes take up several pages to advertise their special offers, especially at sale time. The papers usually have shiny colourful advertising inserts from large stores such as Segmüller or Möbel Biller Erlebniswelt. The newspapers may be delivered to your door, left on the porch of a block of flats, or in the reception area of a firm.

When trying to equip a new home or to get rid of things, your answer could be *Kurz und Fündig*. This publication offers free advertising space and it is not only for tangible items. An Irish friend, new to Munich but fluent in German, found a club through an advertisement in the paper—*Neu Münchner Stammtisch*—around which her social life now revolves.

TELEVISION

Everyone who owns any device with the ability to receive broadcast signals, such as television, radio, VCR or car radio, must pay an annual license fee, currently € 204. This may be paid on a monthly, quarterly or annual basis by direct debit through a bank to the agency, Gebühreneinzugszentrale der öffentlich-rechtlichen Rundfunkanstalten in der Bundesrepublik Deutschland (GEZ). Even if your appliance is not in use or is not used to receive German TV, you will still need to pay for the license. Registered residents in Germany who do not pay this license fee are regularly checked for non-compliance, and if found to own any reception system, a heavy fine may be imposed. The money collected goes towards financing the German public TV and radio broadcasting channels such as First and Second Programmes (ARD and ZDF) nation-wide, plus the Third, a regional channel. By national decree, a third of the material broadcast on these channels must be devoted to news or educational programmes.

The GEZ also finances Bayerischer Rundfunk (Bavarian Broadcasting Corporation). There are many other privately-funded (through advertising revenue) German TV channels available such as SAT1, RTL, and Pro7. These tend to be more downmarket and feature a lot of aging English and American TV material that has been dubbed in German. The public sports channel, DSF (Deutsches Sportfernsehn), covers some British and American sporting events as well as German.

Many people have satellite dishes that can pick up various television and radio programmes broadcast by other countries if they are connected to a suitable receiver. Sky News, ITN News, BBC World, Eurosport, CNN-I, NBC, American news channels, along with MTV and VH-1 music channels (German), and many English shopping channels are available for free viewing from the Astra1, Astra2 and/or the Hotbird satellites.

BBC Prime is the only official English language channel available by subscription. However, it requires a special digital satellite. Additional English channels can be tuned in but require additional equipment and often a subscription fee. Some local satellite companies have procedures in place to assist people to tune into these TV channels that are not normally available to viewers living outside of the United Kingdom because of licensing and copyright issues. Note that TV channels direct from the United States are not available in Europe because the US-based satellite systems do not cover this region.

Many Munich homes have cable television services installed, for which an additional monthly fee is payable. This charge is often included in the rent. The cable TV transmits mainly German programmes, and only CNN-I is available in English.

RADIO

The five main public radio stations in Bavaria, Bayern 1 (traditional German), Bayern 2 (cultural), Bayern 3 (rock, pop, and easy listening), Bayern 4 (classical), and Bayern 5 (news) are available on the FM band.

Newsreaders on Bayern 5 do not read at such a hectic pace, so foreigners may find the news easy to follow even if they only have a little basic understanding of the German language. There are also many private radio stations broadcasting in the large cities or across the Bavaria state, the largest of these being Antenne Bayern based in Ismaning. Teenagers might enjoy Radio Gong on 96.3, Radio Energy on 93.3 or Radio Charivari on 95.5 MHz (FM).

As we found it a necessity to listen to English programmes, we bought a short-wave radio in order to pick up signals from BBC World Service, the Voice of America and 1197 AM.

- World Service, on 9410
  From 6:00 am–9:00 pm
  From 6:00 am–11:00 pm, on 12095
- Voice of America, on 1197
  From 4:00 pm–7:00 pm
  From 4:00 pm–8:00 pm and 5:00 am–8:00 am, on 15205

Please note that all times stated are one hour earlier in summer due to daylight saving time.

From the UK, the BBC radio stations 1, 2, 3 and 4 are available along with the BBC World Service over digital satellite from Astra 2, without any need for special equipment or subscription. All that is needed is an off-the-shelf digital receiver and a correctly installed satellite dish. National Public Radio from the United States is available as a digital transmission from the Hotbird satellite. Their website, www.npr.org/worldwide, provides more information.

Various local companies specialise in the supply and installation of satellite receivers. Try Bavaria Satellite Systems, tel: (089) 9053-9376; fax: (089) 9053-9377; email: info@bavaria–satellite.de. The staff not only speak English but are also experts in all aspects of English and foreign TV and satellite reception, along with telephones, telecommunications and the Internet.

INTERNET

Internet access is becoming more pervasive. Each new month sees more Internet facilities being made available to the general public, and it is unusual to find any company, no matter what its size, without some sort of Internet access. For the public, Internet cafés can be found at:

- Nymphenburger Strasse 145 (open 11:00 am–4:00 am)
- Altheimer Eck 12, in the arcade open 11:00 am–1:00 am; website: http://www.icafe.spacenet.de
- Times Square Online Bistro, Bayerstrasse 10a
- Easy Everything, Bahnhofplatz 1, near Hauptbahnhof

Easy Everything is the largest Internet facility open to the public in Munich. It is not a café in the true sense of the word, but it does serve coffee and light snacks. The prices for using their facilities are given as you arrive, and customers can use one of the 550 computers for up to five hours. The system is 30 times faster than ISDN and allows for burning of CDs too.

If you need Internet connection at home, there are several ways to achieve this. Standard analogue connections are being phased out and ISDN provides the ability to connect to the Internet at 64 kilobytes (bi-directional) and still leaves the phone line free. The latest DSL technology is also available in Germany with asymmetric connections providing 768 kilobytes downstream and 128 kilobytes upstream. Deutsche Telekom is the main telecommunications provider but is losing out to competitors. Bavaria Satellite Systems, listed in the previous section, can help arrange and set up telephone and Internet connections too.

VIDEOS AND DVDS

There are video and DVD rental stores all over town, but these five carry a large selection of films in English.

- British Video Club
  Franziskanastrasse 16
  Tel: (089) 447-0607
- English Video Film Club
  Theresienstrasse 73
  Tel: (089) 542-0524
  Website: http://www.english-video.de
- Filmpassage
  Zweibrückenstrasse 8
  Tel: (089) 296-217
- Video Connection
  Nymphenburger Strasse 79
  Tel: (089)181-858
  The store is open Monday–Thursday, 11:00 am–9:00 pm, and Friday and Saturday, 11:00 am–10:00 pm.
- Millions of Images
  Amalienstrasse 15
  Tel: (089) 8905-9152
  The store has over 7000 videos and DVDs in their original languages.

POST OFFICE

Munich's main post office is at Hauptbahnhof. Open 8:00 am to 6:00 pm, Monday to Saturday, it is closed for lunch 12:30 pm to 2:00 pm. Most, though not all suburbs have post offices and street post boxes are becoming increasingly rare, but what could be easier than posting a letter? After a few weeks of living in Bavaria, the post office staff came to know the lady with a handful of envelopes for England, and I came to realise that I had to put them in standard-sized envelopes! A slightly larger size or an unusual size, even small ones, meant having to pay at least double the basic rate! It was frustrating to have to pay more for postage than the cost of the card inside and it was frustrating not understanding what was said to me as the staff spoke too fast. That was, until I got *the* English-speaking guy one day who enquired if I needed a receipt for the stamps that I had bought.

Before we left England, we had arranged for our mail to be redirected to our German address for one year. Every few days, a large red-edged envelope would arrive containing redirected mail, but it wasn't always meant for us. I guess that we had more post than other *Auslanders* did in our town, so seeing a red-edged envelope, the staff at the post office just presumed that it was for us, without even noting the name or the address. Getting mail that was not meant for us was, strangely, a great way to get to know people. I would write a note on the envelope to indicate where the post had been delivered to and pop it in the appropriate post box after finding the correct addresses on our street plan. Even after our first year ended, we still got post with English or American stamps for other Smith families living around the town. One Schmitz lady and I discovered that we shared many common interests and became good friends as a result. For that, we had to thank the post office for misdirecting the mail.

Post and Parcels

For our first Christmas away from home, our family flew over to Australia to join our elder daughter Caroline for a three-week holiday. When we returned to Germany, there was an official note saying that a parcel was waiting at the post office, with the collection times stated. Post boxes for most homes are quite small here, so it is quite usual to have to collect parcels from the post office. However, because our parcel was not collected within 10 days of the notification, it was returned to the sender.

When collecting a parcel from the post office on behalf of another person, even your spouse, be sure to surrender a specific red card that has been duly signed by the addressee of the parcel. This red card authorises the person to collect the parcel on behalf of the addressee. Anything less than a signed red authorisation card would result in a wasted trip. Even identification to show the relationship between the one collecting the parcel and the one the parcel is addressed to, is not enough, neither is a letter of authorisation with their passport.

TRAVELLING BY RAIL

A safe, reliable way to travel around Munich is by train. From the airport, there are two S-Bahn services, the S1 travelling first to the west, then south, arriving at Hauptbahnhof, 12 stops later. It then crosses town and heads east to Ostbahnhof. The S8 takes the passengers directly south from the airport, through the still countrified small towns of Hallbergmoos and Ismaning, via Ostbahnhof into the centre of town, Marienplatz, on to Hauptbahnhof, then south west to the town of Geltendorf. Connections to most parts of Munich can be made via the U-Bahn somewhere along the stretch of 10 stations in central Munich. Maps are displayed at all the stations and over the exit doors on every train. More conveniently, information is available from the information desks at the main stations or tourist information centres. Beware of old maps as many of the trainlines have been redirected. The final destination of the train, often a long way from central Munich, is displayed on the front of the train and above the platform of departure, so you need to check carefully.

The main train station for Munich is Hauptbahnhof, about 1 km (0.6 miles) west of the centre of Munich. A second smaller station also for international travel, Ostbahnhof, is located to the south-east. There are information centres at each of these stations, and at the DB (Deutsch Bahn/German train) inquiry desk, there is usually someone who can speak English. Be patient as there can be long queues. I have known friends who waited over 40 minutes to get information about international train connections. So if possible, make inquiries before the date of travel. At Hauptbahnhof there is a special office named Euraide where the staff are fluent in English and they will help you to plan the fastest or most cost efficient routes.Their office is open daily from 7:45 am to noon and 1:00 pm to 6:00 pm from June to October, and Monday to Friday from 7:45 am to noon and 1:00 pm to 4:45 pm the rest of the year. See their website at http://www.euraide.com. There are no railway staff at most of the smaller stations, but many of them now have surveillance cameras checking the platforms, so the stations are safe on the whole.

If travelling between German cities, the Inter City Express (ICE) train, is the fastest. But in general, the faster the train ride, the more you have to pay. For example, Hamburg on a day-time first class ICE costs € 79.80 more than a second-class seat on slower night-time InterRegio (IR) or RE train. There are bargains to be had, especially if you book in advance, but usually a higher priced journey is quoted first. If travelling throughout Europe, check out these websites for good deals: http://www.eurail.com and http://www.railpass.com.

Tickets Purchase

Tickets are dispensed from large blue machines, usually under signs displaying a green circle on which is written a white S (for suburban trains). Tickets for train travel within Bavaria or throughout Germany can be purchased here. Recently some press screen credit card machines have been introduced for payment with displays in several languages, including English. Travellers often arrive in a new country with their money in large denomination notes and many machines don't accept € 50 notes, so be prepared. If you buy a ticket from the machine, read all the options. The first option listed on the airport ticket dispensers is a single into Munich, which is the most expensive. For only a small amount more, you are able to get a *Single-Tageskarte,* which gives unlimited travel within Munich until 6:00 am the following day. Be sure to get one that covers all 16 zones as the airport is in the Aussenraum and the centre is zone 1. When staying in Munich you can buy an *Innenraum Tageskarte* ticket. There is also a cheap option for several people travelling together—a *Partner-Tageskarte* or group ticket—that allows up to five people to travel together for below the price of two individual tickets!

If you do not need to go into Munich, a daily ticket can be purchased that just covers the outer regions—a *Single-Tageskarte Aussenraum*—though connecting between areas at opposite points of the compass is difficult without crossing central Munich. Sometimes this card is cheaper than the standard single fare. It is also cheaper to buy a *Streifenkarte* than to pay standard single fares, if you will be taking a few journeys around Munich. These tickets can be bought from the machines by pushing the blue button with black lines on it. The tickets have 10 strips on them, and when looking at the name of your destination on the ticket machine, you can see an adjacent number which indicates how many strips you need to stamp for your journey. Fold over the card until you have the appropriate number displayed on the top of your ticket, then push it into the blue validating machine. Monthly or annual Isar cards can be purchased from the main stations, which work out cheaper if travelling more than four return journeys a week. Check the conditions before purchasing one as they have varied in the past. Some are not valid for discounted travel before 10:00 am, so are not viable for most office workers.

Wherever you travel, any ticket must be stamped to make it valid. This is done by pushing it into a little blue box with a capital E above the slot. These little boxes are generally found on a post about waist height, before you step on to the platform. Ostbahnhof and most outer stations have the validating machines situated on the platform. These machines stamp records of the station travelled, from the date and time. The *Streifenkarte* tickets are valid for three hours from the time of stamping, as long as you travel in just one direction. But you can get off, do your shopping or whatever you want, then get back on again, or on another form of transport going in the same direction.

People are expected to be honest and pay for their rides. Still, there are ticket inspectors patrolling the trains, buses and trams to ensure that commuters pay their fare. There is an on-the-spot fine of € 40 if you are found with a non-valid ticket. The fine can be paid via bank transfer if you do not have sufficient money on you. As the inspectors do not wear a uniform and can look like anyone's dad or granny, it is difficult to identify them. They do, of course, carry identification.

One evening, Amanda had not been paying attention when she stamped her ticket and put it in the validating machine upside-down. The inspector was not sympathetic. Even though the stamp was clearly on the back, it was deemed invalid and she had to pay her fine.

Safety on the Trains

Often at night, one sees pairs of dark uniformed men and women wearing red berets, with truncheons attached to their belts, on the trains. These are the *Bahnschutz* who make sure that law and order is maintained on the S-Bahn trains, and occasionally they ask to inspect tickets too. The U-Bahn patrols wear a dark green uniform and hat. I must admit that though I have seen a few inebriated people on the trains, I have never experienced any trouble at any time. Local people say that it is wise when taking a train late at night, especially if a female, to travel in the front carriage so as to be next to the driver in case of any problem.

There are maps of the S-Bahn and U-Bahn system on every station, and either signs or announcements that tell the destination of the next train. Every train also displays its destination on the front. One must therefore be sure of your train's final destination, even if you are only travelling a couple of stops, as occasionally trains travelling in opposite directions leave from the same platform. One soon learns to recognise the underground stations by the colour or pattern of their wall tiles. Thalkirchen is particularly attractive as the tiles depict animals at the nearby zoo.

Munich has an integrated transport system operated by Münchner Verkehrs Verein (MVV) which, despite the grumbles of the local residents, usually runs on time. When all is running well, buses deposit their passengers at stations a few minutes before a train is due, then waits for arriving passengers from the next train before heading off again. Most of the public transport do not operate after midnight during the week so check the timetables, but there are 11 night-line buses that travel every 30 minutes on Fridays and Saturdays on the main routes.

BUSES, TRAMS AND TAXIS

Buses serve all central Munich and the wider community. If you use more than one mode of public transport to make a journey within Munich, one ticket will cover all. You can buy tickets before boarding a bus, then validate them, or pay the driver directly. Some services use coach companies when there are problems with their own buses, so be aware that the buses do not always look the same. Bus drivers will use a little ink pad and rubber stamp to validate the tickets. There are also long-distance buses connecting Munich to other German cities. Strangely, it is illegal to use mobile phones on the buses but not on the trains.

A tram system still exists in central Munich, with the rails running in the centre of the wider roads. Like all the public transport, it is usual to pay before getting on a tram, and the ticket must be validated by the machine on the tram.

For more information on Munich's integrated transport system, the charges and timetables, call tel: (089) 4142-4344; website: http://www.mvv-muenchen.de.

Taxis can be hailed from the numerous taxi stands in the city, especially at main stations. A standard charge is imposed, and then additional payment is charged by the kilometre, with a small extra charge for cases. To call for a taxi in central Munich, tel: (089) 1941-0 or tel: (089) 2161-0.

LOST PROPERTY

Lost your belongings at the Franz-Josef Strauss Airport? Call the airport's information service at tel: (089) 9752-1370.

If an item is left on a main line train or S-Bahn, their *Fundstelle* (Lost and Found) is at Hauptbahnhof. The items are usually kept there for seven days. It is open Monday to Friday 6:30 am–11:30 pm, Saturday 7:30 am–10:45 pm and Sunday 7:30 am–11:00 pm; for enquiries call tel: (089) 1308-6664; fax: (089)1308-6752.

Items from the buses, trams and U-Bahn are sent to Ötztalerstrasse 17, 81373 Munich (S 7/27, U6 Harras). Open Monday–Friday 8:30 am–Noon, Tuesday 2:00 pm–5:30 pm; or call tel: (089) 2330-0; fax: (089) 2334-5905. This place is not easy to find as it is located on a back street, the entrance is down a small road under a building and there is hardly any parking available. Inside are rooms full of lost items and a board near the door directs you to the room for lost keys, bags, phones, etc. They auction off scores of unclaimed bikes in October. It is helpful if you can give the number of the bus/train/tram where an item was left as well as the time and the date, as each lost item is labelled with this information.

BIKING IN MUNICH

People in Bavaria enjoy the countryside and being active, many choose to cycle to work, to run errands or simply for pleasure. There are over 700 km of cycle paths in and around Munich, making cycling an ideal and cheap form of exercise. There is also a signposted route encircling Munich, but it is too far for an average cyclist to do in a day! Almost all the people I have met here own a bike. Plump old ladies cycle up to collect their shopping, and some less agile ride tricycles for stability. Lycra-clad bodies with well-defined legs zoom past in a flash of bright colour. Children as young as four follow their parents on two-wheelers, with long flexible rods behind them flying flags so they are more visible. Toddlers are conveyed in seats either behind their parents or in front between their arms, while the tiny ones are sometimes transported in a small buggy attached to the back of their parents' bikes.

Buying a Bike

Every town has at least one bike shop, and there are some larger chains with several outlets.

- Der Radl Bauer has helpful assistants and hundreds of bikes. Its city shop is near Hauptbahnhof, at Paul-Heyse Strasse, 25; tel: (089) 5311-09. It also has shops in Pasing and in the Euro-Industriepark at Maria-Probst Strasse, 23; tel: (089) 3169-9441.
- Zimmerman advertises bikes of all prices and often has offers on selected bikes. It has two main outlets, one of which is in Trudering; tel: (089) 4262-21. The other is located in Unterschleissheim; tel: (089) 3109-507, but these outlets are only open from March until September. Their city outlet is at Rumfordstrasse 46, Isatorplatz, but is only open on Friday afternoon and Saturday morning.

The website of the *Yellow Pages*—http://www.gelbeseiten. de—lists two pages of bike shops, so one that is close to home can be traced easily. Of course, if a bike has a few initial problems, it is always easier to take it back to a local shop, though I have been refused service at my local bike shop in a very abrupt manner as my bike wasn't initially purchased there.

Real bargains can sometimes be picked up from the newspapers or from a flea market, especially if you know what to look out for.

Cycling Etiquette

The police expect all bikes to be in perfect working order, including having working lights, day or night! If you are caught cycling with a faulty bike, or cycling without lights at night, you could be looking at a *Geldstrafen* (fine)—the average current rate is about € 15. You can also be fined for cycling in a pedestrian area, though if you are polite and plead ignorance, you may be let off with a warning.

Addressing the Police

Whenever you have any dealings with the police, do be sure to use the formal *Sie* rather than the familiar *Du,* to avoid being regarded as impudent as this could possibly lead to a fine as well. In fact, it may be better to speak English, then the problem does not arise!

If there is a *Fahrradweg* (cycle path), you are obliged to use it. The cycle path is closer to the road than the pedestrian path, but always cycle on the right as many cycle paths carry bikes heading in both directions. Sometimes following the path means crossing a road to continue along the designated route, as a path for both pedestrians and cyclists may suddenly merge to become a *Radfahrerfrei* (pedestrian path) only. The cycle paths are usually, though not always, separated from the pedestrian path by a solid white line. In the city, unaware tourists are always wandering over it but they can be prosecuted if their presence on it causes an accident! Ring the bell well in advance if there are problems ahead, as some people may not be aware of their oversight.

Always follow the small pale yellow signs, or white signs with green lettering and a green bicycle, directing the best route for bikes. They also give the distance to places along the route. Occasionally, the recommended route is not the most direct one but certainly it is the safest, as it may circumnavigate a town centre where there are no bike paths and lots of traffic.

One of the most common accidents occurs when the driver of a car turning right does not see the cyclist on the bike path to his right who actually has priority. Be alert, and always check if something is about to plough into you.

Cycling Carefully

I passed one such accident when the police were seen dragging a mangled bike from under a car's radiator. The car's bonnet was completely crumpled, but as I passed the ambulance with its open door, both cyclist and driver were sitting up, wearing neck braces as a precaution. It seemed amazing that the cyclist had survived. My husband has landed in hospital three times in eight years because of similar situations.

As with cars, bikes must stop and give way to cars entering their road from the right. A cyclist I know was not aware of this, and cycling home from work one Friday, a car suddenly hit him from the right. As he was on the main road, he had presumed that he had the right of way. As there had not been a post with a yellow diamond before the junction, priority therefore was from the right. That was the end of the bike, and he also had to pay for the dent on the car to be fixed.

Some of the bike paths are really long, such as the one through the woods from Munich to Freising. While a great ride, it is a bit bumpy without all-round suspension on the bike. It is a joy to be able to cycle right to the centre of Munich and through the landscaped scenery of the Englischer Garten without having to negotiate motorised traffic, as there are bike underpasses under many of the main roads. Most cyclists starting from the centre of Munich can reach the Tierpark Hellabrunn (zoo) at Thalkirchen, the Bavarian Film

Studios, Olympiapark, Westpark and Nymphenburg easily and quickly. If the ride gets too much, the U-Bahn, S-Bahn and Deutsche Bahn all accept bikes. You pay approximately half the adult fare for a bicycle ticket. The exception is on working days between 6:00 am–9:00 am and 4:00 pm–6:00 pm, when bikes are not allowed on the trains.

The brochure, *Fahrrad am Bahnhof,* gives valuable information about travelling on the Deutsche Bahn with a bike and about renting bikes from stations. If you are not familiar with the routes around Munich, invest in a cyclists' map, available from all good book shops.

Beside the many lovely rides in and around Munich, one will encounter conveniently located beer gardens. To get into some of these beer gardens in summer, you will likely have to fight through acres of bikes. Bear in mind that people can be prosecuted and in extreme instances lose their driving licenses for cycling when drunk. So it is safer to stick to a soft drink or a Radler (beer and lemonade), rather than the stronger brews. One guy I have heard of was trailed by a police car along a road as he wobbled away from a beer garden. He was stopped and found to be twice over the limit. He had to cool off in a police cell and was later fined € 1500.

In winter, there are special tiny snow ploughs to clear footpaths and cycle paths, and they are in action early after a heavy overnight snow fall, so often people can still cycle to work. Sometimes there are also tiny lamp-posts which illuminate the paths when the adjacent road has no lights.

CAR TRAVEL
Car Rental
If you want a faster mode of transport, rent a car. It is better to book a car by phone in advance, as there are certain times of the year, such as when a large exhibition is in progress in Munich or at the Messe, Exhibition Centre, when almost every vehicle is reserved.

There are many places to rent cars around Munich, including the airport where there are desks representing all the main rental companies.

- Avis
  Tel: (089) 9759-7600
- Budget
  Daily 6:30 am–11:30 pm
  Tel: (089) 9759-6705
  Fax: (089) 9759-6706
- Europcar
  Tel: (089) 973-520
- Hertz
  Tel: (089) 978-860
- National
  Open daily from 6:30 am–11:00 pm
  Tel: (089) 9759-7680
  Fax: (089) 9759-7686
- Sixt
  Tel: (089) 9759-6666

Buying a Car
If you bring a car into Germany, it is exempt from tax if you have owned it for more than a year and it is for your

personal use. It should be on the inventory list of items being moved with your household effects.

Whether buying a new or second-hand car, a garage will usually give at least a year's guarantee, depending on the age of the car. This makes life much easier if there are problems, as trying to get help if you do not understand the language can be a nightmare. Buying from a garage close to home has its benefits too, when it comes to servicing as many garages prefer cars to be dropped off before 8:00 am and collected after 5:00 pm. Garages are listed under 'Automobile' in the *Yellow Pages*.

There are many garages selling second-hand cars along the 304, the Wasserburger Landstrasse to the east of Munich and around Trudering and Haar. Another good area to check out is along Landsberger Strasse, west of central Munich. There are dealers for Audi, Fiat, Ford, Mazda, Opel, Peugeot, Renault, Skoda and VW, as well as several leasing companies. Another place to go is the garages on the Frankfurter Ring, to the north of Munich which has almost as many companies represented, including BMW, Mercedes and Smart cars.

Cars and Tyres

Each car needs two sets of tyres in Bavaria, for summer and winter, and these are changed around 1 April and 1 November. If a car has an accident under icy conditions and is found to have summer tyres, the insurance company will not pay out the claim, and you are liable for prosecution, so winter tyres are a must.

When buying and selling cars privately, the official document Kfz-Kaufvertrag, available from stationers for € 3, needs to be filled in by both the buyer and the seller. There are several places around Munich where cars are bought and sold privately for cash. A friend's father went just to look around one Sunday morning and parked close to Landsberger Strasse. He had no intention of buying or selling, but when he arrived back at his own car, a man offered him so much more for it than he thought it was worth he took the money and went home on the bus! Another such place is on the road between Aschheim and Dornach, where on each Saturday morning, real bargains can be had.

We decided to buy a locally-manufactured car—a BMW —as we thought there would be a wide selection and good after-sales service as they are made locally. Having decided to buy second-hand, we went to a large garage—BMW Niederlassung München—told them our budget and they showed us what was available. We had many choices, and the whole process was very easy as the garage also registered, taxed and insured the car for us.

Relocation agents may also do this for you as to have the car registered by an expert can cost more than € 300, although I have heard of it being done for € 80.

All drivers must have *Haftpflichtversicherung* (personal liability insurance) and most drivers also have their cars insured against fire and theft. It is sensible to have *Vollkasko* (comprehensive coverage) for the more expensive cars. When you pay more, the big companies are more likely to be helpful in the event of an accident, whereas some cheaper companies let you muddle through on your own. Both types of insurance also cover damage done to others or their property in case of an accident.

Having lived here a while, we now know that if we had shopped around, we could have got a cheaper insurance plan. But the convenience of getting it from the same garage where the car was bought was well worth it. Though we bought the car near central Munich, we have it serviced at a BMW dealership near our home. Be warned that if one buys an older, less environmentally friendly car, the *Kfz-Steuer* (road tax) is much higher.

CAR SHARING

For anyone who does not need a car all the time, especially if they live in central Munich, Stad-Teil-Auto München could be the answer. It allows people to pick up and use a car just when they want it, rather than having a car parked outside their home unused and depreciating in value each day. You can contact them at tel: (089) 637-7777; website: http://www.stadtteilauto.de. There is a deposit charge of around € 600, a separate insurance charge and a nominal monthly membership charge. There are no repair costs. The rates work out to just a few cents per kilometre, though you can pay a daily rate which ranges from € 2 to € 3 per hour of use, depending on the time of day.

There are six pick-up points for the cars around Munich. They are at Hanns-Seidel-Platz in Neuperlach, Ostbahnhof, Hauptbahnhof, Kolumbusplatz, Rosenheimerplatz and Isatorplatz. If you have further enquiries or wish to join, contact Walter Ernst at Ollenhauserstrasse 5, 81737, Munich. The telephone is manned weekdays between 9:00 am and noon.

A cheap way to travel to another city and share the expense with others heading the same way is to contact the Mitfahrzentrale (website: http://www.mitfahrzentrale.de), who will match and put in touch drivers and passengers, to their mutual benefit. You can reach the agency at tel: (089) 1944-0.

Driving in Bavaria

Speed limits are usually clearly displayed, apart from the suburbs. When you enter a town, the name is displayed on a yellow sign, which automatically means the speed limit is 50 kmph. The speed limit in residential areas is 30 kmph, whereas the limit is 60 kmph for the 2R ring around Munich. Country roads generally have a restriction of 80 kmph, and the official speed limit for the highways is 100 kmph. Closer to Munich the speed limit of the motorways is 80 kmph. There are often illuminated signs displaying restrictions due to heavy traffic, adverse weather conditions, *Unfall* (accidents), or *Baustelle* (roadworks). A recommended limit of 130 kmph is rarely adhered to.

The table below gives the conversions of kph to mph.

Miles per hour	Kms per hour
20	32
30	48
40	64
50	80
60	96
70	112
80	128
90	144
100	160

Whether in a hire car or your own car, it is compulsory to carry a warning triangle in case of breakdown, and a florescent jacket is a must in many neighbouring countries. These can be bought at most petrol stations or car accessory shops. It is also compulsory to carry a basic first-aid kit and a set of car light bulbs. Theoretically, a person can be fined for not stopping to help an accident victim, though not everyone stops for a breakdown.

To join the ADAC or the German Automobile Club, call their information line at tel: (018) 0510-1112. But it may be easier to visit one of its offices office. ADAC has 15 offices around Munich. The main ones are in Rindlerstrasse 35 and Sendlingertorplatz 9, Frankfurter Ring 30 and Elsässer Strasse 33; or check out their website at http://www.adac. de. Their *Pannenhilfe* or 24-hour breakdown service number is tel: (018) 0222-2222.

As in other EU countries, all travellers must wear seat belts, and children under 12 are not allowed to travel in the front seat. All children should have a booster seat or special child-seat according to their size. Anyone found not to be wearing a seat belt can be fined € 30.

Führerschein

To drive in Germany, a valid *Führerschein* (driving license) is of course required. EU licenses are valid until their expiry dates. Other foreign nationals are allowed to drive in Germany for a year using their original license, but it must be accompanied by a translation. You can translate your licence through the ADAC, at Ridlerstrasse 35 München; tel: (089) 5195-0; fax: (089) 519-5257. Some states in the United States have an agreement with Germany for transfer of licenses, but check to see if it applies to your state.

After six months, or at least before the end of a year, all non-Europeans must take a driving test, which includes both practical and written tests. Happily, the written ones can be taken in English, but the whole process is expensive, costing approximately € 500. In order to apply for the test, everyone must take lessons conducted at a *Fahrschule* (driving school), where the tests are also given.

In addition to having proof of driving lessons at a driving school, all applicants for a license must submit proof of an eye test by an authorised optician. They must also have taken a first-aid course. Check with your local town hall, or the Rotes Kreuz Bayer (Red Cross) listed in the phone book. Two passport-sized photographs, your passport and the original driving license with the authorised translation must also accompany each application. All the documentation must be taken to the Führerscheinstelle at Eichstätterstrasse 2 München; tel: (089) 5784-1. It can take a month to have the documentation processed and only then can a test be applied for.

Whoever is driving should carry the *Fahrzeugschein*, car's registration document. Admittedly it is inconvenient if two or more people share a car, to keep passing the document from one to the other, but it is the law.

Car Inspections

Any car that is more than two years old must be tested every two years to ensure its roadworthiness. Called a TÜV, the test is carried out by the Technical Inspection Association. The date of when the test is needed is found on the registration plate on a little coloured disc, the colour of which changes every year. This is divided into 12 segments, one of which has a marker indicating the month the test is due. We were unaware of this until I took the car in for a service and was told that the TÜV was two months overdue. If a car has been well looked after and serviced, there should be no unwelcome shocks from the TÜV.

Mobile Phones and Driving

It is illegal to use a mobile phone while driving, unless it is a hands-free set. If caught using a mobile while driving, a fine will be imposed. But more trouble can be expected if the driver is involved in an accident while using his mobile!

An ASU or vehicle exhaust emission test should be carried out each year, in the same month as the TÜV, even if it is not due that year. A hexagon sticker stuck on the front number plate shows that the car has passed the test. A certificate is also issued which should be carried with your *Fahrzeugschein*.

Traffic Offences

If an accident is minor, the people involved should exchange names, addresses and the names of their insurance companies. Take the registration number of the other car involved and if possible, the names and addresses of any witnesses. Any witness is obliged by law to stay put in the event of an accident. If there is doubt over whose fault it was, the police should be called. In case of injury, the police should also be notified, though once an ambulance is called to a traffic accident, the police will automatically turn up.

It is very thought-provoking for motorists to see the number of small crosses, sometimes with photographs, at the sides of the roads that indicate where people have been killed. It certainly makes you take care there.

Drink Driving

Don't! Allocate a driver for your party and be sure that they stay away from alcoholic drinks. Though the allowed limit of alcohol is two units in Britain, in Bavaria the legal alcohol level in the blood is only 0.05 per milligram. The police do spot checks, especially at holiday time. If you are over the limit, it is an automatic driving ban of a year, possibly a fine of € 1500 and a re-education programme. If you are involved in an accident, the penalties are much higher and the car insurance becomes invalid.

Parking

Parking areas may be marked Pkw or *Personenkraftwagen* for private cars, and Lkw or *Lastkraftwagen* for heavy goods vehicles, such as trucks. If there is space available in a car park, a *Frei* sign may be displayed, but *Belegt* means that it is full. Some car parks have a barrier at the entry point, so that cars entering have to stop to collect a ticket which will have the time of entry stamped. Upon leaving, the ticket must be fed into a payment machine. The pre-paid ticket activates the barrier to enable the car to leave the car park.

Often you need to buy a *Parkschein* (time-stamped ticket) when parking around the streets of Munich. Alternatively, you can feed *die Parkuhr* (the meter). The time spent in most parking bays is self-monitored, using a cardboard clock called *Parkscheibe* which can be bought from newsagents. This must be set to the time you arrive, so the traffic wardens can easily check if you are late returning. I was not aware of the need for the cardboard clock the first time my mother came to stay and I parked the car at the station. We were back within the four hours allowed on the signpost, but there was a ticket stuck to my windscreen. I took it to our town hall to pay and told them that I had kept within the time allowed. It made no difference. I had no clock on display, so had to pay. Needless to say, I bought a clock the next day.

Strafzettel or parking tickets should be paid within the first week they are issued. Payment can be made through your bank, as the payment slip is secured to the ticket. Fines do vary, starting from € 5.

THE ROADS AROUND MUNICH

The very centre of Munich became a pedestrian precinct in 1972, freeing it from noise and pollution. But there are still many small roads you can drive through just beyond the traffic free zone. It does help to familiarise yourself with one-way streets, marked on any good street map, as it is easy to find yourself in the wrong lane and being carried by the flow of traffic to somewhere you do not want to go.

The old city is enclosed by a ring road, built approximately where the city walls used to be. Each section of the ring road has a different name so you should learn each one to help you with orientation. If you need to cross the city, it is much faster to use the ring road rather than trying to negotiate a vehicle across the centre of town, unless you know the area well. A kilometre or two further out from the inner ring, there is another ring road, the 2R, which when fully completed with its underpasses should keep the traffic flowing quite well outside rush hours.

Approximately 5 km beyond the inner ring road is a motorway, the A99. Though three to four lanes wide, it is unable to cope with the current volume of traffic. During non-peak hours, it is a joy to drive along the 99 with the Alps often visible in the distance.

Looking out for Snow
Snow exacerbated the situation in December 2001, when the worst traffic jam in Bavaria's history occurred. More than 60,000 people had to spend the first night of the Christmas holidays in their cars, some for up to 14 hours, as wind blew the snow into drifts.

As with any large city, major motorways radiate from the hub. The A8 which joins the 2R from the north-west, becomes subsumed by it, then reappears on the south-east of the city as it heads for Austria, Italy, Slovenia and Croatia. The A9 is the main highway to and from Berlin and is marked by a statue of a bear, the symbol of Berlin, on the motorway-dividing strip just north of Munich. The A8 and A9 motorways carry so much traffic, especially during the holiday season, that they often have long traffic jams.

ROAD SIGNS
Some road signs can be confusing to foreigners and not all regulations appear to be the same throughout the EU. An

important rule to remember is that unless you see a yellow diamond-shaped sign with a white border or an alternative instruction, traffic coming from the right has priority. In the past, traffic coming on to a roundabout from the right had priority, but this is no longer the case, and appropriate signs have been erected showing that vehicles on roundabouts have priority. Do not use the indicator when entering a roundabout, only when leaving it.

In the late autumn, orange-and-black-striped poles can be found along the sides of the country roads. These are erected as precautionary measures in case of sudden snowfalls. The poles act as visible markers indicating the edges of the road. Some road signs are pictorial, such as the snowflake, which warns of icy and slippery road conditions ahead. Some signs carry one word. When I first saw the sign *Freihalten*, I thought that it meant free parking, when in fact it meant just the opposite, that is, keep the road free from parking! *Anlieger Frei* means that the road can only be used by residents. Usually, these roads are shortcuts to other places, but I have known of people being fined for using these roads. *Bei Nässe* under a speed limit sign means that the speed restriction is in force only when the road is wet, whereas *Strassenschäden* warns that the road surface is damaged. There are often signs over motorways warning drivers of *Stau*—traffic jams due to *Baustelle* or *Unfall*.

BANKING

One of the most prevalent banks in Munich is the Hypo Vereinsbanks, with its 114-m (370-feet) tall futuristic headquarters towering over Arabellapark north-east of the city. The Dresdner Bank with more than 50 branches in and around the city, and the Deutsche Bank with over 60 branches are also well-represented in the city.

The Stadtsparkasse are only to be found within the Munich boundaries, whereas Kreissparkasse are in the surrounding districts, though their main branch is at Sendlinger-Tor-Platz. Sparkassen banks have the advantage of being found all over Germany and you can withdraw cash without being charged whether it is a *Stadt-* (in the city), *Kreis-* (in the

A branch of the Stadtsparkasse bank in central Munich. Stadtsparkasse bank is one of the biggest savings bank in Bavaria.

surrounding district) or *Landes-sparkassen* (in the towns of the countryside). There are many other banks, including the Volksbank, the Raiffeisenbank and the Münchener Hypothekenbank to choose from too.

Bank Accounts

If a foreign family has hired a relocation agent, they would usually recommend a bank, but make sure that it is conveniently located for transactions, as banks in Munich usually keep office hours. Some close for lunch and usually there is only one night in a week, usually Thursdays, when they are open later than 4:00 pm. But it is essential for non-

German speakers to find a bank that has English-speaking staff, as German finances often need explaining. The option of having counter service costs a few euros extra a month but it is well worth it. There are usually charges for setting up *Konto Einrichtungsgebühr* (new accounts).

Almost all companies pay wages directly into a *Girokonto* (current account) with the usual deductions for tax and health care already made. A *Geld(automaten) karte*, cash card and its personal identification number (PIN) usually take a few weeks to come through, so make sure that you have other sources of cash during your first few weeks in Germany. Cash cards usually double up as Eurocheque (EC) cards in Germany. If one is lost or stolen, call tel: (018) 0502-1021 immediately to cancel it so no further transactions can be made. You can withdraw cash immediately as long as you appear in person with your passport.

Some people open an *Einlagenkonto* (deposit account) at the same time as a current account, as it has a higher rate of interest, but deposit accounts normally require a specified period of notice before withdrawals can be made. *Sparkonto* (savings accounts) on the other hand, give immediate access, but earn less *Zinsen* (interest). However, you may be required to place a minimum amount before an account can be opened. Interest rates fluctuate daily, but more can be earned by having telephone banking, with perhaps half a per cent more interest if there is € 50,000 in an account rather than € 5,000.

Cash is King

Until this century, most people around Munich used cash, even when buying high-value goods. Our favourite taxi driver said that she paid for her new taxi in cash, taking the money to the garage in a small case!

For married couples, it is usual to have a joint account, with either person as a signatory. I opened an individual savings account in a Bavarian bank close to home, in which to put my spasmodic earnings and await the tax man before spending the remainder. I had to sign a form that allowed the tax office

access to the saving account records, in case everything was not declared. All the paperwork was completed and I was informed of the princely interest rate of 1 per cent in 1999. But what left me totally dumbfounded was that I had to take a form home for my husband to sign to notify him that I would be earning interest on my account. However, when my husband asked if I had to sign a form if he were to open an individual account, the bank teller just smiled in reply, which I gathered meant 'no'. Apart from that initial irritant, all my transactions have been dealt with courteously and efficiently.

Geldautomat

Geldautomat (ATMs) are found on the outer walls of banks or just in the vestibules. Outside banking hours, the outer door may have to be opened by inserting a cash card first. In the lobby there will be at least a couple of other machines, one labelled *Kontoauszüge* and the other, *Service*. The *Kontoauszüge* machines just accept the card and chug through the process of printing a statement without any other buttons being pressed. Usually, a running tally is not shown, but plus and minus signs are shown next to deposits and withdrawals. At the end of the statement you will see the balance of the previous statement and the new balance. As in the rest of the world, you need to punch in your PIN to be given money at the *Geldautomat,* then after choosing the amount, press the green button. It is polite to stand well back from people collecting money, and a line on the floor often marks the required distance.

Credit Cards

These are a way of life in some Western countries but when we arrived in Munich in 1999, hardly anyone accepted them. Even now, not all the shops accept the most common cards issued in the United States, Britain and Australia. In order to apply for a credit card from a German bank, one must usually have a financial record of several months of transactions with that particular bank, so producing statements from your previous bank won't really help.

MEDICAL CARE

Munich is renowned for having excellent medical facilities, and people come from other countries to seek medical care in the city's brilliant private clinics. Anyone arriving from a European country must bring their form E111, in order to comply with the European Community's Social Security Regulations. The form is available from post offices in Britain, Social Security offices or private medical insurance companies. The form-holder is allowed to stay temporarily in another European country to have medical treatment. If the form-holder needs to see a doctor or needs hospitalisation in Germany, the E111 has to be submitted to the local general sickness fund known as the Allgemeine Ortskrankenkasse (AOK).

Once a person becomes a resident in the area, they must pay into the Gesetzliche Krankenkasse (GKV) German health insurance system including *Pflegeversicherung* (nursing care insurance). The payments for these are taken directly from source, that is, they are deducted directly from your wages and are levied on the first € 3175 of monthly income. The payment entitles the wage earner and dependants to medical treatment; the dependants being a spouse and children up to the age of 23, or 25 if they are still in full-time education. If the spouse earns more than € 400 a month, then he or she must pay for his or her own medical insurance. A spouse earning less than this is covered under the partner's medical insurance. The payment is 13.2 per cent of earnings, though the employer generally pays half of this.

There are two levels of medical insurance in Bavaria: public insurance and private health insurance. Payments to public insurance can be made through several institutions, such as the AOK, BEK, DAK, Kaufmännische Krankenkasse (KKH), TKK Techniker Krankenkasse (TKK) and the Aktive Krankenkasse Schwaben (BKK). You are given a card, which looks like a credit card, that must be presented whenever treatment is needed, therefore be sure to carry it at all times. The doctor then submits the bill directly to the insurance company after treatment. Each quarter there is also an additional levy of € 10 payable directly to the doctor's practice—*praxis*.

Below is a list of a few health insurance companies.

- TKK
  Rosenheimer Strasse 141, Munich
  Tel: (018) 0185-5630
  Fax: (018) 0185-5631
- BKK
  Züricher Strasse 25, 81476 Munich
  Tel: (089) 745-790
  Fax: (089) 7457-9553-99
- AOK
  Landsberger Strasse 150, 80339 Munich
  Tel: (089) 5444-0
  Fax: (089) 544-1919
  Website: http://www.aok.de
- DKV
  Kaiser-Ludwig-Platz 10, 80336 Munich
  Tel: (089) 514-070
  Fax: (089) 5140-7108
  Website: http://www.dkv.com
- Gmünder ErsatzKasse (GEK)
  Elsenheimerstrasse 61, 80687 Munich

Tel: (089) 747-1220
Website: http://www.gek.de

- HUK-Coburg Versicherungen
  Martin Greif Strasse 1, 80222 Munich
  Tel: (018) 0215-3153
  Fax: (018) 0215-3486
  Website: http://www.huk-muenchen.de

As time progresses, it appears that the public health insurance schemes do provide fewer services. In some cases, such as dentistry, the insurance company may not cover all the costs, but the patient should be informed of this before treatment. Estimates for some expensive treatments need to be submitted to the insurance company first, and a second estimate by another practitioner may be asked for. Visits to opticians are paid for by the patient, unless the problem requires a specialist.

Holiday periods are usually bad times to fall ill, as many GPs go on holiday and close their surgeries for the duration of the holidays. Notices about the closures are often found in the newspapers. It is up to the patient to find another doctor in the area if there is an emergency.

To obtain better coverage, additional *Zusatz* (private health insurance) can be taken out and patients may receive more services, such as dental fillings, better hospital rooms or the choice of several different hospitals for treatment. Private patients are also more likely to be able to have a massage paid for under their insurance cover.

Once one opts for private insurance, it is almost impossible to return to the government scheme, even if your source of income dries up. But some people still believe it is worth making the shift for the extra care. With private insurance, the patient must pay all the bills first, then make claims for the amount from their insurance company. Reimbursements are usually done within the month. Having sought the advice of friends and colleagues, I subsequently found that international insurance companies like BUPA and AXA PPP provide private cover in Germany. Some Americans continue to use their American health insurance, valid world-wide, while on a working contract in Germany.

Finding a GP

The list of GPs runs into eight pages in the *Yellow Pages*. Some have their specialities listed as well, such as *Ambulante Operationen* (outpatient operations), *Allergologie* (allergy), *Akupunktur* (acupuncture) or *Psychotherapie* (psychotherapy). If there is no one to recommend a doctor for you, inquire at the local *Rathaus* for a list of local doctors. Your consulate or embassy should have a list of doctors in Munich who speak your mother tongue, though they may not be very close to where you live. Phone the doctors in your area and if you don't speak German, find out if they speak English. We were not sure where to go to find a doctor, but on asking other parents at our daughter's school, we were recommended one who was good, spoke perfect English, did outpatient operations and practised in our area.

At the time of any appointment with a GP, the *Versicherten Karte* (medical insurance card) must be checked through the computer, then every new patient must fill in a brief medical questionnaire. It is advisable to give as detailed a medical history as possible. The GP initially deals with all complaints but if there is a serious problem, they will recommend a specialist. However, you can choose to go directly to a specialist you know or one who has been recommended by others. Sometimes they are available the same day or, if not, usually within the week.

Specialist Care

For children, there are the *Kinderarzt* (paediatric specialists). In Germany, everyone under the age of 18 is regarded as a child. It is, however, not compulsory for all children to go to a paediatrician. Specialists are seen for every aspect of *Gynäkologie* (gynaecology), including birth control. In Germany, a *Frauenarzt* (gynaecologist) does not always have an assistant present when he/she examines a patient, and it is not unusual to be asked to strip completely.

A British woman I know could not conceive after a miscarriage and would have remained childless if she had stayed in Britain as it would have been too expensive for her to have the infertility treatment. She was able to have the treatment paid for by her public health insurance company in Munich and now has two beautiful children.

Everyone should always carry their medical insurance card in case of accidents. When our daughter had an accident on the ski slopes, the hospital needed her insurance number straight away. Unfortunately, she did not have her medical insurance card with her. Frantic phone calls were made home, as it was unlikely that she would have been released without the hospital being able to check the validity of the number given on their computer. We were later billed for the cost of the ambulance from the ski slope to the hospital.

Though it is always wise to consult a doctor, there are some good websites that provide information on medical conditions and medical care. Some of these websites are:

- http://www.healthfinder.gov
- http://www.medlineplus.gov
- http://www.4women.gov
- http://www.kidshealth.org

Hospitals

When you first arrive in an area, finding a hospital is usually not a first priority but it is wise to locate the nearest accident and emergency centre as they are not always easy to find, especially in a crisis situation. If necessary, phone 112 for an ambulance. Signs in the hospitals are usually in German, so have a dictionary with you and be prepared to ask for help and advice from everyone, or you could be waiting unattended in the wrong place for hours. We've heard of it happening!

Many minor operations and examinations are performed in *Ambulanz* (outpatient departments) or *Praxis* (the surgery). Waiting times are often quite short—a week is quite usual for a minor surgery that just needs a local anaesthetic. Patients are given medication if necessary as well as notes about the impending surgery.

Pregnancy and Birth

Some fertility treatments are available with just the basic health cover. A *Frauenarzt* must make a *Uberweisung* (referral), and the couple usually receives counselling first. There are several different clinics in Munich offering treatment for infertility. Typically, the first 10 attempts at artificial insemination and four tries of in-virto fertilisation (IVF) would be covered under the health insurance.

For the majority of her prenatal care, a pregnant mum will see the *Frauenarzt*. She will visit the doctor and be examined every month, and a scan will be taken four or five times during her pregnancy. The pregnant mum will be given a list of hospitals where she could give birth, and it is up to her to contact the hospitals and find out when they have open evenings for her to look round the labour and delivery units. At about 32 weeks, a checking-in appointment should be made at the hospital by the mother.

Not all hospitals have special baby care units, though Harlaching and Rechts der Isar do. In Munich, midwives do not automatically visit mothers after the birth, nor are there health visitors. The *Frauenarzt* must be asked early on in the pregnancy for a list of midwives in the area, and one must contact these midwives to book in the mother for post-natal care. Otherwise the hospital will simply give the new mum a leaflet explaining what to expect and the kind of exercises she ought to do after she and her baby return home.

If a baby is overdue, the mother will be examined at least every other day to monitor the baby's heartbeat. When contractions start, the appointed hospital should be rung to warn them of the imminent arrival. An ambulance can be called and in extreme emergencies, a midwife and doctor will turn up too.

It is preferred that all births in Bavaria are carried out in hospitals, where there will be an obstetrician and a paediatrician. A new mother and her baby usually stay in the hospital for five days, unless a caesarean has been performed, in which case the stay is 10 days. Usually the hospital rooms are for two or three new mothers, but private rooms with their own bathrooms are available.

Geburt

A new baby must be registered within a week of the *Geburt* (birth) at the registry office—usually the town hall—in the district where he or she is born. A resident's permit must also be acquired for the new baby. The registration offices have an official list of acceptable names for children of both sexes. A new mother, or father, is entitled to take up to a year of maternity leave and receive up to 67 per cent of their wages, or to a given maximum. Germany is hoping to rectify the problems of low birthrates with this generous allowance.

There are several health checks that a baby has to undergo from the time of birth. U1 is at birth and U2 before the baby leaves the hospital at five days old. U9 is when the child is five years old and during this time, their fine and gross motor skills are checked and they undergo speech and aptitude tests. There is now a U10 for children in their early teens when a doctor explains the facts of life, contraception and Aids.

Immunisations

Children born in Munich, or who become residents of Munich, have a required schedule of *Impfung* (vaccinations):

- At three months—vaccination against diphtheria /whooping cough/tetanus/influenza type b (DTPHib), hepatitis B, and polio drops.
- At four months—the second diphtheria/whooping cough/ tetanus/influenza type b (DTPHib).
- At five months—the third diphtheria/whooping cough/ tetanus/influenza type b (DTPHib), the second hepatitis B, and the second polio drops.
- At 13 months—the fourth diphtheria/whooping cough/ tetanus/influenza type b (DTPHib), the third hepatitis B, and the third polio drops.
- At 15 months—measles/mumps and rubella, and sometimes a last whooping cough injection is also given.
- At six years—a booster tetanus/diphtheria, the second measles/mumps and rubella.
- At 10 years—booster polio drops.
- Between the ages of 11 and 15—booster diphtheria/tetanus hepatitis B, and for girls, rubella.

Beware

In many parts of Europe including Bavaria, lyme disease which is caused by *Zecken* (ticks) is not uncommon. Ticks are usually picked up on country walks and can also cause encephalitis. If a family is keen on the countryside, it is wise to use a protective spray and check your body after walks. A colleague became very ill after a tick, stuck to the back of her shoulder, went unnoticed.

Elderly Care

There are centres throughout Munich where the elderly can go to meet friends and have a meal too. When people are too old to care for themselves, they may be allocated a place in an *Altenheim* (old peoples' home). However, registration must be made several years before. Every area has a home but some are much bigger and have more space than others.

Hospice Care

There are hospices around Munich for the terminally ill, but the *Pflgeversicherung* does cover home care until death.

Sterbefall

In the unfortunate instance of a *Sterbefall* (death), a post-mortem must be arranged so that a death certificate can be issued. The registrar in the deceased's town should be notified on the next working day. The relatives must then contact a *Beerdigungsunternehmer* (an undertaker), and the *Beerdigung* and cremation or burial should take place between 48 and 90 hours after the death. A listing of undertakers can be found under *Bestattungsinstitute* in the *Yellow Pages*.

GERMAN SCHOOL SYSTEM

In general, the younger the children the easier it is for them to adapt to a new environment, a new culture and a new language. Playing alongside other children in the neighbourhood they start to recognise foreign words without any formal instruction. Having helped infant and junior school children learn a new language, I found that the first month in a school environment, when they did not understand the language, was often bewildering, if not frightening. It can be a difficult time for all concerned!

Family reassurance and friends made all the difference. Within three months, an average six-year-old can understand quite a lot of what is going on when immersed in another language. Within six months, the child will understand almost everything and be able to hold basic conversations. After a year of listening to the new language, they are often fluent. A lot depends on the adaptability of the child and the attitude of the parents towards the new language. Generally, the older a child, the longer it takes to become fluent in the foreign language.

Studies have shown that for an average child who has to take formal examinations in a foreign language, they need to have been learning the language for about seven years in order to attain the level they would have achieved if taking the exam in their native language. Some children may manage sooner. Parents also need to ascertain whether the qualification attained at the ages of 16 or 18 in Bavaria would be recognised in their home country.

Compulsory education starts later in Germany than in the UK, the United States and Australia. If a child returns to his

or her home country at the age of eight, he or she may have received only one year of formal schooling in a German state school compared to his or her peers, who would already have had more than three years of school. Joining a new school can therefore be a trying time for the child. Not only does he or she have to re-adjust to his new school environment, he or she also has to do a lot of catching up to be academically on a par with his or her school-mates. The child's self-confidence may be shaken, unless there is understanding from his or her teachers and some extra tuition.

Formal education is compulsory in Germany for nine years, after which time students can opt to attend a school or college for another three years on either a full-time or part-time basis. Children who are six before the end of the year will usually be admitted up to 30 June of the following year, if a doctor and psychiatrist from the school authority examines them and gives the all clear. Once a pupil starts in Grade 1, the focus is very academic, and few extra-curricular activities are offered.

School hours generally run from 8:00 am to 1:00 pm. There is a six-week holiday in the summer, and a two-week break at Easter, mid-summer and Christmas. Half-term holidays are just long weekends but there are also several other days off for Bavarian holidays. Children may be sent home from school if the outside temperature rises above 28°F (82°F), as the authorities regard this temperature as too hot for children to concentrate. School may also be cancelled if it is too windy or too snowy.

Day-care facilities are available for the very young in both the state and private sectors, but babies need to be registered early. In fact, pre-birth registrations are not uncommon if parents want to return to work in the first few months after birth. The local town hall should have the names of your local *Krippe* (crèche) where children aged one to two may attend before kindergarten.

Nursery School

The *Kindergarten* is for children between the ages of three and six. They are colourful, friendly, caring places and though there is no formal instruction in reading, writing or numbers work, the children are encouraged to interact, sing, play and do handicrafts that enhance their fine motor skills. Most *Kindergarten* are financed by the church or the town, with the parents paying a monthly contribution. It is not always easy to secure a place as there are often more applicants than places and children must be registered several months before. Registration is open only on certain days and at specific times. The dates can be obtained from the city information office, and they are printed on different coloured sheets for the different areas of Munich.

There are many private *Kindergarten* around Munich, some bilingual and some using the Montessori method of learning, but the majority of these tend to be located in central or south Munich. Several of them advertise in the *Munich Found* magazine. *Kindergarten* is an ideal time to learn German, and many children become fluent in the language after only six months.

Starting School

Before starting in a German school, children aged six are given an ability test by a doctor at the infant school to ascertain whether they are physically, mentally and linguistically ready to enter school. The doctor checks the child's health record book and immunisation records. Special attention is given to children who were premature babies. The authorities may decide that a child would benefit by entering school a year later. Children who are to start school in the autumn should be registered at the school in April, but if you are already a resident the school will write to you and tell you that your child is expected.

A *Vorschule* is a school for children whom the authorities think would benefit emotionally or academically from extra help before they start formal schooling. The children are given help in areas such as fluency in the German language, logical thinking, colour recognition and eye/hand coordination. *Ergotherapy* (occupational therapy) is sometimes prescribed for children with poor coordination. This prepares them for writing tasks when they start formal schooling.

School children in Bavaria do not wear school uniforms. Parents are issued with a list of compulsory stationery requirements such as books, pencils and other paraphernalia not supplied by the school. Virtually all primary school children go to school carrying a huge square backpack. The backpacks are quite expensive but do last for several years.

When children start formal education, they are expected to be able to sit and work through the morning, as they have had their time of play at *Kindergarten*. Discipline is quite strict, and children are supposed to have a sensible, positive attitude towards work. School starts at 7:45 am, and for the first year, classes end at 11:30 am every day. As the years progress, the hours spent at school are longer, and the older children usually finish classes at 1:00 pm. There is usually a break of 20 minutes after the first 1.5 hours and a second break of 10 minutes after the next 1.5 hours. Some schools are extending the school day to raise the standard and bring the times more in to line with the rest of Europe.

Grundschule

The *Grundschule* is primary school, which children in Munich attend for four school years between the ages of six and 10. Children are allocated the nearest school to their home. Religious instruction is part of the school curriculum and children whose parents do not wish them to have religious instruction are given classes in ethics. Some children in the last two years of *Grundschule* are offered swimming lessons, sometimes in the afternoons.

No formal examinations are taken in the *Grundschule,* but the parents receive a *Zeugnis* (report) on their child's progress twice a year. Grades are only given after the third year, with one being the best and six the worst grade. There are exams to ascertain academic ability after Grade 4 and then teachers select the type of school most appropriate for the development of each individual child's abilities, based on the marks achieved by the child and also his behaviour in the classroom. Parents can become very frustrated if their children do not realise the importance of these exams and work to attain good marks. The flip side of this is that some children become very stressed before the exams. During this period, local radio stations set up phone-in help lines so the children can talk about their worries. An average grade of two or above must be achieved in order to gain entry to a *Gymnasium* (a selective secondary school), though if sufficient marks are not achieved, there is sometimes a second chance to take the tests the following year.

Choosing a Secondary School

When it comes to choosing a secondary school, parents do have a say and can apply to different schools, if their child is academically suited to them. Different *Gymnasien* concentrate more on certain aspects of the curriculum. A *Neusprachliches Gymnasium* is one that focuses on modern languages, while a *Mathematisch-Naturwissensschaftliches Gymnasium* focuses on science and mathematics. A child who is interested in law and economics can opt for a *Wirt schaftswissenschaftliches Gymnasium*. Sometimes there are more applicants to these schools than there are places, so pupils living closer to the school are given priority.

A *Realschule* is for pupils from Grades 5 to 10. To be accepted, pupils have to achieve an average of 2.66 in general knowledge, maths and German from their *Grundschule*. At the end of six years of secondary education, pupils gain their *Mittlere Reife* (Intermediate High School Certificate), then they may enrol into *Fachoberschule* (a specialised college-oriented high school) for more education and later go on to a *Fach-Hochschule* (technical college) for more practical subjects. They may choose to go to a *Fachschule* (polytechnic university), or some other type of training. There is also the possibility of transferring to a *Fachgymnasium* where they can study for the *Abitur* (the German school leaving examination), and gain access to universities.

A *Hauptschule* is a non-selective school, Grades 5 to 10, where pupils follow a practical work-orientated curriculum. Here pupils study for five years before the *Hauptschulabschluss* (final test), then most pupils go on to some form of training for a trade at a *Lehre & Berufsschule,* a technical college.

The *Hauptschule* and *Realschule* are equivalent to a US junior high school or a British secondary modern school.

A *Gymnasium* is a selective secondary school. After successfully completing six years of education, all pupils automatically gain their *Mittlere Reife.* Pupils usually study for nine years, and then take the *Abitur* at the age of 18 or 19. The *Abitur* is taken in four subjects and is a necessity before acceptance to *Universität* (university) or other institutions of higher education such as the *Hochschule* or *Fach-Hochschule.*

A *Gesamtschule* is a comprehensive school catering for pupils of differing abilities and aims. Some parents seek to avoid what they believe to be an elitist system found in many *Gymnasien,* but *Gesamtschule* are still controversial and the majority of parents still prefer the traditional system. The *Abitur* is also offered in *Gesamtschule.*

The first two years in secondary school are known as *Orientierungsstufe* and throughout this time, pupils are assessed on their suitability for the type of school in which they have been placed. At the end of this period, some pupils may decide to transfer to other schools that are more suited to their abilities.

Special Schools

There are alternative forms of education offered in German, such as the Rudolph Steiner and Waldorfschule, where children are guided in their pursuits rather than seated and taught.

A *Gesamthochschule* combines several kinds of higher education, such as a university, a teacher training college, and an institute of applied science. Students can study for a variety of degrees within the same subject area. This gives the added flexibility to switch courses, an option that may not be readily available in other institutions.

There are schools for children with different types of mental and physical disabilities known as the *Behinderte.* These children are only taught in German. Private schools have not figured large in the German education system but are growing in popularity. Recent European reports on the decline in the general standard of German education shocked German parents, though Bavaria was a top state. As a result many who can afford it are opting for private education. Notwithstanding, the standard of work in the *Gymnasien* is said to be very good.

INTERNATIONAL SCHOOLS

Several schools have been established especially to cater for the influx of foreign workers' children. There are two private schools in the Munich area where English is the main language of instruction.

The Bavarian International School's main building is a palace, built in the French style of over two centuries ago. It is situated on the edge of the village of Haimhausen, to the north of Dachau. Established in 1991, it moved to its present site in 1998 to cope with the rapid expansion of the school. It is popular with both the international community, the majority of whom speak English as their first language, and the German community. The school hires a fleet of private buses to collect the children from their homes all over

The beautiful grounds of the Bavarian International School.

Munich and deliver them back. The school also has a special department set up for the needs of Japanese children. The school can be contacted via email: admissions@bis-school; website: http://www.bis-school.com.

Munich International School E.V. is situated in and around Schloss Buchhof, nestling in the pleasantly undulating woodland just outside Starnberg. The children are mainly German, American and British, but there are many other nationalities represented as well. A recently added station on the S6 at Starnberg Nord has made it more accessible by public transport, though private transport is available for students. For more information, send an email to admissions@mis-munich.de; website: http://www.mis-munich.de.

The European School, at Elise-Anlingerstrasse 21, D81739 Munich, was set up for the children whose parents worked at the European Patent Office. As the office has expanded, the school is rarely able to accommodate other students. Children from all the European countries are educated here, and they are given extra help in their own languages. The children must be competent in German if they are entering secondary school, as by Grade 10 at least half the lessons are conducted in German. The German Mittlere Reifen exam is also taken at Grade 10. The school's home in Neuperlach is close to Therese-Giehse-Allee station (U5), from which it is a short walk to the main building. The school grounds are spacious enough not to feel hemmed in by the surrounding blocks of apartments. For more information visit their website: http://www.eursc.org.

A useful website for children when they need help for their homework or to do research is http://www.homeworkcentral.com. It saves countless trips to the reference library.

LIBRARIES

Every district has its own *Bibliothek* (library), some of which carry English books as well. The largest library, the Münchner Stadtbibliothek, is located at the Gasteig Arts Centre right next to the Rosenheimer Platz S-Bahn station. The library entrance is on the first floor, and all large bags and coats must be handed in at the cloakroom before entry. Anyone

can go in and peruse the four floors of books but bureaucracy comes in to play when trying to get a library card.

All Munich residents must be armed with their passports and resident's permits and fill in their personal details on a green form. The form required so many details, I couldn't help wondering about the relevance. Thinking that I had completed my task, I went back to the desk to collect my card and pay the annual membership fee of € 15. (Short-term residents can opt to pay € 5 a quarter.) Instead, I was told that since I lived outside the city limit, I would also require an *Anmeldung* (registration form), to be collected from my local town hall. At this point, I gave up on being a member and just went to look around. The library prides itself on its large collection of English-language books. There are seven rows of shelves devoted to English books, covering ancient to modern plays and novels. There also Italian, French, Spanish, Turkish, Serbo-Croat and Russian books. But it is the wide array of German books that is magnificent.

The entrance to the Bavarian State Library on Ludwigstrasse is imposing. Inside the 170-year-old building, there is a reading room that has many magazines and newspapers in English. It is open Mondays to Fridays from 9:00 am to

9:00 pm and between 10:00 am and 5:00 pm on Sundays. Foreigners must present their passport on entry, but if you want to borrow books, you must have a Munich City library card.

The Bookshelf e.V., Blumenstrasse 36; tel: (089) 616-227, is an English library run from an old Catholic church. It has children's books, fiction, non-fiction, travel and history sections. Opening hours are from 3:00 pm to 6:00 pm on Monday, Wednesday and Friday, from 11:00 am to 3:00 pm on Saturday. There is a membership charge.

ENTERTAINING CHILDREN

- Cinema visits are often a hit. There are two main English-language cinemas in Munich. Museum Lichtspiele is a small one with four screens near Isartor; website: http://www.museum-lichtspiele.de. Cinema on Nymphenburger Strasse is the other; website: http://www.cinema-muenchen.com/englisch but check in advance to see if there is a suitable film being shown and order the tickets in advance.

- Another place where kids will be well entertained is the circus. Circus Krone is the largest circus in Europe, with 250 animals and a 30,000 sq m marquee. It tours the continent between April and November, though there are some shows at its home in the summer, and people of all ages just love it. Find it at Zirkus-Krone-Strasse 1-6 (S-Bahn Hackerbrücke); tel: (018) 0524-7287; website: http://www.circus-krone.de/en.

- Sea-life is situated at Willi-Daume-Platz 1, in Olympiapark, close to the U3 station. It has over 10,000 creatures in over 30 tanks, showing the underworld of the Rivers Isar and Danube and of the Mediterranean and Black seas. Tel: (089) 450-000; website: http://www.sealifeeurope.com

- A great place to go for an outing with children is the zoo, located at Tierpar Hellabrunn, south of Munich in Thalkirchen. It is accessible by the U3 or bus 52 and is open from 8:00 am to 5:00 pm (6:00 pm in summer). If taking the car, try to get there early as the car parks can get very full. The zoo is beautifully laid out like a natural park and the animals have plenty of space, as do visiting children. There is a schedule of feeding times for the different animals and a day can be planned around these. To be sure of a good view, arrive at each enclosure a few minutes early. There are also food stalls and cafés around the park, so the children can be fed too! The miniature train is great for tired little legs, and there is a children's area where they can stroke and play with the ponies, goats and rabbits and observe newly-hatched chicks.

- East of Munich, just outside Poing (take the S6 train) is a deer park where tame deer roam (almost) freely and can be fed by the children with specially purchased deer food. There are also smaller animals to see such as rabbits and wild boar, and in the summer months, there is a show performed with birds of prey. There is also a brilliant children's playground, from which it can be hard to extricate your charges, though food is a good draw. A picnic area is adjacent, so come prepared. The park is open from 10:00 am to 4:00 pm. In summer, the hours are extended with the park opening its doors at 9:00 am and closing at 5:00 pm.

- Just west of central Munich is the Hirschgarten, a long established deer park. Renowned as a beer garden, it also has a deer enclosure but is somewhat smaller. Another draw in summer is the waterpark. On a fine day, the area is great for picnics, and the children can entertain themselves (supervised) in the water.

- Most museums are open from 10:00 am to 5:00 pm but are closed on Mondays. Though museums do not hold the attention of many children for long, the Stadtmuseum in Jakobsplatz has a toy and puppet section, in which little theatres and moving exhibits are displayed. It is a bit dusty, but there is also a section with gruesome horrors from which screams and groans issue and most junior school boys revel in it. Some children may be interested in the doll house collection, or the film museum, but the photographs and models of Munich years ago can absorb the parents for hours! There is a café attached where cool and trendy types meet.

- The Deutsches Museum between Rosenheimer Platz and Isartor S-bahn stations is a fantastic place, the largest technical museum in Germany. It has several interactive displays, a huge model train layout and aircraft to climb aboard as well as a simulator, several mines and so much more. There are demonstrations at set times throughout the day, so check them out before starting your tour. Check out its website: http://www.deutsches-museum.de/en.

- Most of the museum's aircraft are on display in huge aircraft hangers at Schleissheim airfield, to the north of Munich, where there is also a small restaurant for a full meal or just ice-cream. Not easily accessible by public transport this museum is a delight especially for boys aged three to 93!

- To see real aeroplanes, take the S1 or S8 to Besucherpark, at the edge of Munich's main airport. Here you can observe the runways and terminals and aeroplanes taking off and landing from a large viewing mound, equipped with telescopes. At the base of the hill there are several old aeroplanes, a playground and a visitor's centre.

- The BMW Museum, situated just north of Olympiapark, U3 to Olympiazentrum, houses the BMW brand's earliest and latest models of aeroplanes, cars and motorbikes. An interesting film and informative tapes available in English make the visit more interesting to English-speaking visitors.

- The Bavaria Film Centre, at Bavariafilmplatz, Geiselgasteig, tram 25 from Rosenheimerplatz, does away with the entry fee for the birthday child. There are special family rates too. You can tour round the film sets; there is a stunt show and a film. For more information, tel: (089) 6499; fax: (089) 6492-507; website: http://www.bavaria-film.de.

SHOPPING, MUNICH STYLE

During the times when I visited Munich prior to my move there, I tried to find large supermarkets, like the ones in England. The largest grocery store I found was in the Real Centre at Euro Industriepark, just north of the Frankfurter Ring. The supermarket has a fantastic range of goods.

Apart from food, shoppers can buy clothes cheaply and small electrical appliances as well. An added attraction is its big car park. Nearby on Maria-Probst-Strasse, there is a fantastic Wal-Mart, the big American retail chain. I imagined that I would be buzzing 15 minutes down the motorway every week to load up the car, but that is not the way it worked out.

On the whole, Bavarian housewives shop for just a few items every day at the local shops, often calling at several places for fresh foodstuff. In the last few years, the supermarkets have raised their level of service by extending their opening hours. Many now open as early as 8:00 am in the morning and close at 8:00 pm in the evening. Some corner shops are open at 7:00 am, so you can take a bite of breakfast before rushing off to work. However, many suburban shops still choose to close for lunch, some for as long as three hours. The exception to the usual closing times is Saturday, when most suburban shops close at 12:30 pm. Even in central Munich on a Saturday, 6:00 pm is often the latest closing time. As a general rule, shops do not open on Sundays, although some shops, such as those selling kitchen tiles, are open for viewing.

It is strange for folks from Britain and the United States to turn up to do some shopping only to find a notice on the door saying that the shops are closed for several weeks while the staff take their annual holidays. I know of two village bakers in adjacent villages who often take their vacation during the same week, much to the consternation of their customers. These closures do not happen in the centre of the city but are quite common in the suburbs. Yet despite the closures, trade for the rest of the year does not seem to suffer.

Most of my friends shop locally at family-owned stores or maybe at the small supermarkets such as Minimal-Markt, HL-Markt, Penny-Markt, Plus, Hit, Norma, Edeka, Spar or Tengelmann. Others may drive to an Aldi or Lidl, usually located on the edge of housing areas, to get their basic commodities cheaply. These shops have recently started to accept bank cards, which is great as newcomers used to turn up at the checkout with a trolley full of goods and offer a credit card, which was not accepted, then they would have to dash off with a very red face to find a cash dispenser!

It is worth wandering round local stores to find what the range of products is like. Some have wonderful salad bars or packed dried fruits, others have a large range of eco-friendly products or a counter of varied cheeses. Most offer endless varieties of sausage.

For those who are familiar with daily deliveries of milk to their doorstep, there is no milkman in Munich who calls door to door. Even the price of milk can vary a lot, depending on the amount of fat contained in the milk and the dairy that produces it. If you buy milk in a glass bottle, you will be charged a deposit. Please remember that you are expected to return the bottles. A large cabinet for this is often located near the fresh milk or other bottled drinks section in the shop. Once you put the bottles back into this cabinet, a ticket is dispensed. Bring this ticket to the cashier, who will deduct the given amount from your next grocery bill.

Viktualienmarkt

The natural place to search for fresh fruit in central Munich is the Viktualienmarkt, where produce from around the world,

The Viktualienmarkt is the most famous place in Munich to buy fresh fruit and vegetables.

in excellent condition, awaits your choice. It has a truly fantastic range of fresh fruit, vegetables and herbs, as well as cheeses, wines, sausage, and meat of first-class quality. Prices are however not very cheap. A smaller, cosy market can be found in Elizabethplatz, Schwabing. Both markets are open every day except Sunday.

Organic Food

There is an increasing number of shops selling bio-foodstuffs. The Grünermarkt, located at Weissenburgerstrasse 5 and Rosenheimerstrasse 65, have a huge array, including a bakery and a section for natural cosmetics. Basic, at Schleissheimerstrasse 160 and Römerstrasse 4, is a bit cheaper than other bio shops and also serves organic meals. Vollcorner has three locations at Frundsbergstrasse 18, Arnulfstrasse 134 and Maistrasse 10. Basic AG BioLebensmittel at Westenrieder 35, slightly north-west of Isartor and Öko-Plus Bioprodukte at Rindermarkt 6, close to Marienplatz, cater to environmentally-conscious customers.

Shopping Bags

Wherever you shop, it is expected that you take your own shopping bags, as Germans on the whole are very ecologically aware. Plastic bags are available, but these must be paid for. Some shops do make available brown paper bags, but you always pack the bags yourself.

Asian Palates

For Asian foodstuffs, visit Master Fu at Zenetti 10, southeast of Lindwurmstrasse and Aberle 3, north of Brudermühlstrasse U-Bahn. The Hong Kong Market at Rosenheimer Strasse 30, the Orient Shop at Rosenheimer Strasse 34, and Asia Euro Special Foods at Rosenheimer Strasse 108, have a good selection. The Thai Markt at Albert Rosshaupter 100, Sendling/Westpark and The Indian Shop at Lothstrasse 15, which runs north from Nymphenburger Strasse, also cater to the exotic palate.

If you yearn to cook Latin American food, try Donna Lissy, Häberlstrasse 15A, south of Goetheplatz.

Food Halls

All of the large department stores in central Munich have food halls that cater for international customers. Karstadt at Leopold Strasse 82 and Hertie at Bahnhofplatz 7 offer a good range of quality produce, as does Kaufhof at Marienplatz, Stachus and am Rotkreuzplatz.

The most amazing food shops I have visited in Munich are Dallmayer at Dienerstrasse 14 and Käfer at Prinzregenten Strasse 73. Each shop has small sections for different types of produce, each a little gem when it comes to presentation. Both shops sell their own beautifully-packed presentation boxes and hampers too. The wonderful ambience of the shops and the quality of their goods are of course reflected in their prices.

Bakeries

The *Bäckerei* (bakery) sells a range of different types of bread. But if you are looking for the white, sliced, cuboid variety so common in the United States and the UK, there are not many

Bakeries in Munich offer a wide variety of bread, baked in different shapes and using different grains. Bread is a staple food in Germany.

to be found, except perhaps in the supermarkets where it has recently crept its way onto the shelves. The *Bäckerei* also offers cakes, pastries and doughnuts.

The *Landbrot* or basic loaf is a heavy, dense, flat, darkish bread, and customers who do not need an entire loaf can request to buy a quarter instead. There is a wonderful range of breads, some incorporating different seeds—*Vollkorn* (wholemeal), *Sonnenblumen* (sunflower) and *Kürbiskern* (pumpkin). Rolls that look like large cigars may be flavoured with *Kümmel* (carraway seeds).

In Germany, small rolls are called *Brötchen*, but they are known as *Semmel* in Bavaria. The most usual snack for a toddler is a *Brezel* or *Brez'n,* which is a large, salted pretzel with a soft doughy centre, though people often scrape off the excess salt crystals on top. It has a great shape for little hands to hold and is usually chosen by mums instead of sweets. They are also a favourite with beer drinkers. Sometimes they are sold split and buttered, or as the basis for a very airy sandwich.

Happily, there are often labels on the baker's shelves to help you make your choice. Müller-Brot is the most common bakery chain in Munich, often to be found at stations, where the smell of freshly baked bread is hard to resist, especially if you have a few minutes before catching the next train. Wimmer Bakeries have 36 outlets around Munich and can often be found by the entrances of some supermarkets.

Confectioners

Cakes are bought from the *Konditorei,* which have wonderful displays of cakes and tarts of various sizes often decorated with seasonal fruit. *Lebkuchen* (gingerbread) is a speciality of the area, but traditionally it is only made in the autumn and winter months.

Some of the *Konditoreien* have small cafés attached to them where one can relax over morning coffee, eat a light lunch or a sumptuous afternoon *Kaffee und Kuchen* (K and K). Other *Konditoreien* even close for lunch. One I know of is next to a restaurant that does a roaring lunch-time trade, but the cake shop remains shut for 1.5 hours over the lunch period. Many of the supermarkets actually have bakeries selling bread and cakes on their premises and these do not close for lunch. Several bakeries or cake shops open on Sundays, so their customers can buy fresh bread, call in for breakfast with family or friends, or pop by for their afternoon K and K.

Butchers

A butcher is called a *Metzgerei*. Usually, there are two sections at the butcher, one for fresh meat and the other for cooked meat. Pork is the most common meat in Germany and it also comes in the form of ham and smoked bacon.

Chicken and turkey are also prevalent, but a large chicken is often less than 1.8 kg (4 pounds) in weight. Whole turkeys can be bought at Christmas, but it is more common to buy fillets.

There is also a fair amount of beef, though I have yet to find the larger joints of the roast beef and Yorkshire pudding variety. Braising steak and stewing steak are known as *Gulasch*.

Lamb is not common and therefore is expensive. Large supermarkets sell some frozen meat, but the best place to buy lamb is in one of the farm shops in the suburbs, where the lambs are reared. You can also buy chickens and geese from the farm shops.

Vinzenz Murr is a chain of shops that combines butcher, delicatessen and snack bar.

Delicatessens

Known as *Feinkost,* it is where one finds specially mixed salads, olives, sun-dried tomatoes and rolled herrings. They often have an *Imbiss* attached, which is a cross between a snack bar and café, and where there are small tables around which people stand to eat.

Chemists

An *Apotheke* or the dispensing chemist is usually a smallish outlet that sells medical supplies, whether it is from a doctor's prescription, a homeopathic concoction or another branded medicine, in addition to soaps and perfume. The pharmacists I have met have been kind and helpful, making minor ailments easier to sort out, and the majority of those I've met speak quite good English. When closed, each chemist has a sign on the door saying where the nearest night chemist is. There is a chemist at the main station, Hauptbahnhof, at Bahnhofplatz 2.

There are also shops which sell a range of other items, excluding groceries, that are similar to the drugstores in the United States. The goods range from hair care, foot care and body care products, to baby food, nappies, toys, toiletries, birthday cards and household cleaning products. Schlecker, dm and kd Kaiser's are three major chains of drugstores to be found around Munich. Douglas is a more exclusive chain of perfumeries, selling upmarket cosmetics and perfumes.

Department Stores

In general, the stores are comfortable to browse round and are similar to other department stores around the world. They sell good-quality clothes, shoes, leather ware, jewellery, books, stationery, toys and sports equipment, with the larger stores incorporating hairdressers, restaurants, travel agents and electrical goods departments. They often have food halls in their basements, while the basements in other department stores are devoted to discontinued lines, sale items and cheaper goods.

Kaufhof, which has four outlets, is the most visible. Its flagship store is situated on the south-west corner of Marienplatz. The other three outlets are at Stachus, Rotkreuzplatz and in the Olympia shopping centre. At Christmas, their windows are wonderful to behold with moving tableaux of furry toy animals, where children gaze with rapt fascination.

Karstadt, which is perhaps a little more upmarket, has its main store on Neuhauser Strasse near Stachus, with different departments on opposite sides of the street. At Christmas, their windows often depict scenes from the

Christmas story. Other stores can be found at the Olympia shopping centre, Fürstenried, Giesing, Laim and Nordbad. Their store in Schwabing, towards the northern end of Leopoldstrasse, is the only large store in that locality. A warehouse at Oskar-v-Miller-Strasse in Kirchheim sells miscellaneous goods at very reasonable prices, but this Lagerverkauf is only open on certain days, so check before you go. If you are looking for something specific, it may be better to look elsewhere.

Hertie, at Bahnhofplatz 7, opposite Hauptbahnhof, stretches along a whole block toward Stachus. Customers are entertained by soothing melodies played on the elegant white grand piano as they wander through the different departments.

Kaufring on Orleansplatz, opposite Ostbahnhof, is a good store to look for less expensive clothes, material and haber-dashery.

Kustermann on Viktulienmarkt is the place to go for kitchen equipment, with large departments devoted to cutlery, crockery and glassware. The layout is a little mystifying, but it is worth persevering as it has an invaluable hardware department selling such things as tap washers and sealant for the shower.

Damenmoden

The first place to look for women's clothes *(damenmoden)* is along Kaufingerstrasse and Neuhauser Strasse, the pedestrian precinct that runs west from Marienplatz to Stachus.

At the cheaper end of the range, though few clothes are really cheap in central Munich, is C & A, a department store just for clothes, right on the pedestrian precinct. Another clothes store, but quite exclusive, is Ludwig Beck on Marienplatz, which has a lovely department for glamorous evening clothes. Betty Barclay is the most famous label for women's clothes in Germany and they can be found in many of the shops.

Women's clothes and accessories can also be found in Maximilian Strasse and Fünf Höfe. Escada's main shop is along Theatinerstrasse.

For fashion, Hallhuber, Kookai, Mango, Marc O'Polo, S. Oliver, More and More, and Pharo are favourites with women in their late teens to late thirties. The clothes sold in these shops are up-to-the-minute and exciting, but they are not cheap. A United Colors of Benetton fronts Marienplatz. For teenagers who want cheap, fashionable clothes, Orsay, H & M and Pimkie are the places to go. All these shops are to be found in the city centre.

X-large pap on Zweibruckenstrasse caters for the not so slim and has some really nice designs that are not at all fuddy duddy. The shop carries sizes 42 to 54. Check them out http://www.x-large-pap.de. There is also a shop at the PEP centre.

As a guide, an English size 10 or an American size 8 is equivalent to a German size 36. For other sizes, use the conversion table below as a guide.

German	English	American
36	10	8
38	12	10
40	14	12
42	16	14
44	18	16
46	20	18

Herrenmoden

Herrenmoden (men's fashion) are found in all department stores and in the basement of Ludwig Beck. A popular place with many men is Hirmer in the pedestrian precinct, although the younger set may prefer Gap, just a few shops away. Wormland on Marienplatz is also a favourite. Harry's men's fashion shop at Oskar-von-Miller-Ring 1 (tel: (89) 2800-0482) has lots to choose from as well.

Men's clothes are often sized S, M, L, XL and XXL, but these sizes vary with the design and cut.

Shirts are sold by the collar size, with the equivalent sizes in cm and inches shown below:

Chart of Men's Shirt Sizes							
36	37	38	39	40	41	42	43
14.5	14.5	15	15.5	15.75	16.5	16.5	17

Chart of Men's Waist Sizes								
79	81	84	86.5	89	91.5	94	96.5	99
31	32	33	34	35	36	37	38	39

Kindermoden

While *kindermoden* (children's clothes) are hardly cheap, they are often very colourful. Virtually all the department stores have a children's department, as do the trendier shops such as Esprit and Gap. There are also many privately-owned shops such as Popolino Windelmaus at Sternstrasse 20, Lehel, which is open from Tuesdays to Fridays between 11:00 am and 2:00 pm and again between 3:00 pm and 7:00 pm. On Saturday, it is open from 11:00 am to 2:00 pm.

Children aged two can wear German clothes size 92 cm (the average height of a two-year-old), while six-year-olds wear size 116 cm–122 cm. The average 10-year-old wears size 140 cm–152 cm, and kids of 14 usually take size 164 cm. Many smaller women are able to wear clothes meant for 12- to 14-year-olds as they are cheaper than the smaller sizes of ladies garments.

The special clothes that are worn for christenings and first communion services can be found in several specialised shops such as Dimitra, Schwanthalerstrasse 63. You can also buy these clothes secondhand as they only need to be worn for a day.

Trachten

The *Trachten* (traditional Bavarian clothes) is usually tailored, whereas the *Dirndl* is commercially made and does not have such exacting standards as depth of pleat and length of skirt. The traditional clothes worn in Bavaria are rarely cheap but are sold extensively, with all department stores carrying a selection. So does C & A in the central pedestrian precinct.

The best known name for *Trachten* is Loden-Frey, at Maffeistrasse 7-9. This exclusive store, which sells all types of cloths, uses the traditional *Loden* material, a woollen fabric said to last a lifetime. The range of garments is extensive, all beautifully styled, and needless to say, expensive. Ludwig Beck, in the north-east corner of Marienplatz, sells a wonderful array of *Trachten*.

Trachten Redl, Weltenburger Strasse 17 (website: http://www.trachten-redl.de) also specialises in *Trachten*, as does Trachtenmoden Guth, Müllerstrasse 50 (tel: (089) 266-969), which has an extensive but not too expensive range. Look in the local press for shops close to you with *Angebot* (offers).

SECONDHAND SHOPS

The city of Munich, in association with the surrounding districts, publishes a book that is available from its information office in Marienplatz, entitled *Secondhand-Führer*. It contains a treasure trove of information on different types of goods, including CDs, records, electrical goods, photographic equipment, musical instruments and clothes. Pat's Boutiques have six secondhand clothes shops around central Munich, at Hohenzollernstrasse 44 (the most exclusive), Sendlinger Strasse 21, Tal 14, Sonnenstrasse 2, Dachauer Strasse 20 and Weissenburger Strasse 32.

Schuhwaren

There is a fantastic range of *Schuhwaren* (shoe shops) and shoe styles available in Munich, especially low-heeled and flat shoes. But the majority of shoes are of a standard width, posing a difficulty for people with very narrow or wide feet. The most popular shoe shops carry only a small selection of bags, but the large department stores have separate bag departments. These departments usually sell shoes in the middle and more expensive price range. At sale times, many end-of-season and discontinued lines are sold at good discounts, occasionally for half price.

There are six Tretter stores in central Munich and over a dozen Raab shoe shops, with popular styles that are not too expensive. Salamander is popular, especially with teens and those in their twenties, as is Timberland for the outdoor types. The large sports shops such as Sport-Scheck at Sendlinger Strasse 6, specialises in shoes for outdoor pursuits, as does Outdoor-Schuhe, at Kapuzinerplatz 1, just south of Goetheplatz.

There are also many exclusive shoe shops in central Munich, most of which also sell accessories. Thomas, in Theatrinerstrasse sells beautifully made shoes, as do Charles Jourdan and Bally located on the same street. Bally also has a shop on Neuhauser Strasse. Eduard Meier on Residenzstrasse claims to have one of Germany's oldest shoe shops.

Shoe repairs are often made at Mister Minit, which can be found in many of the larger stores in and around the city. Cobblers are listed in the *Yellow Pages* under *Schuhmachereien und Schuhreparaturen*. For leather accessories, check under *Lederwaren*.

Chart of shoe sizes:

Eur	36	37	38	39	40	41	42	43	44
UK		4.5	5	5.5	6	6.5	7	8	9	10
US		5.5	6	6.5	7	7.5	8	9	10	11

Sportswear and Equipment

Schuster at Rosenstrasse 1; tel: (089) 237-070 and Sport-Scheck at Sendlinger Strasse 6; tel: (089) 21660 are two of the best known sports shops in the centre of town. Both occupy several floors of shop space. As the people of Munich are rather sporty, there are specialist sports shops at virtually every corner.

Spielwaren

Many beautiful toys are available in Munich and the large stores have super departments.

The best known *Spielwaren* (toy shop) for *Auslanders* is the huge and familiar Toys R Us, located on the Euro-Industriepark at Ingolstädterstrasse 66. My favourite shop is Fischer Spiel und Freizeit at Sonnen Strasse 2, tel: (089)

549-1120. Don't be put off by what looks like a small shop, the basement is wonderful.

For model enthusiasts of any age, visit Wagner Model Trains at Rosental 1 and Sendlinger Strasse 1; tel: (089) 266-236; website: http://www.adlergmbh.de. Another store worth taking a look at is Modellbahnprofis, Feldmochingerstrasse 35; tel: (089) 140-3031.

Möbel

There is hardly any hardwood *Möbel* (furniture) sold, apart from in exclusive antique shops. Moreover, to an environmentally aware community like Munich, hardwood furniture hardly qualifies as being friendly to the environment. Most furniture, therefore, is made of pine, either in modern or country styles.

When shopping for upholstered furniture, ask for *Polstermöel*. *Bett* is German for bed, *Tisch* is table, and if you are looking for a chair to accompany that *Tisch,* look for a *Stuhl.* You may also need a *Schrank* (large cupboard) to hold all your clothes.

Comparatively cheap items, often in flat packs, can be found at Ikea. There are two stores, one north up the A9 to the Eching-Neufahrn junction, about 30 minutes by car from Munich on a good run and one to the south when driving in the direction of Garmisch, at Brunnthal. On sunny Saturdays, the queue for Ikea has been known to stretch back down the motorway! The plus side is that if the item you want is in stock and your transport is large enough, it can be carried off immediately.

Möbel Biller is another large furniture outlet, but it is even further away, on the A92 between Freising and Landshut. People are prepared to travel there as it has some very good special offers widely advertised in the Munich newspapers. Find out more from its website: http://www.biller.de.

Segmüller (website: http://www.segmueller.de) along the eastern A94 motorway at Parsdorf also promotes its offers through colourful inserts in the Munich newspapers. These three shops try to make shopping a happy family experience, with places for the children to play, restaurants and toilet facilities. Weekend sales are rarely a joy though!

In and around town there are several large furniture shops. Hess is to be found in Maria-Probst-Strasse on the Euro-Industriepark. It has two stores next to each other, one selling trendier, slightly cheaper furniture. XXL Lutz has a large store in Theresienhöhe, and there is a Kaufhof warehouse—Lagerverkauf—in Eching, close to Ikea, with some excellent deals. Kare has three furniture stores in Munich, in Augustenstrasse, Sendlinger Strasse and Lindwurmstrasse, as well as one at the Olymmpia Einkauf Zentrum (OEZ) shopping centre. The majority of furniture shops around town are smaller family-owned concerns.

Küchen and White Goods

There are countless Küchen kitchen shops around Munich, as kitchens are not usually included in the sale of homes. We bought one in express time from Segmüller, though one should usually expect to wait an average of 10 weeks for delivery and installation after the order has been made. Kitchens are listed in the phone book under *Einbauküchen* or *Küchen,* but it is wise to get several quotes if you have the time as prices vary a lot.

Fridges, deep freezers and dishwashers are sold at outlets that sell kitchens as well as electrical goods suppliers. It is and can still be quite difficult to buy fridges with large freezer compartments. Until about five years ago, all the fridges sold in Bavaria just had a small ice box at the top. Washing machines are not sold with kitchens but dishwashers are. In Germany, washing machines and dryers are found in a laundry room, usually in the cellar, or else in the bathroom. Large appliances are sold with a one-year guarantee, and so far it is not possible to get an extended warranty.

Saturn is the best known shop for large electrical appliances. One shop is at Neuhauserstrasse 39. The staff are friendly and if you ask for someone who speaks English, one will be found. It also has outlets in both the

PEP Einkaufsman Center (PEP) and the OEZ centre. Its Technocenter is in Schwanthaler Strasse 115.

The large department stores also sell electrical appliances, as does + EP (Electronic Partner) on Weissenburgerstrasse and around the suburbs. Media Markt has a store in the Euro-Industrie Park and another close to Leuchtenbergring S-Bahn on Einsteinstrasse

Licht und Lampe

To purchase *Licht und Lampe* (lights) Obi DIY stores are your best bet, especially on a cold day. They have large, cheery departments where you can also buy wires and connectors. Segmüller also carries a large variety of ceiling lights and lamps. There are a lot of modern fittings with small bright halogen bulbs on bars. On the other hand, you can also find heavy wooden Bavarian fittings with linen or thick cotton lace mop-cap lampshades that let out little light.

Teppich

Many of the apartments and houses have either parquet, marble or tile flooring in the hall, kitchen and main living rooms. A few rugs may be strewn on the floor, though some do have *Teppich* (carpet), linoleum or sisal floor coverings. It is usual to remove outdoor shoes when going into a Bavarian home, though new visitors are not expected to. Some visitors even bring their own cloth slippers, so the carpets remain clean longer and do not get worn as quickly. Bedrooms are more often carpeted.

There are many shops that just sell carpets and rugs— from those with expensive foreign imports from Persia, Russia, India, China and America, to those that slash their prices at sale times. Teppichkauf TREND GmbH have shops at Landsberger strasse 294 (tel: (089) 580-1167) and Am Haag at Gräfelfing; tel: (089) 85860; fax: (089) 858-6200. R. Andersen at Pestalozzistrasse 40a (tel: (089) 267-578) has been in the carpet and curtains business for 25 years. Yet again, you will be able to have your pick from one of the many small family businesses as well as the large stores.

Vorhang or Gardinen

The majority of homes and offices in Munich have shutters on the outsides of the windows. They are worked from inside each room either manually or electronically. Some older houses have heavy wooden shutters that close like doors instead. Shutters insulate and cut out the light, so not everyone has *Vorhang* or *Gardinen* (curtains). Sometimes just a thin gauze or net curtain is hung as a decoration or to discourage prying eyes. There are many companies that make curtains as well as sell ready-made ones. Most also sell the *Zubehör* (curtain fittings) too. Here are some curtain specialists.

- Apel & Ness
  Peter-Anders-Strasse 12
  Tel: (089) 606-353
  Website: http://www.apel-ness.de
  Opening hours 10:00 am–7:00 pm (Monday-Friday), 10:00 am–4:00 pm (Saturday).
- H. Pemmerl
  Near Isatorplatz, at Rumfordstrasse 42
  Tel: (089) 226-345
- Faendrl GmbH
  Landsberger Strasse 81
  Tel: (089) 501-061
  Website: http://www.faenderl.de

Kurzwaren

For your sewing needs, you can try the dry-cleaners, who often carry items such as needles, cotton, scissors and patches, as do most supermarkets and especially department stores, which have a wide selection. Kaufering, opposite Ostbahnhof, has a department on the top floor, which also sells curtain material. Ludwig Beck's haberdashery is in a separate shop behind the main store with a fantastic choice of ribbons and buttons, and a good variety of wool. Hertie opposite Hauptbahnhof has a super range and Karstadt has an good department, which also sells patterns and a wide range of materials, some of which can be bought for half price during the sales. Die Wolle is a dear little wool shop at Müllerstrasse 48.

Buchhandel

There are specialist *Buchhandel* bookshops for subjects like medicine, architecture and law, but the majority cater for a mixture of tastes, so anyone can browse happily.

- The Hugendubel stores are found in 12 locations around Munich, including Marienplatz and Stachus. The larger stores stock some best-sellers in the English language, although they cost more than if you bought them in the United States or the UK. They also have departments for every type of published German book imaginable as well as maps. They also have a store that only sells English books at Salvatorplatz, off Theatinerstrasse.
  Tel: (018) 0148-4484
  Email: service@hugendubel.de.

- Words'worth Booksellers sells an extensive range of books, it also has a section on audio-books and a little Pooh Corner.
  Schellingstrasse 21a
  Tel: (089) 280-9141

Garden Centres

There are cheaper family-owned garden centres on the outskirts, but these are among the best known.

- Samen Schmitz GmbH has a large centre in Humboldt Strasse 2, Dornach, off Erdinger Landstrasse, where some of the larger plants are grown. A shop sells tender plants, pots, items for flower arranging and also pet supplies. It is a delight just to saunter through the garden. A smaller outlet is at Viktualienmarkt 5.

- Dehner has a shop just south of the Viktualienmarkt, but its larger outlets are at the edge of town in Forstenried, Germering and Kirchtrudering.

- Seebauer in Ottobrunner Strasse 61, Ramersdorf, is a huge greenhouse that advertises on the U-Bahns as a paradise that offers *Preiswert* (good value). There is a café for those who want to linger. The car park fills up quickly on sunny days.

  If you are actually looking for a gardener, look in your local paper or try phoning someone listed under *Garten und*

Landschaftsbau in the *Yellow Pages.* They are mostly designers of new gardens, but some also tackle smaller jobs.

Several of the farmers who own fields around Munich grow flowers, which people pick themselves. There is always a board propped at the edge of the field with the prices for each type of flower, a knife to cut the flowers, and a large container into which people drop the money. The wonderful thing is that everyone is honest and no one abuses the system.

Bau und Heimwerkermärkte

OBI has its largest *Bau und Heimwekermärkte* (DIY) shop, which covers a vast area off Lerchenauer Strasse 134, just north of the Frankfurter Ring. Its warehouses are like aircraft hangers, and they sell everything imaginable in the DIY line, that is if you can find it. Plants and other garden items are also sold here. There are substantial but smaller stores in the suburbs.

Praktiker is ideal for your needs if there is one near your home. Praktiker has four outlets in town as do both Bay Wa and Toom. Most such shops also have large machines available for tackling the heaviest of jobs.

Electrical Wares

Conrad has a chain of shops throughout Germany, including two shops in Munich. Selling power tools, sound systems, computers, telephones and lights, there are people on hand to offer help and advice. To contact its outlets in the OEZ shopping centre call (089) 143-4170. Those at Tal 29, you can contact at tel: (089) 242-0760. They are open until 8:00 pm on weekdays.

We bought our washing machine from Saturn, which has shops at Schwanthaler Strasse 115, Neuhauserstrasse 39, as well as in the OEZ and PEP shopping centres. Media Markt, at Maria-Probst Strasse 11 and in Solln, specialises in TV and hi-fi systems.

The area around Hauptbahnhof is home to lots of small privately owned shops selling computers and components, watches and audio equipment. My husband just loves to browse in the area, though he says he has never noticed the strip joints and dubious-looking establishments there!

Shopping in the Stations

Hauptbahnhof and to a lesser extent, Karlsplatz/Stachus, have underground shopping facilities, fast food outlets and easy access to adjacent department stores. Ostbahnhof also boasts several refurbished shops. Parts of these complexes are open on Sundays. Rosenheimer Platz has lots of shops inside its western entrance and there are booths selling theatre tickets at Marienplatz and Pasing stations. Most stations have newspaper kiosks and many have bakery outlets, some of which sell coffee too.

Out-of-Town Shopping Centres

The American Mall has not yet hit Bavaria in a big way, but there are a couple of shopping centres not too far from the city centre. Neither has adequate parking to cope with Saturday crowds and visitors at sale times. It can get very frustrating when you spend more time looking for a place to park the car than checking out the shops. Once inside, especially when it is cold and wet, the dividends pay off.

OEZ is situated on Hanauer Strasse, north-west of Olympiapark. Keep a careful eye out for the signs directing road users there as they can be missed. Eventually the U3 will be extended to stop at the centre before continuing its journey to Moosach, but the U1 now takes you there. Alternatively, take the bus, numbers 83, 136,or 143. OEZ is not a huge mall, but it is a great place to shop for clothes in chilly weather.

The PEP centre is on Thomas Dehler Strasse, in the centre of Neuperlach. The red brick edifice is not easy to locate on a first visit, as it is one or two storeys lower than many of the surrounding offices and apartments. But the U2 and U5 stop right at the centre and make it easily accessible from Ostbahnhof. The PEP centre has well over 100 shops, mainly on two floors connected by escalators. The goods available range from fashion to household goods, jewellery to health, travel agents to shoes. The stores are open until

10:00 pm on weekdays and until 4:00 pm on Saturdays. It is an airy and spacious complex with a double-storey, circular central area, under which a stage is erected for special events. There are events throughout the year which are well-publicised locally.

Children and Shopping Centres

Most shopping centres do not as yet have play areas or crèches where the children can be looked after whilst their parents shop.

The new Reim Arcade is spanking new, with food outlets and fashion shops. Situated next to the exhibition centre, the Messe, and a large park, it is serviced by the U2 and there is no lack of parking space.

REFUNDS

By law, goods need only be replaced if they cannot be satisfactorily repaired. A large department store may well replace a pair of shoes, as an act of good will. Some credit card companies will refund the money of defective products. But in general, there is no refund policy in Bavaria.

If you buy over the phone, fax or Internet, an EU directive gives a customer the right to return goods within 14 days. Shops have their own policies on exchanging non-faulty goods, so check before purchasing. Usually, sales items cannot be exchanged, but they should not be faulty unless the fault has been made known and is part of the sales agreement.

The Verbraucherschutzzentrale (Better Business Bureau), at Mozartstrasse 9 can help with customer complaints. It can be contacted at tel: (089) 539-870.

Getränkemarkt

Looking more like small warehouses than shops, *Getränkemarkt* sell mainly bottled drinks. Most people in Bavaria buy their soft drinks and beer by the crate at a *Getränkemarkt*, where a deposit is charged on each bottle, and the customer is reimbursed for each bottle returned. All in all it works out cheaper than buying each bottle individually, but it does mean that a place must be set aside to house the crates. Many supermarkets have a *Getränkemarkt* at the side or behind their main store, but often they are separate shops situated along the side of main roads, with ample parking space.

Wine

Jacques' Wein-depot is an extensive chain of outlets that just sells wines imported from all over the world. Also available are some imported delicacies. They are preferable to supermarkets, as customers are allowed to taste the wines before buying. There are several around Munich, but the two I know well are in Daglfing and Unterföhring, where the proprietor is charming and speaks excellent English.

My favourite salesroom for wine is La Cantinetta di Sergio Bolzan, Neumarkter Strasse 77; tel: (089) 688-2536; website: http://www.bolzan.de. There are huge stainless steel vats of the most popular Italian wines and they fill up the empty bottles the customers bring in, though these can be supplied for a small extra charge. They also sell the more expensive wines from Italian growers. The salami and the truffle ravioli from the delicatessen are exquisite.

Both wine distributors organise special open days, when they invite experts to talk about the wine. Such occasions are fun and a really relaxing way to spend a couple of hours—especially if someone else is driving!

Flea Markets

John has always loved *Flöhmärkte* (flea markets), and the number in Munich delights him. I don't share this love and regard most as *Trödlmärkte* (junk markets) and some actually advertise themselves as such. There are several regular flea markets as well as local ones in the suburbs advertised on posters or in the local newspaper. Often on a Saturday morning, John will cycle off to Riem, where the eastern end of the car parking area close to the Messe, is covered with tables displaying anything the stall-holders think will sell. On a fine Saturday, it can be really teeming. The earlier you go the better. John has found a splendid bike and brand new hiking boots, but bargains are soon snapped up so one should not linger over decisions.

For a change, some Saturdays he goes to the trotting course—Trabrennbahn—in Daglfing where a few stalls are set up on the outside, but in the main building two full floors are taken up with stalls selling antiques, costume jewellery, or military memorabilia. This flea market is also open on Fridays.

My friend Sarah loves to go to Keferloh, near Haar, a few miles east of Munich, where on the first Sunday of the month, except in the coldest weather, there is a flea market specialising in antiques. She managed to pick up an old chest with sturdy locks, which she painted in the traditional Bavarian manner and now it sits in her hall looking wonderful after a few hours of loving attention.

Way north of Munich, but sometimes worth the visit if you fancy a drive up route 13 or the A9, is the market at Pfaffenhofen, which is open only on the second Sunday of the month. I have bought some beautiful lace there and a traditional blouse for a good price. There are also old tools and antiquated farming implements, furniture and lights, and much more.

Two other flea markets worth the drive there are at Kochel am See and Murnau where the backdrop of lakes and mountains offers an aesthetic treat.

ANTIQUITÄTEN

Many Antiquitäten (antique) shops are to be found in the areas around Max-Weber-Platz, Türkenstrasse, Theresienstrasse or Westenrieder-strasse. In the city centre, there is the Auktionhaus Viktualienmarkt, open Monday to Friday, 10:00 am to 6:00 pm and Saturdays, 10:00 am to 5:00 pm. Daily auctions are held at noon, and crowds of people gather round the door to see what lots are being offered by the loquacious auctioneer.

There are also some huge and wonderful antique warehouses. One quite centrally located is the Antik Palast, in the Georg-Elser-hallen on Rosenheimer Strasse, just south of Ostbahnhof. It is open on Thursdays from 2:00 pm– 7:00 pm, Fridays from 10:00 am–7:00 pm, and Saturdays from 10:00 am–6:00 pm. Once you pass the inauspicious exterior, a fantastic array of individual specialised rooms is laid out. There are firms specialising in records, books, shiny dark wooden furniture, elegant clothes, bags and jewellery, perambulators, carpets and chandeliers, and even an old Chevrolet truck. There is another antique warehouse at Dirnismaning on route 11, where the rustic exterior belies the abundance of wares within.

In the autumn, there is the Munich Antique Market, held in several venues, including the Löwenbräukeller. The Haus der Kunst also holds an antique exhibition each October.

RELIGIONS IN MUNICH
Christianity

The majority of the churches in Munich are Roman Catholic, and their spires and towers give the city its distinctive skyline. The austere brick cathedral—*Domkirche*—with its tall old towers topped with green bonnets has become the beloved symbol of Munich. The *Asamkirche* in Sendlinger Strasse with its heavy ornate décor, looks as if it is weighing down on the congregation. St Peter's, the oldest parish church in Munich, had its restoration finally completed 30 years after World War II ended, and the fit and healthy can climb the Renaissance tower for unsurpassed views of the city and on a clear day, the Alps as well.

For anyone who speaks fluent German, it is easy to find a church in which to worship, as there are Roman Catholic churches in every locality. Most areas also have an Evangelical or Protestant church. The majority of Sunday services in the German-speaking churches begin at 10:00 am.

There are several English-speaking churches in Munich, and these usually share a building with the German congregation, therefore the service times may be irregular, in order to accommodate both congregations.

Roman Catholic Services

Some Catholic churches that have services in English are:

- St Kilian's Irish Catholic Mission holds mass at 6:00 pm. The Pastoral Center linked to it is at Landsbergerstrasse 39 and hold its services at 11:00 am.
- Kreuzkirche
  Kreuzstrasse 2
  Tel: (089) 500-3580

- St Bonifaz Church
  Karlstrasse 34
  Tel: (089) 399-081
- St Bonifaz's English Speaking Community Church
  Ainmillerstrasse 5
  Tel: (089) 399-081
- Berkmann College (Mass is held at 10:30 am)
  Kaulbachstrasse 31a
  Tel: (089) 23860

Protestant/Evangelical

The English-speaking Protestant churches are mostly found towards the south of the city, though never very far from a U-Bahn.

- The Munich International Community Church, which is non-denominational, holds a service at 4:00 pm. Communion is celebrated on the first Sunday of each month, after which coffee, soft drinks and refreshments are served. All services have a crèche available and Sunday school for children from ages 2 to 16.
  Freie Evangelische Gemeinde, Mozartstrasse 12 (U3/U6 to Goetheplatz)
  Tel: (089) 4188-9186
- The Anglican-Episcopal Church of the Ascension holds its services in Emmauskirche, Seybothstrasse 4 in Harleching, with communion every Sunday at 9:00 am and a service at 11:45 am. There is a Sunday school, a youth group and a crèche.
- The Gospel Life Center is inter-denominational. Sunday services are in German with a simultaneous translation into English. They take place at Am Kiesgrund 2-4 at 10:00 am. There is a Sunday school for children up to age of 12 and a youth group that meets on Friday evenings.
  Tel: (089) 903-8803
  Website: http://www.gospellifecenter.de.
- The International Baptist Church of Munich is at Holzstrasse 9, and looks from a distance just like any other pale grey Munich apartment block. It holds both

English and Spanish language services at 4:00 pm. Morning services are held in German. The International Café is attached.
Tel: (089) 690-8534

- The Bible Baptist Church is at Balanstrasse 324, tended since 1977 by Wilhelm Falk, who is always available with a sympathetic ear. Sunday services are at 11:15 am, with an international congregation.
Tel: (089) 682-726

- The Peace Church-United Methodist has services at Frauenlobstrasse 5, its heavy dull yellow exterior belying the simple, modern interior. The church's African Choir add wonderfully to their services, which are at 11:45 am for English speakers. There is a crèche, Sunday school and activities for teenagers on the second Saturday of each month from noon to 4:00 pm.
Tel: (089) 2602-3677
Website: http://www.peacechurch.de.

Judaism

- Israelitosche Kultusgemeinde
Reichenbach 27
Tel: (089) 202-4000

- The Kulturzentrum
The Fraunhoferstrasse U-Bahn station is just round the corner.
Tel: (089) 471-067

- Munich Liberal Jewish Community
Beth Shalom, e.V
Tel: (089) 8980-9374

- Ohel Jakob
Reichenbachstraße 27, 80469 München
Tel: (089) 202-4000
Fax: (089) 201-4604
Email: info@ikg-m.de
Website: http://www.ikg-muenchen.de
The new synagogue, bearing the name of its predecessor—Ohel Jakob (Jacob's Tent), was opened at Jakobsplatz in November 2006, 68 years after the previous synagogue

was destroyed. The construction of the synagogue and the new Jewish community centre and museum, cost € 71.5 million, giving a new home to some of the 9,300 Jews who live in Munich. Munich now has the country's second largest Jewish community. Contact the Israelitische Kultusgemeinde für München und Oberbayern via Charlotte Knobloch (President) and Chil Rackowski.

- Jewish museum
  St Jakobs-Platz 16, 80331 München
  Tel: (089) 2339-6096
  Fax: (089) 233-989-96096
  Website: http://www.juedisches-museum-muenchen.de.
  For more information, email: bernhard.purin@muenchen.de at the syngagoge for more information; website: www.juedischeszentrumjakobsplatz.de.

Islam

For Muslims new to the community, the Islamic Centre is on Wallnerstrasse 15; tel: (089) 325-061. It is not easily accessible by train but the 293 bus passes on its way to Garching. If driving, go north up route 11 on Freisinger Landstrasse, and the minaret can be seen peeping over the trees to the right.

FOOD AND ENTERTAINMENT

CHAPTER 6

'Z'essa un tringahäit Leib und Seel beianand.'
'Eating and drinking keeps body and soul together.'
Bavarians can be a fun loving people with a positive
attitude to life.
—A popular German saying

FOOD AND DRINK

The Bavarians are great meat eaters, especially pork, from which the many types of *Wurst,* or sausage, are derived. Heavy loaves of bread or *Brezen* (large pretzels) are consumed for breakfast and supper, with meat and cheese. Historically, the midday dinner was the main meal of the day and tended to be a hearty, if not heavy, affair, as many of the populace were farm workers who needed lots of energy. Potatoes, noodles, or *Knödel* (dumplings) were eaten with meat or sausage, with vegetables or salad served as a separate course. Cabbage—red or white—is the staple vegetable. Many varieties of fish are found in the lakes and rivers around Munich, but they are also reared in fish farms. The traditional way to serve fish is covered with salt and grilled on a long skewer: *steckerlfisch.*

These days, eating patterns have changed somewhat. At lunchtime, some people forgo the meat course altogether and just eat pudding! This can be a strudel filled with apple, sultanas and a touch of cinnamon in a sea of custard, or pancakes sliced up and served with a fruit puree. *Dampfnudel,* a steamed white dumpling occasionally filled with plum jam and swimming in vanilla sauce, is an amazing experience, and one that you can become addicted to, as expanding waistlines will testify!

Being an international city, Munich also boasts restaurants that serve cuisine from all over the world and is capable of satisfying every palate. Eating out in Munich is much more affordable than it is in Paris or London, so people in Munich tend to eat out more often than their counterparts in other big international European cities.

Beer is the beloved beverage of the Bavarian. The three brands of beer most frequently found are *Helles,* a light beer; *Weissbier,* a wheat beer with a rather yeasty taste; and *Dunkel*, a dark beer. Twice a year, breweries produce speciality beers with a higher alcohol content. The best known is the Oktoberfest beer, *Wiesenbier,* which is consumed by the *Mass* (litre-sized tankards) by millions of people. The other is a strong beer, *Starkbier,* produced in March and made originally by monks. This strong beer was meant to help them get through the days of fasting during Lent. Many people wanting a more thirst-quenching drink request a *Radler* (the word actually means cyclist), which is a mixture of beer and lemonade and is an ideal refreshment on summer jaunts. Beer is often presumed to be the most widely consumed drink in Germany. But on average, a German consumes almost 190 litres of coffee a year, compared with just 150 litres of beer.

Generally, the coffee served in Munich is stronger than in the United States (and I haven't come across instant coffee

here yet), but tea is weaker. Tea is placed only seventh in the order of preferred drinks in Munich; water, milk and fruit juices are more widely consumed. A cup of tea is usually a Darjeeling, Ceylon or Earl Grey tea bag floating in a cup of hot water. Another kind of tea—Schwarz Tee—is usually served with a slice of lemon instead of milk. If you cannot do without your tea in the English style, bring it with you as it is very difficult to find in any of the shops here. Fruit or herb teas such as nettle, camomile or peppermint, are just as popular, as well as the more unusually flavoured Rooibos.

BAVARIAN CUISINE

Historically, the Bavarian diet was rather limited. The influx of foreigners from all parts of the world into Germany has led to a far wider diversity of cuisine available in the country. Today, Munich offers a cosmopolitan culinary spread. Pizza, spaghetti bolognese or lasagne are standard fare in Bavaria as they are in Britain and the United States.

For breakfast, the commuter rushing in to Munich may nowadays grab a quick bowl of cereal, often muesli, or buy a roll from the bakery near the station. Traditionally, breakfast was a family occasion, heralding back to the days when a farmer and his extended family lived together and ate together. Those types of breakfast are still eaten in many Bavarian homes today, when there is time. A typical hearty breakfast consists of several types of cold meat such as *Schinken* (ham), *Speck* (bacon) which is always smoked and very thinly sliced, *Wurst* (sausage) and several types of *Käse* (cheeses), eaten with *Brot* (bread) or *Semmel* (rolls). Occasionally, there will be tomatoes or fruit if they are in season.

The most traditional breakfast food though is the *Weisswürst*, a pale veal sausage seasoned with parsley and served in pairs with sweet mustard. Customarily they should be consumed before 11:00 am but now they are often served as a light lunch too. Do not attempt to eat the tough skins. Traditionalists bite off one end and suck out the contents, but that requires a special technique or the entire process can become very messy!

A plate of salad often precedes the main meal of the day, which may begin as early as 11:30 am. When we first visited a Bavarian restaurant, we were unfamiliar with this fact and waited for our main course to eat the salad with. The waiter, on the other hand, was waiting for us to eat the salad before he brought out the main course. Needless to say, it turned out to be quite a long meal!

Soup may also be served. *Pfannkuchensuppe* is a clear soup with pieces of chopped pancake added, and *Leberknödelsuppe* is similar but has small liver dumplings cooked in it. Some people make vegetable soup, and bundles of root vegetables and *Suppengemüse* (herbs) can be bought specially-prepared in the shops. A warming, meaty goulash, not heavily spiced with paprika, is usual in winter, and *Eintopf* (a stew) can have beans, peas or lentils as the main constituent.

Schweinefleisch (pork), *Kartoffel* (potatoes) and *Kraut* (cabbage) are the standard Bavarian foods, as is the dense pale brown bread. Germans are one of the greatest pork consumers in the world and they prepare the meat in many ways. *Schweinebraten* is carved roast pork, whereas *Schweinshaxe* is a joint of meat from the bottom of the leg covered in crunchy crackling skin. Either of these may be accompanied by *Kartoffelknödel*—dumplings the size of tennis balls made from potatoes. An alternative is *Semmelknödel* that is made from stale bread (bought in bags at the supermarket), sometimes mixed with semolina, giving the dumplings a more slippery, rubbery consistency. It tastes great with rich gravy once you get used to the texture—some people never do. *Wiener Schnitzel* is known internationally as a thin fillet of pork coated in breadcrumbs that is fried. An alternative would be *Putenschnitzel*, also called *Truthahnschnitzel*, which uses turkey instead of pork. It is sometimes served with *Kartoffelsalat* (potato salad), which may be served either lukewarm or cold.

Spätzle is a home-made egg pasta which is grated rather than rolled. Each piece is about 3 cm (1.2 inch) long and more solid than Italian pasta. It is sometimes served as an accompaniment to meat and in a huge mound sprinkled with cheese, necessitating lots of vigorous exercise afterwards.

Pork sausage abounds in all its diversity: boiled, grilled or fried, thin or thick, served hot or cold with sliced fried potatoes or in a roll. *Currywurst*, a favourite of teenagers, tastes like a *Frankfurter*, but it has curry powder sprinkled over it and is served with dollops of tomato ketchup and *Pommes frites* (chips). *Leberkäse* is a meatloaf that also tastes like a skinless *Frankfurter* with a crispier top. *Leberkäse* is often served as a snack at kiosks and in beer gardens.

Hendl and *Hähnchen* are different names for chicken. The birds are much smaller here than those I've seen in other countries, so being served half a roast chicken is not as daunting as it sounds. *Ente* (roast duck) is another Bavarian favourite, often served with *Blaukraut* (red cabbage) and usually cooked with apples to make it sweet. It is unlike *Sauerkraut*, which is white cabbage cooked with vinegar and often caraway seeds.

Rehfleisch (venison) and *Keiler* (wild boar) are found on the menus quite often, and some restaurant owners actually hunt the animals themselves. Rabbit is another animal that occasionally pops up on a menu. Game and pork are often

served with *Preiselbeeren* at the side. Looking like a blob of red jam, *Preiselbeeren* is made from a tiny local berry with the sharp taste of cranberry. Several dishes have a *Spiegel Ei* (fried egg), a topping of crowning glory.

The fish most commonly seen on the menus is the locally caught *Zander*, which is a tasty white fish, a type of pike or perch. *Matjes* (young herring) is also a Bavarian favourite, served with salad, in a roll with *Zwiebel* (onion), or in mayonnaise salad with apples and onions and served with boiled potatoes.

Two vegetables that are especially celebrated when they come into season locally are *Pfifferlinge,* which are small yellow mushrooms and *Spargel* (asparagus). Then they appear on every menu, in sauces or as part of a dish to complement their particular tastes.

Rote Grütze is quite light—a mixture of morello cherries, red currants, blackcurrants and raspberries cooked in syrup, though a bit tangy nevertheless. Often served with *Schlagsahne/ Schlagrahme* (whipped cream), it is really delicious. For really hungry souls, or those who are feeling greedy, there is *Kaiserschmarrn*—a plateful of chopped pancake with sultanas, drenched in icing sugar; *Apfelstrudel*—filo pastry wrapped around stewed apple with cinnamon; or *Dampfnudel*—a huge sweet white dumpling served with vanilla sauce.

Desserts

Puddings are not a star feature of Bavarian cooking, as the portions of the main courses are usually so huge that no one can eat the desserts.

As in Austria, coffee and cake, often referred to as K&K, is an afternoon institution, served any time between 2:30 pm and 5:00 pm. All restaurants and cafés have a wide selection of mouth-watering *Gateaux* (cakes) to choose from, as well as *Torte* (fruit flans). Many an afternoon I have seen friends in cafés and restaurants around Munich chatting over huge slices of *Gateau*. It is no wonder that many of the people who come to live in Bavaria put on weight! A moment on the lips equals a lifetime on the hips. Luckily, those *Dirndls* (traditional skirts) cover a multitude of sins!

Many annual celebrations are associated with specific foods. As Easter time approaches, rounds of sweet bread are baked. These are similar in taste to a French brioche. Plain or with dried fruit and sprinkled with sliced almonds or icing sugar, *Osterfladen* is sold in all bakeries. Traditionally, heavy sponge cakes in the shape of small lambs, *Oster Lamm*, are baked for the Easter weekend, though Easter hares are now quite common too. As in most Western countries, small chocolate eggs are hidden in the house or garden for the children to find.

Each family has its own Christmas recipes, but in this area, a large, crispy goose is the highlight of the meal served on Christmas Day. A lighter meal, usually consisting of sausage, being served on Christmas Eve. Pink sugar pigs, a symbol of good luck, are often exchanged among friends. Traditional Christmas biscuits are baked, *Lebkuchen* being the most famous. *Stollen*—a long fruit cake with marzipan in the centre —is greeted with great enthusiasm.

RESTAURANTS AND CAFÉS

Most people arriving in Munich for the first time head for the city centre, and Marienplatz is an excellent meeting place for people from different parts of town. Having travelled on foot, by train, tram or bus to get there, most people want some form of refreshment, and there are several cafés and bars overlooking the square, each with a different character. They may be slightly more expensive than cafés further afield, but are still cheaper than in many large cities around the world. In 2007, smoking remains acceptable in most restaurants. Some patrons light up before the meal and between courses. A few places are beginning to introduce no-smoking areas, but these are small in comparison to the main areas and are not usually screened from the rest of the room.

Do check at the door before entering a restaurant whether credit cards are accepted, as not all places do so. It would be embarrassing to have to dash off to a cash point for money, leaving a partner as a hostage.

Dining al fresco at cafés and restaurants is very popular amongst the residents of Munich.

Tables with *Reserviert* signs are to be avoided though sometimes they state a time too, and if you can be up and away before then, you can eat there. But beware of tables that have either a flag on them or a notice above with the word '*Stammtisch*'. These are reserved week in week out for a specific group of people, usually a club, who meet there to eat and chat and you will be turned away if you are not part of their crowd.

When you arrive at a table, drinks are generally ordered first and brought to the table. If water is asked for, bottled carbonated water is served, but the *Munich Leitungswasser* (tap water) is fine and usually complimentary. The *Brezen* (pretzels) found in baskets on the table are charged for and you will be asked at the end of a meal how many you ate. Every dish is brought to the table as soon as it is ready, and people start to eat as they are served rather than wait for everyone to start together. In some instances the first served have almost completed their course before the last on the table are given their meals.

At the end of the meal, the diner may be asked *"Hat's geschmeckt?"* which means "Did it taste good?" The polite answer is *"Sehr gut, danke"* or *"Ja, danke."* Individual diners are then asked what they have eaten and drunk, so that a total charge can be calculated. If there are two of you, the question may be *"Zusammen?"* that is "Are you together?" What it really means is whether two bills should be made out instead of one. Tax is included in the bill but not usually a service charge or tip. Check the bill if you are given one. Tourists often give a 10 per cent to 15 per cent tip, which is the practice in the international hotels. It is, however, acceptable just to round it up to the nearest euro or € 5 for a larger bill. This is given directly to the waiter or waitress when the bill is paid and not left on the table.

Central Munich

The *Rathaus* has its own restaurant tucked in the basement of the building. Access is by a narrow staircase in the front of the building. The restaurant is decorated in typical Bavarian style with lots of wood, flower arrangements and subtle lighting. The food is also typically Bavarian, but there is a wide variety on the menu, and a good meal, surprisingly, is not too expensive for this prime location.

Ludwig Beck has a small coffee shop on the first floor of its prestigious store, which is a good place for people-watching while the oblivious shoppers peruse the merchandise downstairs. It is only a small café, so it can get crowded quickly. Rischart's is on the south-east corner of Marienplatz, towards the Viktualienmarkt. Bread, sandwiches, *Brezen* and doughnuts are sold at the front of the shop but inside, there is a wonderful range of *Gateaux* that can be bought by the slice. To the left of the shop is an unobtrusive staircase leading up to the modern, light and airy café, which has nine windows overlooking the square. Of course, the tables near the windows are snapped up as soon as any are free. All the clientele, from trendy teens to aged dowagers, always appreciate the delicious breakfasts, morning coffee, light lunches and afternoon refreshments here.

Café Glockenspiel has its entrance down a little alley on the left of Rosenstrasse, which leads off Marienplatz. From here, a lift can be taken to the fifth floor, though there is a spiral staircase for the more energetic. There is a Bavarian bar that can become rather smoky but has a wonderful view overlooking the square. There is also a café at the back of the building overlooking a car park but as that is five flights above, it does not really detract from the ambience. In summer, the area can be opened to a welcome breeze.

A quaint, elegant tea room which also provides light meals is Woerner's Café am Dom. Like Rischart's, it is also on the first floor above a cake shop, but under the arcade on the west of the square. It has crisp tablecloths, small crystal chandeliers, polite staff and if you are lucky, a table by the window. Bohne und Malz is down a small passage to the left as you walk up Theatinerstrasse. It sells thirst-quenching beers like *Löwenbrau* and *Franziskaner Weissbier*.

The Ratskeller Weinstube is part of the *Rathaus* building but its entrance is round the back facing Marienhof. Several times a year, there are wine-tasting days when vintners from all over southern Germany encourage people to sample and buy their wines. Every Sunday there is a special family lunch, which is very good value.

A few steps further north and you find yourself stepping into the traditional atmosphere of a 200-year-old coffee house. Open for breakfast, Tambosi at Odeonsplatz, 18, lets one sit and soak in the morning sun on their terrace facing Odeonsplatz, or go through the arch in the adjacent wall and shelter in the shade of their parasols in the Hofgarten as the summer heat rises.

Away from the central square, one can find more expensive restaurants in which to wine and dine. The top hotels all have exclusive restaurants that serve international cuisine, but though the food is very good, they do not generally give the flavour of the area.

Reservations must be made in all the restaurants as people in Munich often eat out. Most restaurants are full by 8:00 pm.

American

The Hard Rock Café is familiarly like the rest of the worldwide chain with its glass cases of pop memorabilia and chunky burgers. Tables cluster on the square on sunny summer days, facing the Hofbrauhaus opposite. It is located at Platzl 1.

Edison & Co, at Schulstrasse 28 (tel: (089) 1303-9393), specialises in making Americans feel at home, especially at Thanksgiving, as does the California Grill in the Marriott Hotel, Berliner Strasse 93; tel: (089) 3600-2809. Here they serve authentic American food and put out the Stars and Stripes during Thanksgiving.

Café Atlas is one of my favourite places to hang out for lunch. On a bright day, their west facing sun terrace is packed, protected from the noise and pollution of the road by a glass screen. It serves great breakfasts with bagels and huge salads served on colourful chunky plates. Find it at Innere Wiener Strasse 2; tel: (089) 480-2997.

Bavarian

The Spatenhaus an der Oper Bräustuben at Residenzstrasse 12 (tel: (089) 290-7060) is the place to eat before or after going to the Nationaltheater. Traditionally Bavarian with an international clientele, the service is excellent as is the food and the prices are not wildly expensive.

The Asam-Schlössel, Maria-Einsiedel-Strasse 45, Thalkirchen (tel: (089) 723-6373) is a Bavarian restaurant with a wonderful ambience and truly Bavarian menu. Weisses Bräuhaus, Tal 10 (tel: (089) 299-875) also has excellent Bavarian fare served at large tables under ornate old light fittings.

Chinese

Win-Wah, Zschokkestrasse 55 (tel: (089) 5701-222) in Laim and Fuh-Guei, Boschetriederstrasse 51 (tel: (089) 7809-099) in Obersendling are open for lunch at 11:30 am. They do a great Sunday buffet brunch and remain open until 11:30 pm. Both have conservatories and provide underground parking for their customers.

The Shanghai Restaurant, Sonnenstrasse 3 (tel: (089) 592-744) is open daily from 11:30 am till 11:00 pm and serves good authentic Chinese food.

English

The Victorian House, Frauenstrasse 14 (tel: (089) 2554-6947) is an English enclave where one can have afternoon tea and scones at 4:00 pm. But one can also drop by for breakfast from 9:30 am and dinner until 11:00 pm.

French

Chez Philippe, Holzstrasse 16 (tel: (089) 266-199) is a cosy restaurant with friendly French staff. It is not far from Sendlinger Tor. A short bar provides before-dinner drinks while waiting for a table, but it is better to book ahead. It is open from 7:00 pm to 1:00 am.

Le Faubourg, Kirchenstrasse 5 (tel: (089) 475-533) is open Monday to Saturday from 6:00 pm to 1:00 am though the kitchen actually stops cooking at 11:00 pm. The décor is a little sparse but the wonderful food and great service more than make up for that. The waiters and waitresses take time to explain the menu in German, French or English.

Indian

Shiva, Augustenstrasse 96 (tel: (089) 523-2888) is the favourite of our Swedish and Argentinian friends, with lots of dark red furnishings and candles. My husband, John, however, thinks Maharani, Rottmannstrasse 24 (tel: (089) 527-912) and also at Baldeplatz 1 (tel: (089) 776-713) has the best Indian food in town. Swagat, Prinzregentenplatz 13 (tel: (089) 4708-4844) is the favourite of our Pakistani and Dutch friends. It is located in a cellar, serves good food and provides deferential, attentive service. Be warned—the cigarette smoke can spoil one's enjoyment when the place gets very busy.

Italian

Bei Mario, Adalbertstrasse 15 (tel: (089) 280-0460) is great for the students' special night out. Serving delicious Italian dishes and perfect pizzas, it also offers a good choice of wines as accompaniment to the food. During summer, tables are set up in their inner courtyard so that diners can enjoy their meal outdoors. It is open from 11:30 am to 12:30 am.

Piazza Linda, Elizabethstrasse 12 (tel: (089) 2727-2201) is owned by an Italian-American singer, who has made this cellar restaurant a mix of both cultures, with live music most evenings and great food.

Japanese

My friend Doris loves Japanese food, and one of our favourites is Tokami. It has four restaurants in Munich specialising in seafood and sushi. They are sophisticated, expensive but excellent.

- Rablstrasse 45
  Tel: (089) 448-9526
- Kanalstrasse 14
  Tel: (089) 2194-9970
- Theresienstrasse 54
  Tel: (089) 2889-6760
- Wurzerstrasse 18
  Tel: (089) 2554-6942

I also love the atmosphere of Sushi and Soul, Klenzestrasse 71; tel: (089) 201-0992. The food is ok and there's good music for the young and trendy. Sushi Duke Restaurant, Platzl 3 (tel: (089) 2280-7500) is where our daughter chose to have her 21st birthday dinner and the food was absolutely delicious. Another firm favourite is Matoi, Hans-Sachs-Strasse 10; tel: (089) 260-5268.

Mexican

Enchiladas at Gabelsbergerstrasse 97 is fun and noisy and definitely a great place to go for a drink with friends. It has good food and great cocktails. Booking ahead is a must. Its opening hours are between 6:00 pm and 1:00 am. Tel: (089) 522-297.

Slovenian

The Dalmatiner Grill is a family-run business north of Prinzregenten-Strasse, at Geibelstrasse 10; tel: (089) 470-4415. There is a garden at the back and it boasts good food and friendly staff. It is a favourite of the expat community and a great place for family parties.

Vegetarian

For her 18th birthday celebrations, Amanda chose Prinz Myshkin, Hackenstrasse 2; tel: (089) 265-596. The décor is modern and stark, and unusually for Munich, there is a good-sized non-smoking area. There are great pasta dishes and enormous salads on offer. It is open from 11:30 am till midnight.

A really great place to wander is the Schrannenhalle—a new venue in the converted warehouse to the south of the Viktualienmarkrt. There are lots of different food experiences under one roof including a typical Bavarian bar, as well as small shops selling everything from toys to *Trachten*. In the centre is a stage for gigs and when there is a big football match a wide screen comes down to show it.

There are cafés in the larger stores and many along the shopping streets, as well as those tucked away in corners that only the locals know about. It is always good to get recommendations from people who have lived in Munich for a while.

BARS

There are Irish, English, American and Australian bars in Munich where the English language is spoken behind the counter and by many of the regulars. Feeling lonely or just a long way from home? Pop into one of these and strike up a conversation.

Günther Murphy's, Nikolaistrasse 9 (tel: (089) 398-911) is a favourite of our friends in their twenties and thirties. It is open 5:00 pm to 1:00 am, Monday to Friday; 2:00 pm to 3:00 am on Saturday; and noon to 1:00 am on Sunday, when you can order brunch. Serving good pub food, it gets packed by mid-evening, especially at weekends. So if you want a seat, go early. Visit their website: http://www.gunther-murphys.com.

Shamrock Irish Pub, Trautenwolf Strasse 6 (tel: (089) 331-081) is just off Leopold Strasse and close to Gisela Strasse U-Bahn. It operates from 5:00 pm to 1:00 am on Monday to Thursday and is open till 3:00 am on Friday and Saturday.

On weekends, it starts earlier at 2:00 pm. There is live music daily from 9:00 pm, while an Irish folk session takes place every Sunday. Student night is on Mondays when drinks are cheaper. It is a great place for friends to gather to watch televised soccer matches from the English Premier League and the Bundesliga, and other sports such as Gaelic football and hurling. An added bonus is that it serves Newcastle brown as well as Beamish, Murphy's and Guiness Irish beer. Its website can be found at http://www.irish-pub-munich.com.

Molly Malone's, Kellerstrasse 21 (tel: (089) 688-7510) is open from 5:00 pm to 1:00 am on weekdays and from noon till 1:00 am on weekends. Close to Gasteig, the pub attracts the local Germans as well as *Auslanders*. Good Irish food is available, as well as the usual quick pub grub and a comprehensive range of Scotch and Irish whiskey.

Kilians Irish Pub, Frauenplatz 11 (tel: (089) 2421-9910) opens 11:00 am to 1:00 am daily. It publishes a programme of events to inform guests of the many different live band performances—from rock, blues, Irish and American folk to the oldies. It claims an international menu of Irish, Mexican and American food. The sunny terrace is just behind the Frauenkirche.

Ned Kelly's Australian Bar (tel: (089) 2421-9910) shares the same staircase as Kilians. Ned Kelly's is an Aussie sports bar that screens the Bundesliga, English Premier League and Aussie Rules football. It specialises in Australasian food.

Outland, The Australian Bar, is at Weissenburger Platz 3; tel: (089) 4899-7880. With an Aussie-based menu, we have eaten here several times, and they have great fish and chips, but not of the English variety. There are two unobtrusive small screened TVs permanently tuned in to sports programmes, but the larger screens are brought in for important football games.

Barfly is an American-Latin bar and restaurant. Sunday and Monday are fondue evenings, served with baguette and pickles. Simply scrumptious! It is located at Sternstrasse 21; tel: (089) 224-491; website: http://www.barfly-munich.de.

The Big Easy–New Orleans bar and restaurant at Frundsbergstrasse 46 (tel: (089) 1589-0253), at the corner of Ruffinistrasse, north-east from Rotkreutzplatz U-Bahn is open 5:00 pm till 1:00 am. Happy hours are from 5:00 pm to 8:00 pm. There is a huge list of cocktails. On Sundays and holidays, it opens at 10:00 am for a jazz-filled brunch. It has a brilliant atmosphere where we always feel mellow and relaxed.

BEER GARDENS

Unlike the past, meals are now served in most beer gardens at tables that are covered with clothes. The plain uncovered wooden tables remain available for those who

The Chinese Tower in the Englischer Garten is a popular beer garden.

bring their own picnics or who buy meals from the self-service windows in the beer gardens. Tables are shared with whoever comes along regardless of rank or creed. *"Ist hier noch frei?"* meaning "Is this free?" is asked by newcomers when seeing an available seat. Beer is generally served at wooden kiosks, labelled *Ausschank*, by the *Mass* though some do serve *Halbe* (half-measures).

When paying for the food or beer, often at a separate kiosk, you will find the cutlery. But a *Pfand* (deposit) must be paid for the plates and glasses. Proof of payment of the deposit is sometimes a plastic disc that you return to another window labelled *Pfandrückgabe* with the dirty crockery at the end of the meal. Your deposit is then returned. Some beer gardens have people clearing the tables, so be careful that your crockery is not whisked away if you have paid a deposit for them and not had a disc.

The legal drinking age is 16, so beer gardens are popular places for teenagers to gather in the summer. As many beer gardens are in residential areas, the closing times are strictly adhered to. Usually last orders are served at 10:30 pm, though I have known some that stop serving much earlier.

Driving round Munich one passes several breweries with their huge copper vats displayed, so you know a beer garden must be close by. Then again, there is one close by wherever you are as there are more than 180 in the vicinity!

A very popular garden is the Augustiner Keller, Arnulfstrasse 52; tel: (089) 594-393. Though not far from Hauptbahnhof, it is far enough away from the centre of town to attract just locals and tourists in the know. It still gets really busy on a warm day, and there are lots of tables inside too for the cooler evenings. It is open until 1:00 am every night.

The Paulaner brewery's Salvatorkeller is situated on the top of Nockerberg in the Au district. In November 1999 its great hall burnt down, but it has since been rebuilt and is a magnificent place to get views over the bustling city if you can escape on a quiet afternoon.

The Chinese Tower beer garden, Chinesischer Turm is open in the Englischer Garten from 10:00 am to 11:00 pm; tel: (089) 3838-7327. You can get there by taking bus 154 or 54 or tram 17. It has a seating capacity for 7,000 and a variety of different fare. Behind the seating area is an old-fashioned carousel for the children as well as some modern play equipment. A brass oom-pah band often plays in the tower to entertain the visitors. It is a great place to end an early evening or weekend stroll. Adjacent is a more sophisticated restaurant with lots of tables outside and attentive waiters.

Munich's Beer History

In 1516, Munich was the first city to have a Law of Purity for its beer. By then lots of beer was being brewed, especially in the monasteries. But when leaders of the Roman Catholic Church announced in 1539 that no one could produce beer between the saints days of St George and St Michael, which fell on 23 April and 29 September respectively, ways had to be devised to keep the beer fresh throughout the hot Munich summers.

In winter, great pits were filled with ice and snow to keep the beer cool, a precursor to the storage cellars dug in the grounds of the breweries. Though the beer kept better in the cellars, chestnut trees with their broad hands of leaves were planted to shade the cellars and any beer stored above the ground. The beer still grew warm as it was transported from the breweries to the drinkers, so the breweries encouraged the drinkers to come to them, by placing tables under the shade of the trees. At first the beer gardens also served food, but the local restaurateurs whose business was affected complained to the king. Ludwig I then declared that if a person drank in a beer garden, they would have to bring their own food. While there were scores of breweries in and around Munich in the past, today there are only about six large breweries in town, but they supply countless beer gardens.

Further north in the Englischer Garten is the Seehaus beer garden on the banks of the Kleinhesseloher See; tel: (089) 3816-130. Take the U3 or U6 to Münchener Freiheit to get there. It is open Monday to Friday, 11:00 am till midnight, opening an hour earlier on Saturday and Sunday. With no residential housing close by, it closes late.

Right at the north end of the Englischer Garten is Zum Aumeister, Sondermeierstrasse 1; tel: (089) 325-224. It has a sizeable car park and is not far from the U6 at Studentenstadt. There is a great playground to keep the children occupied while the parents carouse. It is open until 11:00 pm.

The Hirschgarten or deer garden is near the Liam S-Bahn, and open 9:00 am to 11:00 pm; tel: (089) 172-591. It can seat 10,000 revellers at any one time. There are lots of play apparatus for the kids and a large enclosure of deer, hence its name.

Hofbräuhaus am Platzl, Platzl 9 (tel: (089) 221-676) is the oldest and most famous brewery in town and is often packed with tourists. Open 9:00 am to midnight, it often has a brass band performing, which is great for the atmosphere. It seems to be the only place open in town after lunch on Christmas eve, so a good place for foreigners to congregate.

Hofbräukeller, WienerPlatz, Haidhausen (tel: (089) 459-9250) has an extensive garden outside and several large dining rooms, including a 60-seater for non-smokers inside. It is very popular with the city dwellers.

The Max-Emanuel-Brauerei can be reached via U3 or U6 to Universität; tel: (089) 271-5158. A small but very trendy beer garden, it is situated next to the university at Adalbertstrasse

33. It throngs with students but closes at 9:00 pm, so the locals can get their sleep.

The Viktualienmarkt has several areas set aside as small beer gardens, where shoppers can quench their thirst whilst appreciating the aroma of exotic spices, flowers, fresh fruit and cheeses.

Outside the City

Waldwirtschaft Grosshesselohe situated above the River Isar at Georg-Kalb-Strasse 3, Grosshesselohe (tel: (089) 7499-4030) is a short walk from the S7 Grosshesselohe Isartalbahnhof. Open 11:00 am to midnight, the restaurant has been in existence for over 200 years. On summer weekends, a jazz band performs in the garden to as many as 2000 drinkers. Kugler-Alm, Linienstrasse 91, Deisenhofen on the S2 is a lovely beer garden to visit in the south of Munich. Lots of people make it a designated stop while on a country bike ride, or make it their destination after the short pedal from the station.

ENJOYING THE BAVARIAN CULTURE

CHAPTER 7

'Mir san mir.'
'I am me.'
Bavarians are proud of being Bavarians and feel special.
—A popular German saying

VACATION SPOTS NEARBY

Munich is a wonderful hub for holidays in Europe. The pretty old Bavarian towns of Regensberg, Garmisch-Partenkirchen, Erding and Landshut are close enough to visit in one afternoon. Impressive Passau, at the confluence of the rivers Inn, Ilz and Danube is only a couple of hours drive away, as is beautiful Salzburg, associated with Mozart and the 1960s film, *The Sound of Music.* The eastern end of Lake Constance, Bodensee, takes a similar amount of time to reach if you travel south-west, whilst Prague takes just over three hours. We have driven back from Lake Garda, Vienna and Slovenia in four hours. Berlin is less than six hours directly up the motorway.

With an overnight stop, Paris can be reached in comfort and also the French coasts, either on the North Sea or the Mediterranean. Friends drive to Spain with just two overnight stops. These are average journeys by car, though when holiday traffic crawls, it can at least treble the length of a journey. So it is best to avoid travelling on the first weekends of the school holidays and the month of August unless you travel by train or plane.

MUNICH'S CULTURAL HERITAGE

Is there any other city in the world with a greater love for its cultural heritage coupled with such an appreciation of new ideas and art forms than Munich? The diversity of venues and the range of interests catered for in Munich are truly amazing for a city of its size. Many local people frequent the cultural centres not just at weekends or on special occasions but as part of their everyday routine. Prices of cultural performances and venues are often lower than in the cities such as London, Paris or San Francisco.

Realising the abundance of interesting places awaiting me after coming to live in Munich, I decided to try and sample a different cultural experience at least once a month. Three years later I had barely covered all of the museums, galleries, theatres and concert halls found in Munich. I found out about places primarily by word of mouth and from tourist books. Information about individual performances can be gleaned from the local press and the KULTUR i SZENE i information posts dotted around the city. These are cylindrical boards approximately 3 m (about 10 ft) in height where posters about cultural performances are pasted. Carry a pen and diary as you may want to jot down the date of an antique fair in Planegg or a concert at the Muffathalle.

Interest in the arts has been fostered in Bavaria by generations of rulers. An art gallery in what later became the Central Mint in Hofgraben was erected between 1563 and 1567 in the Italian Renaissance style to house the Ducal Art Collection. In 1565, Duke Albrecht V decreed that the treasures of the Wittelsbachs must never be sold, laying the basis of today's magnificent Residence Treasury and the State Collection of Egyptian Art. In 1571, Maximilian I instigated the building of the beautiful Hall of Antiquities in his palace, the Residenz, to house works of art. His descendants continued to pour money into architecture, painting, sculpture and music.

The northern part of the Hofgarten arcade was built to accommodate the art collection of Elector Karl Theodor, but the most beautiful décor was created in the late 18th century when Francois Cuvilliés the Elder designed his small court theatre, which has been called 'a jewel among the few surviving European court theatres.' Opera and drama are still performed in this theatre and in the Herkulessaal and

Max-Joseph-Saal rooms in the Residenz, the royal palace where everyone can feel like an aristocrat. For reservations, call tel: (089) 296-836.

MUSICAL LEGACY

To encourage people to listen to classical music, the Munich Philharmonic Orchestra performs open-air concerts in Odeonsplatz under the summer skies. Seats can be paid for and reserved, but the music drifts far beyond the seating area. Try the website: http://www.klassik-am-odeonsplatz. de for more information. On some summer evenings, an opera performance is shown free of charge on wide screens in Max Joseph Platz, as it is being performed in the adjacent opera house. People who have been before bring stools to sit on and wine to sip.

A Love for Munich

Music is held close to the hearts of most Munich people, and the performers return their appreciation. I once met an internationally renowned conductor on the S8 train, dashing up to rehearsals in Unterföhring. He had turned down what seemed to me a fortune offered by an American orchestra so that he could remain conducting in Munich and Salzburg.

Munich has links with three great composers. Mozart was invited to Munich, and between 1780 and 1781 he composed his opera *Idomeneo* while living in Burgstrasse. The opera was premiered in the Cuvilliés Theatre.

Richard Wagner lived on Brienner Strasse under the tutelage of Ludwig II and made many of his musical debuts in Munich, including the *Mastersingers, Rhinegold, Tristan and Isolde,* and the *Valkyrie*. Five of his operas were first staged at the Nationaltheater.

Richard Strauss' opera, *Salome,* was first acclaimed in Munich's Nationaltheater in 1906, though it was banned in other countries. Subsequently, he also premiered *Friedenstag* and *Capriccio* in the same theatre.

WORLD-CLASS THEATRES

The Prinzregententheater, Prinzregentenplatz 12 (tel: (089) 218-502), which was completed in 1901, was built to emulate the democratic, amphitheatre style of the Bayreuth Theatre that Wagner had instigated. The Prinzregententheater soon became famous for its Wagnerian productions, and the Munich Opera Festival was founded here.

The classically styled Nationaltheater, Max-Joseph-Platz 1 (tel: (089) 2185-1920), which seats almost 2,100 people, now puts on 360 performances a year with an average audience attendance of over 90 per cent. During the Opera Festival, the hall is often over 99 per cent full, amazing numbers for any theatre. Except for a six-week break between 1 August and 14 September, it is open all year round. This repertory theatre performs all operas in their original language. Employing over 1,000 people per day, the theatre is always bustling with people clearing and cleaning the whole stage area each night so that the next stage set can be constructed from 7:00 am the next morning. The magnificent chandelier hanging over the auditorium still sees most of the audience dressed in style. I was told by a local man that though seats at the opera were not cheap, the money collected did not even meet half the costs of production, and the Bavarian government usually steps in to subsidise the shortfall.

The Theater am Gärtnerplatz is a heavy grey building built in 1865 in the Italian neo-Renaissance style. It is another venue much loved by music lovers. Besides orchestral productions, ballet, opera and operettas in German are regularly staged. Tel: (089) 201-6767.

The Deutsches Theater, Schwanthalerstrasse 13 is tucked away in a cobbled courtyard, where pre-theatre wine and ice cream is served in summer; tel: (089) 5523-4444. Many popular Broadway shows, such as *Grease, Evita* and *Jesus Christ Superstar,* have been staged here, sometimes in English. The lighter operas, such as *Carmen*, have also been performed at the Deutsches Theater. The fact that most musicals are translated and performed in German should not be a problem if you know the stories beforehand.

The glass and brick construction set on the hill at the north-west end of Rosenheimer Strasse is the Gasteig Arts Centre, built in 1985. With its stark exterior and towering windows facing the city, it is the home of the Munich Philharmonic Orchestra. The main auditorium, which has wonderful acoustics, is decked in wood, giving it a cosy feel, though I do not find the seats particularly comfortable. The music is splendid and the audience appreciative. Having gone along on the spur of the moment mid-week, John and I felt like country cousins wearing woollen jumpers when compared to our neighbours wearing linen or silk! People in Munich make a grand occasion of attending a musical performance. The Carl Orff Hall, the second largest hall in the centre is the venue for drama productions.

The America Haus in Karolinenplatz has no frills but puts on good performances. It intersperses English and German performances. The plays span the decades, and *The Importance of Being Earnest, 1984* and *Moon Palace* were all produced in one season.

Münchner Kammerspiele on Maximilianstrasse 34-35 is only visited by native or fluent German speakers, as the performances in this quaint art nouveau theatre are always in German. Built in 1901 and restored in 1970, it has staged performances of *Waiting for Godot* and *The Crucible.*

There are also a couple of English-speaking theatre companies in Munich, and details are often available in the press. Munich also holds concert seasons in three dazzling palaces:

- Nymphenburg
  Tel: (089) 179-080
- Blutenburg, Seldweg
  Tel: (089) 834-4945
- Schleissheim, in Oberschleissheim
  Tel: (089) 315-8720

There are many other theatres in and around Munich that give praiseworthy performances, but these three are the most well-known, and they feature English productions as well.

Getting Tickets

Tickets for all concerts in Munich can be bought in advance from the individual venues. They are also available from ticket booths around the city. The most central venues are in the tourist information office in Marienplatz and the kiosk in the underground station in Marienplatz; tel: (089) 264-620. There is another ticket kiosk inside Pasing station (tel: (089) 820-6242) and one at Ostbahnhof. Karstadt supplies tickets in their shops in Schwabing (tel: (089) 3366-59) and Karstadt Oberpollinger (tel: (089) 2902-5499). You can also purchase tickets at WOM at Kaufingerstrasse 15; tel: (089) 2699-942. Seven of the main Aral garages sell tickets, and the ticket office in the Olympia-Eissportzentrum sells tickets for all events in the Olympiapark; tel: (089) 5481-8181.

MARCHING TO THE BRASS BANDS

Of course Munich is not only famous for classical music. Most areas and many of the trades have their own brass bands or *Blaskapelle*. Musicians from other countries are often welcome to join, as long as they wear the individual uniform

Outdoor musical performances, like this free concert in a park, abound in Munich.

by which each band is identified. One guy we know said that he found playing his trumpet more fun in Bavaria than in his native country, as the bands were not as competitive. The emphasis was as much on the fun as on the music making, and the beer drinking sessions after rehearsals added to the relaxed atmosphere and overall enjoyment.

There are always street performers around the centre of Munich. On summer weekends after the shops close, these performers often congregate so close to each other that operatic arias mingle with the sounds of Hungarian violins, or South American pipe bands with rock musicians. It all makes for a wonderful, musically stimulating environment.

MUSEUMS

On a gloomy October day four months after arriving in Munich, a visiting friend and I decided to investigate the Deutsche Museum. Built on an island in the River Isar, it lies between Isartor and Rosenheimer Platz S-Bahn stations. Engineer Oskar von Miller conceived the idea for the museum in 1903, but it was not until 1925 that the museum was inaugurated and it is now billed as the best science and technology museum in Germany. What fantastic foresight!

The museum has evolved with time and houses some brilliant modern exhibits, as well as older ones. Not just hours but days could be spent inside visiting the different areas. It is a wonderful place to visit with older children, friends or just on your own. There are timed tours, lectures and demonstrations each day; it is worth joining as many of these tours as possible if only to see the visual effects.

My friend loved the exhibits on the evolution of the different types of machines, as well as of computers, telephones, aeroplanes, cars and motorbikes. I loved the international collection of musical instruments and listening to some of them being played by talented artists. The bridge building section was surprisingly interesting and the glass blowing demonstration fun. On the sixth floor, right at the top of the museum and next to the garden of sundials is a planetarium. For a short rest and some refreshments in between tours there are two cafés, including a nice coffee shop at the top with panoramic views of the surrounding areas on a sunny day.

Next door to the Deutsches Museum is the IMAX cinema, which screens films on nature or technology on a huge screen. Some of the films are in 3D format, creating such a visual impact that the text takes second place.

I adore the ancient Greek and Roman sculptures found in the Glyptothek—one of the 'Greek temples' facing each other in Königplatz. Although the collection is not huge, it is beautiful and well displayed. Windows looking on to a central courtyard allow light to filter through the building and one can sit out there in the summer with coffee and cake from the cafeteria before feasting one's eyes on more antiquities. The Corinthian 'temple' opposite houses the State Collection of Antiquities.

The Münchner Stadtmuseum buildings, a little south of Marienplatz in Jakobsplatz, were built to house the armoury in 1431. Although the weapons are still displayed here, they are just one facet of the popular city museum. Here visitors are given an insight into the development of the city. It is fascinating to be able to pick out present-day landmarks on models depicting the city centuries ago, to see paintings of bridges swept away in floods, and to have a window into life as it was in the poorer Au district two centuries ago. The original statues of the 10 Morris dancers by Erasmus von Grasser, often represented on souvenirs, are displayed here. But what I enjoyed most are the costumes, everyday wear and elegant evening gowns worn by people in Munich in the past. Others may find the film museum and the puppet museum, both within the same building, of great interest too.

ART GALLERIES

When I first came to Munich on a visit, I spent much of my time familiarising myself with the delights of central Munich. One of the galleries I was impressed with was the Kunsthalle, on Theatinerstrasse, where I saw a spectacular exhibition of artifacts from the Medici family. The gallery was imposing and gloomy, but the exhibits were beautifully lit, creating an air of mystery and splendour. When I eventually settled in

...unich, I searched for the gallery but had no luck as I could not remember its exact location. Two years later, however, it emerged from the chrysalis in which it had been hiding. The dark old building was transfigured into a glass edifice as part of the Fünf Höfe shopping complex. The entrance now looked to me like a large ticket booth for a sporting fixture, exacerbated by the fact that it was packed with people and there was only one lady selling tickets. There was no large sign announcing what it was and my friend and I had to ask a security guard where to find the Kunsthalle der Hypo-Kulturstiftung, while standing just outside the gallery's shop and back entrance! The name is in fact etched into the glass of the window. A quite narrow, wooden staircase with a slender wrought iron handrail led to the first floor, where the cloakroom and cafeteria are located. We trudged up another staircase to the actual gallery (there was a lift available too) where a few dark blue bucket chairs in the vestibule comforted those weary from the stairs. Headsets were available to guide you round the exhibition of inter-connecting rooms. At the time of our visit, the exhibition was on paintings from the 1920s by artists from many countries, including Germany, Italy and the United States. The Kunsthalle holds many differing exhibitions, each lasting just a few weeks' long. Those that I have attended have been exceptionally good and as it is so close to the centre of town, one can easily pop in for the odd hour, if you do not mind slightly expensive entrance fees.

 The Städtische Galerie im Lenbachhaus, Luisenstrasse 33, is an art gallery housed in an exquisite Italian villa that was completed in 1891, which was the home of painter Franz von Lenbach. It has two wings sheltering a peaceful garden replete with sculptures and fountains. It is now the home of many paintings by The Blue Rider group, which was headed by Wassily Kandinsky, but it also includes works by his former pupil and mistress Gabrielle Münter, and friends Franz Marc, Paul Klee, August Macke and Alexei Jawlensky. The colourful walls enhance the vibrant paintings, where more contemporary works are also on display. The small café has an inventive, delicious menu for light meals as well as snacks.

The best-known art galleries in Munich are the Pinotheken. The Alte Pinakothek, the Neue Pinakothek and the Pinakothek de Moderne are situated on Barer Strasse 27 and 29. The Alte Pinakothek and the Neue Pinakothek were so severely damaged during World War II that it was not until 1957 that the first building was reconstructed with some modification. The other had to be completely demolished and re-built. In its place stands a wonderfully modern gallery completed in 1981. The type of art exhibited in the Alte Pinakothek is mainly religious, but there are also splendid works by Old Masters such as Raphael, Rembrandt, Rubens, Brueghel, Tintoretto and Tiepolo. By contrast, the Neue Pinakothek displays 19th and 20th century paintings in light and airy rooms. Works by Paul Gauguin, Francisco de Goya, Vincent van Gogh, Paul Cézanne, Max Klinger, Gustav Klimt and Franz von Stuck are just some of the amazing paintings to be found here. There is also a lovely little restaurant that has friendly service, a bonus to each visit.

The glass and metal Pinakothek der Moderne opened in Autumn 2002 on Gabelsbergerstrasse, is itself a work of art. It is home to contemporary and modern art in all its forms. Another favourite of many for modern art is the Haus der Kunst at the southern end of the Englischer Garten. Built to exhibit Nazi art, its corner stone was laid by Hitler, but now it mainly displays international art of the 20th century.

Outdoor Art

Art does not end at a gallery's front door in Munich. There are ancient and modern works of art displayed in the streets all over the city—some abstract and some delicately realistic. One of the tallest must be the five-ton 'Walking Man' erected in 1995 in Leopoldstrasse. The smooth white lines of this faceless, genderless giant outside the Münchener Rückversicherung offices is shielded from the traffic's gaze by a row of poplar trees.

Another more subtle work is the 'Man on Construction Beam' above the entrance to Kaufinger Passage. It was a couple of years before I noticed his precarious balancing act, as he is high above most people's line of vision. A fountain in the shape of a huge tuba makes people smile as they enter the Gasteig Centre.

Fountains and waterfalls are usually covered with custom-made wooden hoardings for the winter to protect them from damage by frost and ice. Not all works in Munich are permanent—the Nationaltheater once had a yellow ring of neon light encircling its main façade, which was used to promote the performance of Wagner's *Ring Cycle* when it was performed.

CINEMAS

The largest venue that shows English-language films is The Cinema at Nymphenburger Strasse 31, west from Stiglmaierplatz U1; tel: (089) 555-255; website: http://www.cinema-muenchen.de. It is the place that seems to get the new releases first, so you can forgive the limited snacks of drinks, tacos and popcorn.

Museum Lichtspiele is at Lilienstrasse 2, between Isartor and Rosenheimer S-Bahn stations. For reservations, call (089) 482-403 or visit their website: http://www.museum-lichtspieler.de. It has four screens with tiny auditoriums. You have a choice of films but for popular films you should book ahead. It has a small counter serving drinks, sweets and popcorn.

The Mathäser cinema complex opened in 2003. Located halfway between Hauptbahnhof and Karlsplatz Stachus, they have 14 screens and can seat more than 4,000. Some of the films are shown in the original version (OV), which generally means English. Bayerstrasse 5; tel: (089) 515-651; website: http://www.mathaeser.de.

The Neues Arena is a tiny venue, seating only 110 and showing non-blockbuster films. At Hans-Sachs-Strasse 7, take the U1 or U2 to Fraunhoferstrasse. For bookings, call tel: (089) 260-3265 or visit their website: http://www.arena-kino.de.

Circus

Circus Krone is the home of its namesake for the winter and advertises itself as the greatest circus in Europe. During the summer months, the circular building is host to visiting celebrities, such as the Chippendales, the Irish Folk Festival and the Beatles musical. Be careful when booking tickets as only the rows directly in front of the stage are assured of a good view. Located at Zirkus-Krone-Strasse 1-6, you can take the S-bahn to Hackerbrücke; tel: (089) 458-000; website: http://www.circus-krone.de/en/munich.

PARTYING THROUGH THE NIGHT

The nightlife of Munich can seem very tame compared to that of many other big cities. But once you know where to go, every evening can buzz until the small hours of the night.

Kultfabrik at Grafinger Strasse 6 (tel: (089) 4900-9070) claims to be the largest party area in Europe. Formerly a factory area, it was converted into 33 trendy bars, clubs and discotheques. The crowds poured in, making it the most 'happening' place in town. Ask those over 16 where they spend their nights out and it could well be Kultfabrik. With different theme nights, such as the Majorca Special or the Deep Space Night, the huge disco attracts thousands of people in their teens and twenties. They flock in from the suburbs via the Ostbahnhof, astounding the older wide-eyed passengers by their attire—or lack of it in the summer. And if one feels like something to eat, some eateries are open throughout the night.

Pacha at Rosenheimerstrasse 145 (tel: (089) 4902-6633) is a club for the sophisticated and *Schicki Michis,* the term given to the upwardly mobile who like to be seen in all the best places. *Shick* means smart. There is a restaurant, sushi-bar and club where music ranging from R & B to electro is played.

Another favourite club is P1, at Prinzregenten Strasse 1, under the Haus der Kunst art gallery. It has a strict dress code, but some sleepy-looking guys I met heading for the airport then London early one Sunday afternoon said it was one of the best clubs they had ever been to.

Other sophisticated friends find the Nachtcafe at Maximiliansplatz 5 the place to see and be seen. There are often brilliant musicians performing, and the bar never seems to close.

The Bayerischer Hof Hotel at Promenadeplatz 2-6 has a night club with international performers playing from 9:00 pm. It is open for reservations from 7:00 pm. Tel: (089) 2120-0.

While nightspots are widely advertised, it is not easy for a foreigner to find the smaller clubs that are frequented by locals in the know. Often, word of mouth is the most reliable way of finding good places to go.

A better known 'happening' venue is the Muffathalle, at Zellerstrasse 4 (tel: (089) 587-5010). It is in a converted steam generation works, complete with chimney. Sitting on the bank of the Isar, it is tucked just behind the Müllersches Volksbad, so is not immediately visible from Rosenheimerstrasse. The Muffathalle has been a cultural centre since its conversion in 1992. It often plays host to concerts by groundbreaking musicians and artistes. In addition, it holds book readings and festivals for both dance and theatre, and shows football matches on the big screen. Young people flock to Muffathalle to see their favourite bands and DJs, who may be playing anything from hip hop, funk or techno to Japanese or Jamaican music. As the city of Munich pays for the upkeep of the Muffathalle, it is also the venue for their functions and other cultural events. It also has its own beer garden.

✄

PARKS AND WILDLIFE
Englischer Garten

A local Munich newspaper surveyed the public on their favourite activity on sunny spring days. The answer was unanimous—a walk in the Englischer Garten. Said to be the largest park in Europe at over 5 km (3 miles) long, it is a magnet for the community—a bit of country right in the centre of town.

People cycle, skate, stroll, play games and music at the Englischer Garten. Bands and individual musicians practise in the park or give free concerts to entertain passers-by. In several areas of the park, one may come across nude sunbathers at any time from March to October. Germans are not reticent about discarding their clothes as soon as they get to the park or onto a pebble beach on the banks of the Isar. In summer, there are occasional police patrols to make sure that the bounds of propriety are not overstepped.

Annual Japanese Summer Festival

While cycling in the Englischer Garten one Sunday, John and I stumbled upon the 16th Japanese Summer Festival. It was

Japanese children wearing their traditional costumes for the Annual Japanese Summer Festival in Munich.

unlike other festivals that we had been to in Munich as it was an annual celebration of Japanese culture. A small garden of raked gravel, smooth stones and bamboo created a tranquil scene as we walked through the wooden gateway. It struck me as unusual that among the Japanese instructors teaching *die Japanische Kalligraphie-Shodo* (the art of Japanese lettering) in one tent or *Ikebana* (flower arrangement) in another exquisite area, there were several German instructors as well.

Grounds of Nymphenburg Palace

A favourite area for a stroll in the west of the city is the park behind Schloss Nymphenburg. The first part of Nymphenburg Palace was completed in 1675, built by Ferdinand Maria for his wife, Henriette, to celebrate the birth of their first son Maximilian Emanuel II, after a 10-year wait. The palace and surrounding parks were extended in the 18th century under the direction of builders and artists such as Cuvilliés, Fischer, Effner and the Assam brothers. The grounds, now open to the public at no charge, were designed to emulate Versailles, with formal gardens, canals, ponds and fountains close to the palace and in the wilder areas. In winter, people love to skate or have games of curling on the canal, though they are officially frowned upon because of the danger of cracking ice.

Westpark

An area of parkland almost divided by the 2R road is Westpark, which came into existence as the site of an International Garden show in 1983. The park still contains an exotic exhibit—the Thai Pagoda—and several small ponds, Seebühne being the largest.

Westpark also has a brilliant water playground for the kids in the summer, with little wooden houses, rope and tyre swings, caves, rocks and beaches. Much of the eastern part of the park is devoted to sports, and there are sections for *Kleingartenanlage*—plots of land that can be rented from the council. Many Munich folk and *Auslanders* live in apartments but long for their own little gardens where they can visit in the evenings or at weekends, to potter among their flowers and vegetables or just sunbathe on their little lawns. These *Klein Karten* serve that purpose and are found all over Munich apart from the old city.

Ostpark

Ostpark, south-east of Michaelibad U-Bahn station, is also a favourite area to get away from the city and enjoy the tranquillity of walking alongside water. Or to indulge in strenuous exercise in the tennis court, swimming pool or ice rink.

It may sound strange, but the old cemeteries such as Alter Südfriedhof and Waldfriedhof are also interesting places in which to saunter and gaze at the varied memorials, and to find peace watching the birds.

CELEBRATING NATURE

The Bavarians are particularly careful of protecting their natural flora and fauna. In the summer, it is usual to catch a glimpse of red or black squirrels chasing each other in the trees and hedgehogs scuffling in the leaves at twilight. There are large tracts of land that are designated as wildlife areas.

Summer crowds take advantage of the warm and sunny weather to lounge on the shores of a Munich lake.

While waiting in the car one evening to collect our daughter from her friend's home, I got a real shock as an animal the size of a small fox jumped onto the car bonnet. It peered at me through the windscreen, then having surveyed the locality for a few moments, jumped off and disappeared. I had never seen a pine marten before, let alone had eyeball contact with one, but I am told that there are lots of them living in the trees along the banks of the Isar. People may mistake the muddy paw marks on their cars for those of cats but more often they belong to pine martens. Sometimes, they cause problems by wriggling under warm cars in winter and nibbling the insulation from around the cables.

There are also foxes, and skinny long-eared hares can still occasionally be seen dashing across the diminishing areas of rough grasslands on the edges of Munich. Though there are a few protected deer in Munich parks, the majority of the larger wild deer do not venture under or across the encircling motorway. Instead, small groups of them can often be seen grazing at dawn not many metres beyond the rushing traffic. Smaller species of deer hide in the denser tree cover during the day.

In the winter, birds of prey can often be spotted perched on posts near the quieter roads. Some are really big birds and look ferocious with their curved beaks and speckled breasts. Spring is heralded by the singing of blackbirds balanced on the apex of roofs. Bluetits and chaffinches can be seen flitting between the trees, and flocks of sparrows make a habit of diving in the hedges. A tiny long-tailed tit makes a piercing noise like a squeaky wheel in early spring and in early summer, and house martins start to build their nests under the eaves of many houses. Jays and woodpeckers visit suburban gardens, and big black crows or rooks are in noisy evidence all year round, as are the arrogant magpies.

So much water makes the Munich area a playground for waterfowl, and ducks of all varieties can be seen paddling on lakes and streams. Swans rear their cygnets on the banks of canals and lakes and as many as 10 in a clutch may be seen swimming beside their regal parents.

The best known tree in Munich is the stately horse chestnut, which shades almost every beer garden. Originally planted to shade the cellars where beer was being stored, in recent years they have been under attack from the larvae of the chestnut leaf miner. The leaves turn brown and start to die in August, a couple of months before other trees shed their leaves. It is not yet clear if the city will lose these beautiful trees. Pine trees, several varieties of oak and maple, as well as ash and silver birch are also common. In early summer, the heady scent of the linden trees suffuses the air of the suburban streets. Old trees are pruned in the winter and often traffic is inconvenienced, but it decreases the risk of limbs being blown off during storms and injuring passers-by. Tremendous trouble is taken over the planting of new trees, with two or three thick stakes and ropes securing them until the roots take hold, and carts turn up to water them throughout the drier periods.

Dandelions for Sale

As a keen gardener, I've been amused to see packets of dandelion seeds for sale in the shops around Munich. Many Bavarians love dandelions for their colour, and I wonder if their native name—lions' teeth—endears people to the flower, as the lion is a traditional symbol of Bavaria. Daisies and clover often thrive in the suburban lawns too, and mowing takes place around the wild flowers in the parks.

During my first summer in Munich, I found the 'Alter' Botanical Gardens on the map and so went to lift my spirits with the promise of the scent of a thousand flowers. To my dismay, I found I was 84 years too late! The main gardens had been moved and though there is a prettily laid out garden between Sophienstrasse and Elisenstrasse, which was a wonderful place to relax for a few minutes near Karlsplatz/Stachus, it was not what I was looking for.

Botanical Gardens

For those who love formal gardens or who just want to see what will grow in their own patch of Munich, visit the 60-acre botanical gardens on the northern edge of Schlosspark

Nymphenburg. You can get there by taking tram 17 from Hauptbahnhof. It drops you off almost at the gate on Menzinger Strasse, where the entrance is to the side of the Botanical Institute of the university. Though a little dreary in winter, there are always things to see in the heated hothouses, where orchids grow in profusion. The stationary turtles look like bumpy cobblestones until they plop into the pool under the dripping ferns. Children love the turtles even though they are not allowed to touch. There are cacti and succulents in desert conditions, palm trees and exotic flowers even when there is snow outside.

Sometimes there are special exhibitions focusing on different plants, such as coffee or cocoa. To the far left of the gardens, plants are laid out alphabetically so visitors can see what monsters their little 15-cm (six-inch) cuttings will become. The arboretum provides wonderful shade on a hot day, whilst the alpine garden with its natural looking stream makes one feel as if in a country glade. In the centre of the grounds are beautifully tended formal gardens adorned with brilliant roses in the summer. Between these gardens is a glass-covered restaurant with crisp linen cloths and waiter service. Or you can opt for the self-service area on the wide stone terrace. The staff is friendly and relaxed. The garden has worked its charm on them, as it does on all visitors.

OLYMPIAPARK

Olympiapark, with an area of more than 2.8 sq km (1 sq mile), is the largest sports and recreation area in Europe. It was built for the 1972 Olympic Games and thanks to its modern facilities, it is still the focus for many of the main sports events, as well as the venue for a day of fun and frolics for the family. The Olympiapark can easily be reached on the U3 from Marienplatz or by car. Be warned that if there is an international star performing in the park, there will be long traffic jams and the car parks to the north-west of the park will soon fill up.

The site, which covers 640 acres, is where the debris from the damaged city was dumped after World War II. This was then carefully sculpted to create an undulating site with 10

The summer festival at Olympiapark, a favourite venue for families with children.

main buildings, under futuristic silver tiles. The whole area is open to the public, and people jog, cycle, exercise their dogs or just take a stroll around the landscaped park. The paths are either covered with tarmac or cobbled, allowing access to wheelchairs, though it would be difficult for most of them to reach the summit of the almost 60-m (200-ft) high Olympiaberg on their own, even though the hairpin bends make the slopes a little more gradual. The view from the top is fantastic on a clear day, with Munich laid out beneath and the Alps in the distant south. An equally panoramic view can be seen from the Olympic tower, which is more than 290 m (950 feet) tall. It has a swift lift to a revolving restaurant and observation platform.

Olympiapark is the location of the Eissportzentrum, home for the ice hockey team the München Barons, who call themselves 'The Champions of the Ice'. In the vestibule are showcases displaying their photographs and trophies and a booth selling tickets for the matches. The ice rink is open for skating sessions between 10:00 am to 10:00 pm. Skating lessons are also available, and there are several young champions who learnt how to skate here. Entrance fees for adult: € 3, fees for youths under 16: € 2.50, and children under six: free. For more information, trying calling them at tel: (089) 3067-2150; website: http://www. olympiapark-muenchen.de.

Adjacent to the ice centre is a centre for sports action—an indoor arena filled with ramps and bumps on which youths jump, slide and skid on a variety of wheels. Roller blades, skateboards, scooters and bikes all share the space.

During the summer months, there are lots of outdoor pursuits for individuals and families. A mini-golf course is set out where all ages are seen playing together. The opening hours are Monday to Friday from 11:00 am to 9:00 pm, and Saturday and Sunday from 11:00 am to 10:00 pm.

Paddle-boats can be hired at the artificial lake. A small enclosed area, easy to overlook but adjacent to the swimming pool lawns, has been set up with trampolines, on which the kids have tremendous fun under supervision. Another treat for youngsters is a ride on the blue and white train around the park, which stops conveniently close to the restaurant and ice cream stand. From April to October, there is an Adventure Tour of the park, which takes place at 2:00 pm. Fans are shown not only the outside of the stadium but also the dressing room once used by FC Bayern Munich and TSV 1860.

The three halls in the park host a variety of acts, from Holiday on Ice to concerts by famous pop stars and operas to the annual general meetings of BMW and Siemens. Olympiahalle is the largest of the three halls. It is so huge that artistes holding their performances there have their images projected on multiple vast screens set up at the sides of the stage so that the audience are able to see the performance.

In August, a Sommerfest is held in the park between the main buildings. There are rock concerts in the Theatron, which has a semi-circular auditorium next to the lake and firework displays. Fairground rides, including a big wheel, a magic carpet, twirling octopus, scooter cars and roundabouts keep the crowds hankering for more. Also dotted everywhere are countless stalls selling items from Africa, Asia and Australia as well as toys, clothes and jewellery. There are shooting galleries and lucky dips, kiosks for snacks and tables for those with bigger appetites. Everybody usually has a fantastic time at the Sommerfest.

SPORTS FOR EVERYONE

People in and around Munich spend a lot of time on recreational as well as competitive sport. It is a good way to meet people, and there are many sports facilities, both indoors and outdoors, in and around Munich. The great thing about sports is that as the rules are generally the same in every country, participation does not require fluent German.

As the winters are long and usually very cold, there are lots of opportunities for winter sports, especially as the Alps are in such close proximity. Winter sports enthusiasts were given a boost in 2002 when Germany topped the medals tally in the Winter Olympics in Salt Lake City, bringing home 12 gold, 16 silver and seven bronze medals.

For information on all the available sports facilities in Munich, there is a thick tome published by the Landeshauptstadt München called *Sport in München,* available from the Civic Information Office in Marienplatz for around € 8. There is also a free seasonal booklet entitled *Freizeit Sport,* but in the meantime, here are some pointers on the sports commonly enjoyed in Munich. To get more information on local sports clubs, contact Bayer. Badmintonverband which is located at Georg-Brauchle-Ring 93; tel: (089) 1570-2302; email: info@msj.de.

Badminton

Many local sports clubs offer badminton, and groups are often organised through companies or clubs, such as the German-English Association. One club specialising in the sport is the Badminton club München 1954, at Adam-Berg-Strasse 115h, 81735; tel: (089) 6809-3580.

Baseball

The above address for badminton is also the one to contact for baseball and softball, though there are several clubs around Munich, such as the Taufkirchen Smelly Sox, the

Garching Atomics, the Munich Tigers in Waizenegger and the Munich Ambassadors. The Munich Ambassadors' home ground, at Säbenerstrasse 61, has been the centre of the Munich baseball scene for many years, hosting not only the Ambassadors but also their co-tenants, the Munich Carribs. Email: info@ambassadors.de.

Basketball
Information for all the Oberbayern area can be obtained by writing to Heinz Reible, Postfach 40 02 24, 80702 Munich; tel: (089) 3077-7376; email: gs-obb@bbv-online.de.

Billiards
Billiards is a popular pastime for many teenage boys I know and they often frequent a billiard hall in Ostbahnhof station.

There is a club for young people in Schwabing west at Theo-Prosel-Weg 16; tel: (089) 1215-6730; email: info@cvjm-muenchen.org.

Bella-Pool-Billiard Center GmbH is not far from the Silberhornstrasse U-Bahn station at Martin-Luther-Strasse 22, and opens at 10:00 am; tel: (089) 692-8080.

Boules
In summer one can contact people playing Boules in the Residenz-Hof, the gardens under the arch north east of Odeansplatz.

Bowling (Ten-Pin)
Olympia-Bowling at Klopstockstrasse 4 just south of the Petuelring and north of the Schwabing hospital (U2/U3 Schneidplatz), looks unassuming from the street level, but once downstairs you will notice a different atmosphere. There are tables with cotton tablecloths and tapestry upholstered chairs where you can enjoy a meal and attentive waiters are ever ready to replenish your empty glasses as you play. The scoring is mechanised so no mental dexterity is needed. Altogether it is a good night out for people of all ages, it is not cheap if you play all night. For more

information, call tel: (089) 360-4840; website: http://www.olympia-bowling.de.

Other places to try are:

- Bavaria Bowling
  Lazarett Strasse 3
  Tel: (089) 121-5390
  Website: http://www.bavaria-bowl.de
- Hollywood Super Bowling
  Forstenrieder Allee 74 (U3 Forstenrieder Allee)
  Tel: (089) 753-921
  Website: http://www.hollywood-super-bowling.de
- Isar Bowling
  Martin-Luther-Strasse 22 (U2, Silberhornstrasse)
  Tel: (089) 692-4512
  Website: http://www.isarbowling

Climbing

On a clear day, the Alps beckon climbers, but there are facilities for practising *Klettern* (climbing) within Munich.

Heaven's Gate, Grafingerstrasse 6, is run by the IG-Klettern München & Südbayern e.V., and is easily accessible by U- or S-bahn to Ostbahnhof. It is open from 10:00 am to 11:00 pm daily. Contact them at tel: (089) 4090-8803.

Kletterhalle im ESV, Herthastrasse 41, in Laim is open weekdays (except Tuesday) from 6:00 pm to 9:00 pm and Saturday from 10:00 am till 5:00 pm. Visit their website: http://www.indoorclimbing.com/bayern.html.

MTV München von 1879 e.V. has been a sports centre for 125 years. Located at Häberlstrasse 11, on U3 and 6 at Goethplatz, it is open daily from 10:00 am to 10:00 pm.

High-east Kletterhalle is at Sonnenallee 2, Heimstatten, S2; tel: (089) 9279-4796; website: http://www.High-east.de.

Cricket

This particular sport is not widely known in Bavaria. Indeed, *Sport in München* has a drawing of croquet next to the information on cricket! There are three clubs in Munich.

- For Lufthansa Sportsclub, write to Hans Neubauer, Am Hedernfeld 21, 81375 Munich; tel: (089) 703-514.

- Munich Cricket Club began life in 1982 and training sessions take place in the summer at their home ground at the Hirschanger, Himmelreichstrasse, every Friday (May-Sept) from 4:30 pm to 7:00pm. Write to Knut Haenelt, Loichingerstrasse 6, 81245 Munich; tel: (089) 3800-3285; website: http://www.munichcricket.net.
- For the Pak-Orient-Cricket-Club, contact Naeem Malik, Fasangartenstrasse 129, 81549 Munich; tel: (089) 699-0233. This club meets every Wednesdays from 6:00 pm to 8:00 pm at Eduard-Spranger-Strasse 17 (U2/8 Hasenbergl). For more information, visit its website: http://www.cricinfo.com/link_to_database.

Curling

Known as *Eisstockschiessen,* curling takes place during the winter months at almost every large frozen area of water around Munich. The curling area is prepared by brushing the ice so that it is free of snow and debris. At any one time, several games may be in process on the Nymphenburger Canal, but there are also several local clubs that play, one of which can be found practising on Tuesday evenings at the Ostpark ice rink. People also play in Olympiapark but only in winter.

Cycling

November sees the spinning wheels of 6-Tage Rennen (cycling's six-day race) at Olympiahalle. Top racers of *Radsport* or *Radwandern* (cycling) from all over the world converge on Munich where they compete in elimination races, sprints and laps to earn points toward the final total, with the winner being announced on the final day. The event is surrounded by all the hullabaloo of a festival, with stalls, sideshows, international cuisine and live performances by musicians.

There are many clubs for serious cyclists. Try the Bayer. Radsport-Verband e.V. by writing to Ternus, Georg-Brauchle-Ring 93, 80992 Munich; tel: (089) 1570-2371; email: brv.bayern@t-online.de; website: http://www.radsport-aktiv.de.

In contrast to Radsport, Radwandern is not so hectic. Try the ADFC Allgemeiner Deutscher Fahrrad-Club; tel: (089) 773-429; email: info@adfc-muenchen.de.

Fishing

Under German law, no one is allowed to inflict pain on any creature with a backbone, which of course includes fish. This means that fishing for the joy of the pursuit, to subsequently release the fish, is not allowed. Anything caught must be killed quickly and then eaten.

Munich is surrounded by lakes, rivers, streams and canals, and children can often be seen waving their fishing nets around in the water. But fishing is only allowed if you are under 11 years of age. Anyone older than that must have a fishing licence and in order to get one, a written exam must be passed. The course leading up to the exam is 45 hours long and includes practical experience, plus aspects of biology, chemistry, botany and ecology, as well as knowledge of the laws on fishing. One must be able to recognise 70 species of fish and know their individual spawning seasons and feeding habits. The exam is only held once a year, so be well prepared or you will miss out on another year of fishing.

Football/Soccer

Every village and suburb has its own football team, and the listing of clubs around Munich takes up around 16 pages in the *Yellow Pages*. Usually, junior and youth teams train in the week, so go along to watch and inquire. I know of one suburb on the edge of Munich whose junior team is two-thirds British and several of the younger teams include girls. It amused us to see a local club halving its entrance fees for women and children to watch a game.

The Irish Rovers, registered with the Bavarian Football Association, has over 70 active members and train Wednesdays and Fridays between 7:00 pm and 9:00 pm at the Parkstadt Solln, Herterich Strasse 141. You can get there by buses 64, 65 or 66. League games are played on Sundays at 12:45 pm for the second team and 2:30 pm for the first. For more information, visit their website: http://www.munichirishrovers.de.

For spectators wanting to see professional players, the two big clubs are FC Bayern and TSV 1860. They share the spectacular Allianz Arena stadium, inaugurated in May 2005, in Fröttmaning, just north of Munich. It cost € 340 million and the façade of the huge curved structure is made up of 2874 foil cushions. Its capacity is 69,901 spectators, most of whom are protected from the elements by a curved roof. A great website which tells you all you want to know about the stadium is http://www.allianz-arena.de/en/fakten/allgemeine-informationen.

Golf

Golf is gaining popularity in Bavaria, but it is not a cheap sport. To play in the clubs, one must be a member and be willing to pay fees starting from several hundred euros a year. An internationally renowned 18-hole golf course is the München Nord-Eichenried, located in the north-west of Munich, on the road to Erding. It is closed on Mondays but is open on other days between 8:30 am and 12:30 pm and between 2:00 pm and 6:00 pm. To reach the club, call tel: (081) 239-3080; website: http://www.gc-eichenried.de.

For a day in the country, Golf MangfallTal e.V. located in the south-west of Munich, on the way to Saltzberg, offers beautiful views; tel: (089) 1570-2231. Membership is currently € 1800 a year.

For information on Bavarian golfing, try http://www.golf.de/bgv or contact bgv@golf.de.

Gymnastics

Virtually every sports club around Munich offers lessons in *Turnen* (gymnastics), so find out where your closest sports centre is and go along to ask about times.

- ESV München e.V.
  Tel: (089) 1271-1020
  Email: esv-muenchen@t-online.de
- Männer-Turn-Verein München von 1879 e.V.
  Werdenfelsstrasse 70 (Holzapfelkreuth on the U6)
  Tel: (089) 5388-6030
  Email: info@mtv-meunchen.de

- Turnerschaft Jahn München von 1887 e.V.
  The club meets at Freisinger Landstrasse 60, U6 Freimann
  (Bus 293 to Emmerigweg)
  Tel: (089) 915-294
  Email: geschaeftsfuehrer@tsjahn.de

Hockey

There are three large clubs in Munich. For more information, in German, visit this website: http://www.bayernhockey.de.

Horse Racing

The main racing stadium, Rennenplatz, is in Reim, and there are races several weekends a year. These are advertised in the local press. Just up the road in Daglfing is the Trabrennbahn where smaller, more lithe horses race pulling two-wheeled buggies.

Horse Riding

The *Reit und Fahrsport* (horse riding) association can be contacted at tel: (089) 9269-67250, or via email: BRFV. LKBayern@t-online.de.

Close to the centre of town is the Akademischer Reitclub ARC Munich e.V., Königinstrasse 34, which is the university riding school (U3/6 to Universität); tel: (0160) 182-2837; website: http://www.arc-muenchen.de.

For the Reitclub Isartal e.V., write to Gross, Schönstrasse 89, D81543 Munich; tel: (089) 662-159; website: http://www.rc-isartal.de.

The further you are from the city centre the more stables you will find, but horses can often be seen trotting through the Englischer Garten on the bridle paths.

Ice Hockey

The Munich Barons, winners of many ice hockey awards, practise and play at the Olympiapark rink. Tickets for their games can be obtained in advance from the kiosk there. But if you want to play, there are lots of clubs, including the Olympia-Eissportzentrum—take the U3 to Olympiazentrum; tel: (089) 3067-2150.

The are two ice hockey associations in Munich. Bayer. Eissportverband is one of them (tel: (089) 157-9920). The other is Deutscher Eishockey-Bund e.V.; tel: 089-8182-0; email: info@deb-online.de.

Ice Skating

All skating rinks usually have skates available for hire. The most visible venue is at Karlsplatz/Stachus where an outdoor rink is erected from the end of November until the end of January. Decked in fairy lights with music playing, it is fun to watch and even better to join in.

Olympiapark has one of the largest ice rinks in Europe. Skates can be hired, and lessons can be booked. There are freestyle sessions, some of which follow a specific type of music—rock, classic or beat. Spiridon-Louis-Ring 21 is open from 9:30 am–noon, 1:00 pm–4:00 pm and 7:00 pm–10:00 pm; tel: (089) 3067-2150; website: http://www.olympiapark-muenchen.de.

- Ostpark has both outside and inside skating facilities at Staudingerstrasse 17 (U5/U8 Michaelibad), daily from 9:30 am.
  Tel: (089) 6301-9145
  Fax: (089) 6349-7100
- Eis-und Funsportzentrum München West is a rink between Laim and Pasing, at Agnes-Bernauer-Strasse 241. There is a varied daily timetable so be sure to check before going.
  Tel: (089) 689-007
  Fax: (089) 689-657
- The Prinzregentenstadion was renovated in 2001 and 2002 and now provides very modern facilities in winter. It is located at Prinzregentenstadion, Prinzregentenstrasse 80.
  Tel: (089) 236-150

Many people just pick up their skates in January and February when the ice is usually thick and enjoy free skating on their local lake. Sometimes the chilly winters bite early and it is possible to skate in December.

In-Line Skating

Roller-blading is actively promoted by the city. Several city streets are closed to traffic one evening a week during the summer so that skaters can indulge in their sport. The largest club is ESV Sportfreunde München-Neuaubing e.V., Papinstrasse 22, D81249 Munich, on the U5; tel: (089) 873-870. More information is available from Deutscher Inlineskate Lehrer Verband e.V.; tel: (089) 8208-4599; email: info@dilv.de.

Judo

The Judo World Masters was held in Munich in 2001, inspiring enthusiasm in the many local clubs. Contact their association, Bayer Judoverband; tel: (089) 1570 2442; website: http://www.bayer-judo-verband.de.

Rugby

München Rugby Football Club trains each Wednesday at 7:00 pm, at Görzerstrasse 55, Perlach, near junction 92 on the A8 and each Friday at 6:30 pm in the Bezirkssportanlage, Grosshadern; tel: (089) 3547-1028; website: http://www.munich-rugby.de.

The other club is smaller and always on the look out for players. Studentenstadt München Rugby Football Club meets at the Sportplatz at Grasmeierstrasse, U6 to Studentenstadt; tel: (089) 3220-9526; email: profi33@gmx.de.

Running

The Munich half-marathon takes place in June every year. There are two groups of participants—one running the full distance of about 21 km (13 miles) and the other competing in the 10-km (6.25-mile) race. The first race for the half-marathoners starts off at 8:00 am. They are followed soon after by the second race. Unlike the more serious runners in the longer race, participants in the 10-km run are of varied ages and come in all shapes and sizes. You can spot a 10-year-old as well as a 70-year-old from among the crowd of runners. There will be a few who will be displaying ankle and knee supports, at least a couple in wheelchairs, and babies in prams being pushed by a mum or dad. Adding to the colour and fun of the event will be a dog or two accompanying their masters on their run.

Medien Marathon München

A more serious race is the Munich marathon that takes place in October. It had a four-year break a few years ago, but came back with a new route and better organisation. The 11,000 competitors assemble well before the start time of 9:00 am at Spiridon-Louis-Ring in Olympiapark. The participants come from all over the area, from sports clubs and companies as well as several individuals racing against their own previous records and athletes from other countries. What will be missing this time are the dogs and trolleys. The route traces an erratic 42 km (26.25 miles) and circles around stunning sights, streets and parks, and is watched by about 200,000 spectators!

In conjunction with the marathon, a kid's run is usually organised. There are several categories—a family run and categories for children between 10–12, 12–14 and 14–16. The run is just 400 m (0.25 mile) from Coubertinplatz, Olympiageläde to the stadium of the central high school.

The Munich City run is a hugely popular event that sees thousands of participants each year.

The assembly time is 8:45 am, but the actual race starts at 9:30 am.

Enrolment for the runs must be made in the preceding weeks, but if there are places available last-minute applicants are accepted. The cost, to cover the organisation, is about € 50 per participant. But if you submit a late entry—within the last two weeks—the entry fee is € 60. There are leaflets at the civic information centre in Marienplatz, but information is also available from Verein für City-Marathon München e. V., Postfach 150640, D-80044 Munich; tel: (089) 7483-5794; fax: (089) 748-3579; email: presse@muenchenmarathon. de; website: http://www.medienmarathon.de.

Sailing
There are so many lakes in and around Munich that it is only natural that *Segeln* (sailing) is a popular sport here. The clubs give coaching but also train supervisors and instructors. The biggest lakes are up to an hour's drive from Munich. They are Starnberg in the south, Ammersee in the west and Chiemsee in the south-east. The association Bayer. Seglerverband e.V. has information about sailing clubs in Munich. The association can be reached on tel: (089) 1570-2366; email: bsv@bayernsail.de; website:http://www. bayernsail.de.

Skateboarding
The main centres are in:
- The Olympicpark, Baureferat-Gartenbau at Fröttmaninger Berg (U6 to Fröttmaning)
- Garchinger Strasse (U6 to Alte Heide)
  Email: gartenmuc@compuserve.com
- Euro Skate Leopoldstrasse 250 (U3/6 to Munchener Freiheit then bus 43/85 to Griegstrasse)
  Tel: (089) 3506-2910
  Fax: (089) 3506-2911
  Email: info@euro-skate.de
  Website: http://www.euro-skate.de

The sports centres in Perlach and Pasing also have facilities for skateboarding enthusaists.

Skiing

If *Skisport/Skigymnastik/Skibergsteigen/Skilanglauf* (skiing) is your kind of sport, the nearest ski slopes are at Blomberg, more than 50 km (31 miles) south of Munich, and many go to Lenngries. Wear appropriate clothing as it can get very cold on the slopes. Skis and poles can be hired from most of the larger resorts but remember the price of a daily ski pass can be very expensive, depending on the resort, and the traffic jams back to Munich can be torturous. I've known some Germans who have stopped weekend skiing because the four-hour traffic jams on the way home were too much to bear. There are lots of cross-country ski trails *(Loipen)* in and around Munich. One trail goes right through the Englischer Garten. Floodlights enable night skiing in the Sendlinger Wald and at Fasaneriesee. The longest trail is through Isarauen Süd, a 12-km (7.5-mile) distance. Maps showing the trails are available from the Umweltladen, Am Rinderberg. The organisations to contact are:

- Bayer. Skiverband e.V.
  Tel: (089) 1570-2325
  Email: info@bsv-ski.de
  Website: http://www.bsv-ski.de
- Skiverband München e.V.
  Tel: (089) 8997-9723
  Website: http://www.skiverband-muenchen.de
- Deutscher Alpenverein e.V. Tal 42 Munich
  Tel: (089) 290-7090
  Website: http://www.alpenverein-muenchen-oberland.de
  Although the most popular slopes for snowboarding are further south in the Alps, you can find lots of action in Olympiapark whenever there is snow. The Snowboard World Cup, held at Olympiapark, attracts thousands of fans in February.

Squash

Many health and fitness clubs have both squash and tennis courts but the following ones are for squash only:

- Park Club Nymphenburg, Stievestrasse 15
  Tel: (089) 178-2055
  Website: http://www.parkclub.de

- Squash-Centre Schwabing, Winzererstrasse 47b
  Tel: (089) 308-3516
- Racket Park, Höglweg 7, Haar
  Tel: (089) 464-647
- Sports 4 you, Zielstattstrasse 61
  Tel: (089) 786-970
  Website: http://www.sports4you.org
- Squash and Badminton Insel Taufkirchen, Birkenstrasse 169, Taufkirchen
  Tel: (089) 614-1620

Swimming

Swimming pools are often called *Hallenbad* on maps and signs in Munich. In summer, several of the indoor pools stay open until 11:00 pm. Many of the pools have solariums and provide massages as extras. The sign FKK stands for 'textile free', meaning it is a nude area. Most pools have a small café attached for those who have expended all their energy and need refreshments. A strange idiosyncrasy with suburban pools is that many close during the school summer break, as people are expected to be on holiday or to swim in the local lakes. The cleanliness of the lakes is monitored closely, though I have yet to venture in next to the ducks. The daily temperatures are recorded in the local newspapers, and the larger lakes often have lifeguards in attendance at peak times.

Swimming clubs usually make use of the pools and sessions are held during term times.

- Cosimabad has a large wave pool and a very small pool indoors, as well as an outdoor pool with a tiny terrace area. The pool is open daily from 7:30 am to 10:00 pm. The sauna is open from 9:00 am.
  Cosimastrasse 5 (Buses 37, 87, 89, 90, 154, 187 will take you there).
  Tel: (01801) 796-223
  Website: http://www.swm.de
- Giesing/Harlaching's opening hours are 10:00 am to 6:00 pm, except Tuesday to Friday, when the pool opens at 8:00 am and closes at 8:00 pm.

Klausenerstrasse 22 (Trams 15 and 25, bus 51, U1 Mangfallplatz)
Tel: (01801) 796-223
Website: http://www.swm.de

- Michaelibad's pool has been refurbished and reopened in 2001. There are clean, open cubicle showers. Part of the larger pool is often divided into lanes for faster swimmers. It is a wonderful experience to swim in the very warm outdoor pool at sunset, even when the air is chilly.
Heinrich-Wielandstrasse 24 (U5 Michaelibad)
Tel: (01801) 796-223

- Müllersches Volksbadis on the banks of the Isar, across the Ludwigsbrucke from the Deutsches Museum (Trams 18, 19, 20 S1-8). It is the oldest swimming pool in Munich, built over 100 years ago in the art nouveau style as an all-male establishment. It has two ornately decorated pools. The smaller one, which is a little warmer, is found by walking along the side of the larger pool. There are wooden cubicles for changing but I wandered around the corridors for ages before I found them. It also has a sauna and steam baths (both nude, Tuesday and Friday being women's days) as well as massages on offer from a delightful team. It is open Tuesday to Sunday from 7:00 am to 11:00 pm and 7:00 am to 5:00 pm on Monday. There is a café to the left of the entrance and lots of people use it as a lunchtime rendezvous.
Rosenheimerstrasse 1
Tel: (01801) 796-223

- Nordbad has a terrace on which to rest and recuperate, a night swimming area, a whirlpool, a children's warmer pool, solarium, steam cabin and massages on offer.
Schleissheimerstrasse 142 (Trams 12, 27, buses 33, 53 or U2 to Hohenzollernplatz)
Tel: (01801) 796-223

- Olympia-Schwimmhalle. Make a day of it in a complex that has a huge Olympic-sized pool, a small pool and a fantastic diving pool, where you can see some

accomplished divers train. Apart from a terrace surrounding the water, there is access in the summer to the grassy area outside, which is lovely for families. A 'Sauna-Paradise' is available from 8:00 am to 11:00 pm, and the solarium is open from 7:00 am to 11:00 pm.
Olympiapark (U3 to Olympiazentrum, tram 20, 21, bus 36, 41)
Tel: (089) 3067-2290

- Südbad opens at 8:00 am on most days.
  Valleystrasse 37 (Midway between Harras station U6/S7 and S27 and Implerstrasse U3/6 Tram 16, 26, bus 31)
  Tel: (01801) 796-223

Outdoor Pools

Entry is free for children under six. For keen swimmers, it is worth buying a *Streifenkarte* for 10 visits, as it reduces the overall cost of buying individual tickets. The water temperature is kept at a constant 24°C (72.5°F). The outdoor pools are open from 1 May until September, usually between 9:00 am and 6:00 pm, though on fine days they may remain open until 8:00 pm. To be sure, check with the individual pools.

- Sommerbad Allach
  This site also has a beach volleyball area.
  Eversbuschstrasse 213 (S2-Allach, bus 75 to Kleselstrasse)
  Tel: (089) 2361-2861

- Dantebad
  Open from 9:00 am to 10:00 pm. Although this is an outdoor pool, it can be enjoyed for much of the year because the water is heated to between 30°C and 35°C (86°F and 95°F)—a fantastic combination of warm water and cool air when it is not at the height of summer. There are also a sauna, a steam room and a solarium on site.
  Postillonstrasse 17 (U1 to Gern or Westfriedhof, tram 20, 21, or bus 8 or 177)
  Tel: (01801) 796-223

- Georgenschweige-Bad, Belgradstrasse 195 (U2, 3 or 8 to Scheidplatz)
  Tel: (01801) 796-223

- Maria Einsiedel, Zentralländstrasse 28 (U3 Thalkirchen,

Bus 57). Set in a lovely area next to the Isar canal, there is a nude area for women and a trampoline for anyone.
Tel: (01801) 796-223

- Michaelibad, Heinrich-Wielandstrasse 24 (Buses 93, 94 and 137, U8 and U5). This place has the highest water slide in Munich, children's play facilities, water area, a trampoline and an area for playing beach volleyball.
Tel: (01801) 796-223

- Sommerbad West, Weinbergerstrasse 11 (Tram 19 to Westbad or bus 72 to Gräfstrasse). It has a children's play and water play areas, trampoline, volleyball court, and nude area.
Tel: (01801) 796-223

- Schyrenbad, Claude-Lorrain-Strasse 24 (Bus 52, 58, 220 to Claude-Lorrain-Strasse or to Humboldtstrasse, U1 or U2 to Kolumbusplatz).
Tel: (089) 653-715

- Ungererbad, Traubestrasse 3 (U6 or bus 4 to Dietlindenstrasse). It has a nude area for families, a water play area, trampoline and sandpits for the children.
Tel: (01801) 796-223

- Erding Therme. The swimming experience we enjoy the most is several miles north east of Munich at Erding, where they have huge thermal pools surrounded by natural palm trees. Set under a sliding dome, the indoor area has several jacuzzis, a steam room, small mineral pools, a light therapy room and a café. Outside, there is a large landscaped area with different water slides and an extension to the pool. It is wonderful to swim there when there is snow all around and be wonderfully warm. It is located at Hot Spring Avenue, Erding.
Tel: (081) 2222-9922
Fax: (081) 2222-9929
Email: willkommen@therme-erding.de
Website: http://www.therme-erding.de.

Tennis
In summer, the thwack of tennis balls resounds round most parks and sports complexes, though there are many indoor

courts around Munich too. Most sports clubs have tennis coaches who give lessons. Look for your local courts in the *Yellow Pages,* under *Tennisanlagen.*

- Sports4you, Zielstattstrasse 61
  Tel: (089) 786-970
  Website: http://www.sports4you.org
- FBayer. Tennis-Verband e.V.
  Tel: (089) 1570-264
  Fax: 089 1570-2665
  Website: http://www.btv.de

Table tennis

Lots of people play *Tischtennis* (table tennis) seriously but introduction to the sport often takes place in the local park where permanent tables are often provided for whoever comes along with bats and a ball. Most sports centres have facilities but if you want to join a club, contact an association.

- Bayer. Tischtennis-Verband e.V.
  Tel: (089) 1570-2420
  Website: http://www.bttv.de

Volleyball

A sport that requires two to six players, volleyball has an enthusiastic following in Bavaria with volleyball clubs in most suburbs. Munich hosted the Eurogames 2004 Beach Volleyball Championships, so try the local sports centre to see if there are teams there.

Walking

Well, walking sounds easy, you may say, but you need stamina to be a real hiker. The Munich Wanderers is a sub-division of the Deutscher Alpen Verein (DAV) and caters to people who enjoy mountain walking. Monthly meetings are held at the Unionsbräu; website: http://www.alpenverein-muenchen-oberland.de. There is a book that provides information about the programmes available each season.

People who meet at the German–English Association go for a gentler Sunday walk of about 15 km (9 miles or so) rain

or shine, always meeting at an S-Bahn station at 1:30 pm.
Email: info@gea-muc.de; website: http://www.gea-muc.de.

FESTIVALS AND CELEBRATIONS
Festivals and Parades
Bavaria has the highest number of *Feiertage* (official holidays) of any state in Germany. Being a Roman Catholic state, it celebrates many religious holidays as well as the secular holidays laid down by the German government. On the religious holidays, churches often hold services and sometimes processions.

Always ready for a holiday, Munich workers will often take the Friday off if a *Feiertag* falls on a Thursday, making it a long weekend. Most *Feiertage* are fun, although some are regarded as more serious occasions and other holidays are just days off work. The festival most associated with Munich is the Oktoberfest, which is always celebrated during the weekend.

January
New Year's Day
The New Year begins with flashes of noise and colour. People are out on New Year's Eve for Silvester parties and as midnight approaches, many head for the streets to let off fireworks. The sale of fireworks is strictly controlled and they can only be bought by those over 18 years of age in the three days leading up to New Year's Eve. To the uninitiated, the period around midnight can be a bit scary as rockets shoot in all directions, especially in Marienplatz. All over the city and its suburbs, groups of people head for the parks and open spaces, often with wine or beer in hand to toast the beginning of the New Year. The Olympiaberg is a good place to watch the fireworks of Munich. Another site offering a good view is the Monopteros hill in the Englischer Garten. The noise and colourful celebrations often last an hour.

New Year's Day is a national holiday, so most people can sleep off the effects of the festivities. At midday, a brass band performs from the tower of St Peter's Church.

Christian Feast of the Three Kings

The Christian Feast of the Three Kings falls on 6 January along with another Bavarian holiday. On this day, children in groups of three tour round the town, dressed as kings Kaspar, Melchior and Balthasas, and bless the houses for the following year. Having done this, they chalk the date on the top of the front door with the initials of the kings: K + M + B. The initials also represent the first letters of the Latin phrase, *'Christus mansionem benedicat'* which means 'bless this house'. The children are rewarded with money and sometimes sweets and small presents. Usually they only call on houses where they know that they will be welcome.

People traditionally take down their Christmas decorations on the sixth day of the new year. The council sends around a lorry within a day or two to collect the discarded trees from the streets, from the recycling bins or from designated car parks. Without doubt, the trees will be recycled.

February
Fasching

The time of Fasching (carnival) is known as the fifth season in Munich. The period starts from 7 January but really begins in earnest towards the end of January, depending on the date of Easter.

In pagan times when people were tired of the cold, dark winter days, they tried to scare the dreary days away by donning masks and costumes. The word carnival comes from the Latin *'carne, vale'*, meaning 'meat, farewell'. Before Lent, when devout Christians give up meat for 40 days in remembrance of the suffering of Christ, they indulge in celebrations and revelry.

Over the years, pagan and Christian festivals appear to have been integrated and in Munich this is the season for balls and other festivities. Costumes are sold in all the big stores or are made at home. The Deutsches Theater is the venue for some of the most glittery events. The Ball der Silbernen Rose (Silver Rose Ball) is a spectacular event, where international musicians entertain graceful and stylish dancers. The afternoon before the Ball der 1000 Torten (Pastrymakers'

Ball), the locals can usually view the decorated cakes in the Silbersaal. These are raffled off during the evening. The final ball of the season is the Bal Classique. Many other venues, such as the Olympia Hall, the Bayerischer Hof Hotel, and many of the breweries hold balls throughout the season.

Women's Day

Carnival Thursday, the week before Ash Wednesday, is called 'Altweiber' (old women) or 'Wieverfastelovend' (the women's day). It is the day that by tradition, women take control.

Women are given the liberty to get into all sorts of mischief. They may take the keys to the town hall and lock some of the doors but most commonly, they creep up on men and cut off the ends of their ties with a swipe of the scissors. So it is wise for the men not to wear an expensive tie but a very old one, on Women's Day. Ignorance of the practice is no insurance against it!

The most important evening for balls is Rosenmontag, the Monday before Ash Wednesday. There are around 20 balls for those who choose to attend. Some areas of Germany declare Rosenmontag a holiday, including some businesses in Munich.

Throughout the fifth season, there are activities for children as well. Apart from balls and parties organised for the children, there are also puppet shows and mask workshops.

On the final Sunday of Fasching, there is usually a theme parade through Sendling-Westpark, which is great fun to watch or participate in.

Faschings-Dienstag

Faschings-Dienstag (Shrove Tuesday) is a half-day holiday around Munich for schools and for many Bavarian companies, though it is not official in all companies. Crowds assemble early in the Viktualienmarkt to see the female stall holders dance with gay abandon in their Fasching costumes. By lunchtime, Marienplatz and the Viktualienmarkt are a heaving mass of bodies, with almost everyone in fancy dress and hearts, freckles and flowers painted on the women's cheeks. Music blasts from loud speakers and people dance. Lots of people shower passers-by with confetti. Everyone is happy and smiling, apart from those trying to get served a beer when several hundred other orders are ahead of theirs.

Local street festivals in the afternoon are usually much safer for the children. Usually a DJ plays the music and families and friends of all ages, looking crazy in their costumes, dance in the roads that are closed off to traffic. There is always an ample supply of beer and food, especially the traditional Fasching Krapfen—doughnuts filled with jam, fruit, or chocolate. Leberkäse in rolls, Weisswurst, chips and sweets are also eaten in the street by revellers of all ages.

March
Starkbierfest
As Lent arrives, so does the Starkbier season. When monks brewed their own beer, they used to make it extra strong during Lent to fortify themselves during the period when meat was not eaten. The local breweries took up the tradition and the results are looked forward to with eager anticipation by all beer drinkers. The beer is dark but not bitter as well as being strong and really delicious. The most famous brewery for Starkbier is the Paulaner Brewery (Am Nockherberg in the Au district), where local politicians tap the first barrel. The Löwenbraukeller also has a large beer hall where the season is celebrated much like Oktoberfest, with a band and lots of singing and traditional food but fewer tourists. All the large breweries brew especially for this period and the beer names always end with —tor. It is hard to limit oneself to just two *Mass* (litres) in an evening, but 'just one more' can result in very unsteady legs and an aching head the following day.

St Patrick's Day
The St Patrick's Day Parade takes place in the afternoon of the Sunday closest to 17 March. Organised by the Deutsch-Irischer Freundschafskreis Bayern (DIFB) since 1996, the parade marches from Münchener Freiheit to Odeonsplatz.

Each year, the parade crowd gets larger. It is often a chilly day but the warmth of the participants makes up for it. Orange, white and green striped flags are seen everywhere, painted on faces and clothes, as well as waved by friendly people, the Irish and some Germans. There are Americans, Australians and English mingling and laughing together. The parade is preceded by police cars clearing the way, followed by St Patrick and a huge loping Irish wolfhound. Irish bands and dancers perform, followed by bands and dancers of different nationalities. As the parade ends, there is music, dancing and food for sale in Odeonsplatz. After, the crowds drift, often to one of the local Irish pubs.

Easter Markets

It seems that as soon as one celebration is over, people in Munich start preparing for the next. It certainly makes the long winter days pass faster. Not long after Fasching, the spring or Easter markets begin. These markets sell, among other things, traditionally decorated eggs of all sizes, from humming bird to ostrich eggs. A splendid market with wonderful craftsmanship takes place annually in the town hall at Gräfelfing. Not only are beautifully painted or lace covered eggs for sale, there are also traditional crafts such as Klosterwork. These are religious scenes decorated with ornate lace and beads that have been crafted by nuns for centuries.

Easter Eggs

The egg is a Christian symbol of new life and resurrection. The more expensive eggs are often painted with scenes of spring or Bavarian landscapes.

In the days leading up to Easter, most homes in Bavaria are decorated with branches of pussy willow, flowers and ornaments of rabbits, ducklings, chicks and eggs. Most households herald the arrival of spring by hanging real, porcelain or plastic eggs on a tree outside or branches inside. Some houses appear to be as well adorned as at Christmas. Many also have a spring wreath hanging on the door.

Palm Sunday

Palm Sunday, which may fall in either March or April, is celebrated in all the churches with special services. People go to church carrying small bunches of evergreen and pussy willow, though the children may carry staffs topped with greenery and decked with ribbons to celebrate Christ's triumphant entry into Jerusalem over 2,000 years ago. These staffs are taken home afterward and displayed in front of the houses throughout the following week.

April
Good Friday

On Karfreitag (Good Friday), many Christians attend church services. The day is a public holiday.

Ostern

The night before Ostern (Easter), some Christians keep guard *(Oster Wache)* in their churches until dawn when they celebrate Christ's resurrection. Some of the outlying farming communities have special early morning church services. It is still dark when the services begin at 6:00 am, and each member of the congregation takes a candle. Outside the church there may be a brazier of fire, and as dawn breaks, the fire is brought into the church and used to light everyone's candles. If there are any babies in the congregation, it is the time for them to be christened. During the service, the priest blesses the baskets of food brought in by each family and places them in front of the altar. Inside these baskets are bread, salt, eggs and ham. Afterwards families and friends join together in the dawn light for an Easter breakfast, made with the blessed produce. All the churches throughout Munich hold special services.

The zoo always organises a special Easter egg hunt in a designated area of the park for children under the age of 12 on Easter Sunday and Monday. There are also other activities for kids such as face painting and special rides.

Easter Monday is another holiday for friends and families to celebrate.

Munich ballet week

This annual event takes place some time in April and showcases the talents of the Bavarian State Ballet. In recent years the company has joined the Munich Philharmonic and the State Opera as an internationally recognised ensemble. Performances take place at the Nationaltheater.

Spring Festival

From late April to early May, the Frühlingsfest or Spring Festival takes place on the Theresienwiese, home of the Oktoberfest. There is a great fair, with lots of side stalls and beer tents, but it is not on the scale of Oktoberfest.

'Free Night'

The evening of April 30 is known as 'Free Night' for the 'betweenagers'. Groups of children, generally aged between 10 and 14, tour the streets and get up to mischief, singing and laughing. People make sure that their cars are safe in the garage, or they may find their vehicles swaddled in toilet roll or covered with shaving foam the next day. The police turn a blind eye to the high spirits just as long as things do not get out of hand.

May

May Day

On 1 May, everyone has a holiday. Every four years, each town or village has a new Maypole, usually painted in the Bavarian colours of blue and white, and there are great festivities as a new pole is erected. Traditionally this is done by the young men of the town using ropes and poles to control the immense length, though some towns now bring in a crane to do the work. The local band plays, and there are stalls in the street or square and of course a beer tent. In some suburbs, people can be seen dancing in front of their village Maypoles, but often the pole's position makes it impossible to dance round it. Each pole is usually adorned with metal or wooden models or plaques, depicting the interests and activities of the locality.

The Maypoles are officially inspected every year, and if they are deemed unlikely to last a year safely, they are taken away. The night before a new pole is erected, it is often guarded by some of the townsfolk in case it gets stolen by a neighbouring town's mischief makers. It may sound like a major undertaking but I have been told that Maypoles have been spirited away before.

Asparagus Season

May is *Spargel* (asparagus) season, waited for with eager anticipation by the local gastronomes. The event is celebrated throughout Bavaria as the shoots are harvested. Stalls soon spring up at roadsides selling all varieties of asparagus from long thin green to short fat white ones. Restaurants have special menus devoted to the vegetable, and everyone eats their fill for the year.

Mai Dult

The traditional Auer Dult—the fair in the Au district of Munich—is held three times a year and has been recognised for over 200 years. The Mai Dult falls at the end of April or the beginning of May. The fair opens in the area around Maria-Hilf-Kirche, which is south-east of the centre, across the river. There are rows and rows of stalls. Just keep searching and you may find something you just cannot go home without.

Ascension Day

Ascension Day is a holiday, known as Christi Himmelfahrt.

Pfingsten

This day of celebration is always on a Sunday, known as Whitsun or Pentecost to English-speaking Christians, and followed by Pfingstmontag. This is a Bavarian holiday that may occur in May or June and is usually the time of a two-week break in the state schools. Many children take their first communion at this time.

Feast of Corpus Christi

On the second Sunday after Pentecost is the Feast of Corpus Christi, or Fronleichnam, another holiday. A traditional procession takes place in the city.

Men and women dance around a blue and white Bavarian Maypole.

Maibockausschank

The Munich breweries have yet another beer festival in May—the Maibockausschank. Make up your own reason why!

There is hardly a week at this time of year when one has to work all five days of the working week.

June
Stadtgründungsfest

The second weekend in June is the Stadtgründungsfest or Munich Founders' Day Celebration. Founded on 14 June 1158, the city now celebrates with events and stalls from Marienplatz to Odeonsplatz. Marienhof holds entertainment for children, and there is usually at least one brass band, dancing displays, people dressed in medieval costume, jazz and rock concerts and local artistes showing off their talents.

Tollwood Festival

Theatre, music and art are featured at the festival that is held in the south of Olympiapark, accessed from Ackermannstrasse. It is quite a walk from public transport, but there is a free shuttle bus from Scheidplatz on the U2. This festival includes many different types of performing arts, including performances by internationally-acclaimed artistes. Small kitchens prepare international fare as diverse as sushi, burritos and fish and chips, and stalls sell a variety of mainly ethnic goods. There is something for almost everyone, so book in advance to see the performances, which usually begin at 5:30 pm.

Munich Film Festival

In 2007, Filmfest München (Munich Film Festival) celebrated its 25th anniversary with a razzmatazz celebration of all that is new in the film world. Taking place towards the end of June, there are approximately 200 films shown on 15 screens portraying a widely differing range, including documentaries, experimental and quirky films, films from America, Asia and Latin America as well as European films, and films for children. There are glitzy premieres attended by international stars where awards are given out. Tickets to such films cost no more than at other times, and are screened at several locations around Munich. They can be booked before the festival begins at IMAX or Gasteig. The festival's website can be found at http://www.filmfest-muenchen.de.

July
Christopher Street Parade

Mid-July sees the Christopher Street Parade for the gay community. A large stage is erected in Marienplatz and an amazing sound system is suspended from above so that everyone can hear the bands or speeches. The whole square is a flood of colour with rainbow flags and even before 11:00 am, the square starts to fill up. The parade assembles early for its 1:00 pm start, stretching from the east of the square down the Tal.

There is a buzz of excitement that is really infectious. The most outrageously dressed are the men in drag, decked out as brides or princesses with lots of lace, jewellery and the longest false eyelashes imaginable. Others turn up in a variety of costumes. As 1:00 pm approaches, the excitement mounts. The square is absolutely packed, the drum beat starts, claps and whistles take up the beat and the leading huge American car pulls slowly away. Behind come dancers and lorries festooned in balloons the colours of their clubs or organisations, while their occupants throw out leaflets or confetti or just wave to the crowd.

The parade travels a short route around central Munich, but as the end of the parade leaves the square, so do most of the onlookers. Some gay couples do not join the parade but are happy to just roam about freely displaying their affection in public. Not that they can't at other times but this is a special day for them. For more information, the website is http://www.csd-munich.de.

Munich Opera Festival

The highlight of the cultural year for many is the Munich Opera Festival that takes place throughout the month of July. Most of the performances by the Bavarian State Opera, the Bavarian State Orchestra and international stars take place at the Nationaltheater, the Cuvillies theatre in the Residenz, and the Prinzregenten theatre or Allerheiligen Hofkirche. 'Opera for All' is the phrase now synonymous with this festival. New operas, such as *Alice in Wonderland* as well as more traditional ones are performed during the month. There are also free live open-air broadcasts displayed on a vast screen in Max-Joseph-Platz. These broadcasts are tremendously popular and it is wise to arrive early to secure a place. The festival also includes concerts, ballet and individual singing performances. The programme is available from the festival box office, Festspielkasse, Maximilianstrasse 11, but it is best to book early as many performances sell out quickly. To find out more about the festival, send your queries via email: festspiele@st-oper.bay-ern.de.

Jakobi Dult

The Auer Jakobidult fair and market is held in Mariahilfplatz.

August
Bundesfeiertag/Maria Himmelfahrt

Bundesfeiertag (Federal Celebration Day) falls on 1 August, followed by Maria Himmelfahrt on 15 August. The latter marks the Roman Catholic Church celebration of the Virgin Mary's corporeal body and soul ascension to heaven. At this time of the year, many people are already away on holiday, though a significant number do stay in Munich and enjoy the summer sun.

Hans-Sachs-Strassen-Fest

Another weekend of celebration is the Hans-Sachs-Strassen-Fest in mid-August, centred around one of the main gay areas in Munich. It first started in 1990 in a street south of Blumenstrasse, perpendicular to Müllerstrasse. Since then it has grown to encompass other areas of central Munich. The weekend kicks off with a gay and lesbian party at the Park-café in Sophienstrasse, behind the old Botanical Gardens. The main events are in Ickstattstrasse and Frauenhofer, on the corner of Klenzestrasse.

Summer Festival

This festival is held in the northern part of Olympiapark, with events staged in some of the pavilions, fairground rides to stimulate and food and beer to relax with.

September
Oktoberfest

To many people throughout the world, Munich and Oktoberfest are synonymous. As many as six million people pour into Munich during the 2.5 weeks of the festival, filling every hotel room and guesthouse for miles around. Since 1810 when Crown Prince Ludwig married his bride, Therese, the populace has been celebrating in the meadow named after her—Theresienwiese. Presiding over the fair is an enormous iron statue of Bavaria, looking like an Amazon, though attired in Roman robes, standing in front of a Doric temple built between 1843 and 1853 to celebrate the victory over Napoleon.

The festivities have been brought forward a couple of weeks since then as the weather in September is a bit warmer for outdoor celebrations. Three months before the festival, work on building the huge wooden framed tents on each side of a wide central promenade begins. The Bürgermeister of Munich opens Oktoberfest on the next to last Saturday of September, which is attended by local dignitaries. As he taps the first barrel, he calls *"Ozapft is!"*, a Bavarian call meaning "It's open!"

Each brewery has its own tent, decorated in individual styles and colours, and different brass bands play. Outside the Löwenbrau tent is a huge mechanical lion, the symbol of Bavaria. Some tents are very traditional, while others are more raucous.

People sit cosily close on long wooden benches lining long wooden tables. The food and drinks are ordered from waiters or waitresses, attractively clad in *Trachten*. Some appear to be mere slips of girls, but they can carry as many as 10 one-litre glasses of beer at a time! Even if you do not know the beer songs, many of the tunes are recognisable American folk songs and it is easy to join in with many of the Bavarian choruses. As the day wears on, everyone becomes your friend and as the evening progresses there is dancing in the limited spaces between the tables and often on the benches.

As well as the beer and *Brez'n*, each tent offers a variety of foods. But the most frequently served are half a roast chicken, pork sausage or roast knuckles of pork. Radishes with salt are a usual accompaniment to the beer. Outside the tents are more tables, as all the participants cannot be accommodated inside. Along the thoroughfares are stalls selling souvenirs of the occasion, such as T-shirts and tankards, sweet roasted almonds, and gingerbread hearts on ribbons decorated with sugar icing.

To the south and east of the beer tents is a wonderful fairground with amazing rides to delight the revellers. Oktoberfest is a family tradition and although huge quantities of alcohol are consumed, you rarely see unpleasantness or fights as each tent has its own security force, and there are plenty of police keeping an eye on things. The rides open

The Hacker-Pschorr brewery wagon makes its way to Oktoberfest.

at 10:30 am, so mornings and early afternoons are a good time to take the children before the crowds get there, or the last Tuesday of the fest, which is the day designated for children.

The morning after Oktoberfest opens there is a spectacular international costume parade, the *Trachtenzug*, the largest of its kind in the world. It starts from the triumphal Siegestor arch, at the end of Ludwigstrasse at 10:00 am and lasts almost two hours, as it makes its way to the Oktoberfest grounds, accompanied by many different bands. The route is packed with spectators, so it can be difficult to watch the parade. But if you take the U3 or U6 to Giselastrasse and arrive at about 9:15 am, you can watch the parade assemble and walk among the participants.

October
Day of German Unity/Herbst Dult
On 3 October, the Day of German Unity is celebrated as well as the autumn Auer Herbst Dult, which takes place in Mariahilfplatz.

Die Lange Nacht der Münchner Museen
The third Saturday in October is really fun for those who want cultural nourishment. In the afternoon, from 2:00 pm til

6:00 pm, children between the ages of six and 14 have access to 16 different museums, one price covering the entrance to all. In the evening, about 80 museums, galleries, art collections, palaces and churches are open to the public from 7:00 pm until 2:00 am the next morning.

On Die Lange Nacht der Münchner Museen, the local transport system provides buses on four different routes around the city, taking in all the venues, and it is easy to link from one route to another. One payment, a little more than the entrance fees to visit two museums, covers access to everything. Everyone on the buses is there to enjoy themselves, and all the excited chatter is about places they have just seen. Many of the larger museums have refreshments available, and quite a few have bands, orchestras or individual musicians performing in their entrance areas. It is best to plan a route beforehand, so you can utilise the time well and maximise enjoyment. Only those with tremendous stamina can make it right to the end of the evening. Do use public transport to get in to Munich on the night as every available cranny already has a car parked in it.

Halloween

Halloween celebrations can be witnessed on 31 October, which are becoming more and more popular with the children. Houses are often decorated with pictures and figurines of spooky ghosts, witches and spiders, and black and orange are the colours of choice. Pumpkin lanterns with gruesome faces can be seen touring the streets, carried by 'witches' or 'skeletons' who go from house to house trick or treating in the American way.

November
All Saints' Day

All Saints' Day is commemorated on 1 November. The holiday is a celebration started by 9th-century Christians as a defence against evil. Services are held in the churches and graves are newly decorated with dried flower arrangements and candles in small red pots that flicker through the winter nights. When out walking in town, most of the older generation are dressed in sombre clothes, as if for a funeral.

Bonfire Night

On the Saturday before 5 November, some of the English community celebrates Bonfire Night in the village of Mariabrunn, north-west of Munich, close to Dachau. Stamping feet to keep out the encroaching winter chill, warm drinks, jacket potatoes and parkin are consumed while waiting for the fireworks. The fireworks are followed by the lighting of the bonfire, upon which Guy Fawkes is engulfed yet again. For information on the celebration, contact the German English Association through their website: http://ww.gea-muc.de.

St Martin's Day

St Martin's Day is celebrated on 11 November. On this day, children gather their extra toys and put them in a box to give to less fortunate children. Young children make paper lanterns in school and parade through their towns at twilight holding them on long sticks. Martin was a soldier and on one bitterly cold night, while he was out riding on his horse, he met a scantily clad beggar. He immediately took his sword, cut his own cloak in half and gave half to the beggar. Afterwards he dreamt that the beggar was Christ in disguise, who thanked him for his kindness. Martin became a Christian shortly afterwards, and later a priest. On hearing the news that he had been made a bishop, he felt so unworthy that he hid in a farmyard, but the geese cackled and gave away his whereabouts. Hence the tradition of eating roast goose on St Martin's Day. He is now the patron saint of the poor.

Jewish Culture Days

Jewish Culture Days, aimed at integrating the Jewish community to Munich life, have been held here since 1987, usually in late November. There are concerts, readings, documentaries and theatrical performances held at Gasteig and the Spanish Institute for Culture.

Repentance Day

Repentance Day or Buss-u. Bettag is a holiday that usually occurs on the third Wednesday of the month, but only in a few places now.

Thanksgiving

Thanksgiving is not a Bavarian festival but some Americans feel bereft without it and continue to celebrate it even when far from home. There are a few restaurants in Munich that cook special roast turkey menus complete with cranberry sauce, mashed potatoes and pumpkin pie. Try contacting Luigi Malone's, Leopoldstrasse 28a, decorated like an East Coast pub, tel: (089) 39501, or Edison & Co., Schulstrasse 28, tel: (089)1303-9393; fax: (089) 303-9292; email: EdisonCo@aol.com. Another restaurant to try is the California Grill in the Marriott at Berliner Strasse 93, which is 4 km from the centre of Munich. You will need to make bookings well in advance to be sure of a table.

December

Advent

The Advent season begins four Sundays before Christmas. Most families in Munich have an advent wreath in their home, and there is one in every church, heralding the birth of Jesus Christ. The wreath is usually made of evergreen foliage, sometimes decorated with ribbons or baubles on which are placed four candles, one of which is lit each Sunday until Christmas.

The first weekend of Advent sees the opening of Christmas markets around Germany. Marienplatz is magically transformed into a twinkling, bustling market of little wooden huts beside a huge Christmas tree. Short concerts are held on the *Rathaus* balcony each day at 5:30 pm.

The tradition of putting up Christmas trees began in Germany, and one story tells of the German Protestant preacher Martin Luther walking home from church one Christmas eve and being so overcome by the beauty of the countryside, he felt compelled to share it with his family. According to the story, he dug up a small fir tree and took it home where he decorated it with stars and small candles, thereby starting a world-wide tradition.

Christmas Markets

Christmas markets in different parts of Munich have their own unique atmosphere, attracting different types of people. Of course in Marienplatz, the Christkindlmarkt in the centre of Munich attracts the most tourists. Some stalls sell decorations made of straw, others sell wooden toys, hand-painted glass baubles or Christmas wreaths and flower arrangements. Still others sell an assortment of Christmas delicacies, such as cinnamon biscuits or sweets, and suffusing the air is the smell of *Glühwein*—warm, spicy wine that chases away the winter chills. There is another market a short walk away in Rindermarkt, the Krippenmarkt, which just sells figures for the nativity scenes. Everyone wants a crib scene in their own home, and here the choice is overwhelming. People can also buy individual items, an extra shepherd or another ox to add to their own collection.

Another lovely market is held at Weissenburger Platz, close to Rosenheimer Platz, where the small market is located on a large roundabout. Münchener Freiheit has a different market, specialising in crafts such as pottery, paintings and *objets d'art*. In fact almost every open square around Munich has a market for at least one day during Advent, with the ones in the suburbs often selling goods produced locally.

Tollwood Festival

Tollwood's biannual festival, which started in the early 1990s, is usually held from early December until New Year's Eve. Theriesenwiese, the site of Oktoberfest, is the present location for the festival. More than a million people come to the festival each year to view the cabarets and enjoy the many different types of music and dance from all around the world. There is also a Christmas market. As dusk approaches, the stalls and tents are illuminated with countless glowing lights, adding an extra touch of magic. More information about the festival can be obtained from this website: http://www.tollwood.de.

The Rathaus hosts many concerts during the Christmas season.

Saint Barbara

On 4 December, you may see people cutting a branch from their fruit trees and taking it into their house. Cherry is usually the tree of choice. It is said that if the branch blossoms by Christmas, it is a good sign for the future year. The tradition is based on the story of Saint Barbara, who died in AD 306. The daughter of a pagan emperor, Dioscorus, he would lock her up whenever he went away to ensure that she remained a virgin. Sad and lonely, she found a dried-up cherry branch and shared her drinking water with it, until eventually it blossomed and consoled her with its beauty. When Dioscorus discovered that his daughter had become a Christian, he had her beheaded. Soon after, he himself died, struck by lightning. Saint Barbara is now the patron saint of miners, artillery men and firemen.

Saint Nicholas' Day

Saint Nicholas' Day falls on 6 December. According to legend, he was a man especially kind to children. On passing a poor family's home one day, he left three gold coins for the family's three daughters on the windowsill. The girls' stockings were hanging up to dry and the coins fell into them, and so began the tradition of hanging up stockings to receive presents. Tradition has it that during the day, Saint Nicholas tours the streets carrying a book in which he has documented any bad deeds of the children. He is accompanied by his helper Knecht Ruprecht who carries a sack of presents for all the good children, and a birch rod with which to beat the bad ones. Now more often children leave out their shoes to be filled with little presents and sweets.

Christmas Eve
On Christmas Eve, all shops usually close by 2:00 pm, as Bavarians celebrate Christmas on the eve. Traditionally they decorate the tree, have family lunches of something simple, such as sausage, and open the presents which have been brought to the house by Christkindl (the Christ Child). Many families finish the evening by attending midnight mass at their local church.

Christmas Day
Christmas Day (25 December) and 26 December are holidays devoted to family, friends and relaxation. The dinner is on a grander scale and often consists of roast goose and red cabbage.

New Year's Eve
New Year's Eve (31 December) is a time for wild celebration, when orderly, sensible Bavarians travelling in to central Munich abandon their natural reserve to usher in the New Year amidst the cacophony of fireworks, laughter, singing, popping of champagne bottles, and the ringing of bells of the Frauenkirche.

'Wer ko, der ko!'
'Who can, can!'
—An expression of admiration after someone has shown
bravery, power or ability.

LEARNING THE LANGUAGE

Before we came to live in Germany, John and I went to evening classes in England for a term to learn basic German. He then came to live in Munich while I saw Amanda through her GCSE exams, continuing to attend evening class once a week for the rest of the year. The teacher was impressed with our class, or so she told us, and we could hold basic conversations by the end of our third term.

I was horrified, however, when I came to live in Munich as I could not understand a thing that was being said. There are many words that are only used in Bavaria and not in the rest of Germany. On top of the dialectal differences, the Bavarian accent is very thick, with broad vowels. The pitch is also lower than I was accustomed to hearing. A Bavarian friend came to dinner with five English female friends and said that we sounded like a tree full of sparrows in comparison to a group of Bavarian women.

As the majority of people living here were not born in Munich, High German is understood by almost everyone. Several Germans have told me that only a few kilometres outside Munich, there are some old folks with such a strong local dialect that people from other areas have difficulty understanding them.

Not understanding the language was not a big problem at first, as the people I met through Amanda's international school and John's firm all spoke English. It did mean though that whenever we had a problem, we could not go to the official bodies, even if we knew where to go, as we could not speak German well and the office workers rarely spoke English. Actually, most people under the age of 35 do speak some English, as it is taught in all schools, but many do not like to attempt speaking it for fear of being misunderstood. It is the same with some expatriates, who claim that they can manage fine in Munich without having to speak German.

Happily, the most important word for anyone—toilet—is very similar to the English word. We can manage without food or drink in town but certainly not the toilet. *Wo sind die toiletten?* (Where are the toilets?) will be a necessary phrase. There are clean toilets in Hauptbahnhof and Ostbahnhof, although the ones in Marienplatz are best avoided in summer. The symbol WC is used in shops and restaurants, with *Damen* for ladies and *Herren* for men marked on the doors. They may be abbreviated to D and H, or *sie* and *er*.

In the city centre, English is understood by most of the people in the shops, particularly in the larger department stores. It is a different story in the suburbs where English-speaking shop assistants or staff working in the local *Rathaus* are uncommon, so learning some German is a necessity.

"SCHOOL GERMAN"

"BAVARIAN GERMAN"

Entschuldigung or 'excuse me' is used to get someone's attention, or when you accidentally bump into somebody, which is quite common during the busy tourist season.

One of the best ways to learn German is through the television news. The newsreaders tend to speak a little slower than the people on the soaps and other shows. Many of the English-language films shown on TV are dubbed, which is rather frustrating as we never realised how often we watch lips move. Some people say that they find watching children's TV programmes beneficial too, as the language used is simpler.

Of course, the best thing to do is to attend lessons in Germany and to make friends with Germans. John and I went to 'in-house' lessons after work, but there was quite a high dropout rate. After a term, there were just two other students left in the class, both of whom had German partners. Naturally their progress was more rapid, and having difficulty keeping up, we dropped out the following term. However much you intend to study on your own, in most cases it just does not happen. Once you have gained certain lazy habits, such as not giving the nouns their proper gender, it becomes harder to overcome these bad practices. There are many private language schools located in the centre of Munich where you can learn German, either individually or in groups. Alternatively, you can enrol in one of the night schools that offer German as a foreign language. Night schools are usually cheaper.

After two years, when people asked if I spoke German, my reply would be "shopping German". I became familiar with the names of all types of food, even the likes of lobster and pumpkin, as they were labelled. I was also able to understand and order from a menu. However, active participation in a conversation in German still held many challenges for me. I could often understand the gist of the conversation but not every word, and by the time I had thought of a rejoinder, the topic had changed! Today, I still carry a small dictionary with me and look up words I am not familiar with—words that I see on advertising hoardings and street signs, or words I overhear in the street.

Having lived in Munich for the past eight years, I still find it easier to travel several kilometres to meet someone on official business rather than try and converse over the phone. Facial expressions and body language say so much. I still find it disconcerting though when a German answers his or her phone, whether at home or in the office, just by announcing the surname, "Schmit!"

Language Schools
The facilities in the language schools vary. Some have language labs with tapes but you tend to get more individual attention the more you pay.

- ASL München, Leopoldstrasse 62, Munich
  Tel: (089) 332-825
  Fax: (089) 398-718
  Website: http://www.aslsprachen.de
- Goethe-Institut, Sonnenstrasse 25, Munich
  Tel: (089) 551-9030
  Fax: (089) 5519-0335
  Email: muenchen@goethe.de
- Tandem München e.V., Kurfürstenplatz 5, 80769 München
  Tel: (089) 280-370
  Fax: (089) 280-371
  Email: info@tandem-muenchen.de
- DESK (Deutsch English Sprachkurse), Blumenstrasse 1, Viktualienmarkt, Munich
  Tel: (089) 263-334
  Email: info@desk-sprachkurse.de
  Website: http://www.desk-sprachkurse.de
- Meeting Point, Löwengrube 10, Munich and at Haupt-Strasse 4, Haimhausen
  Tel: (089) 2090-0500
  Fax: (089) 2090-0501
- FOKUS Language School, Brienner Strasse 48, Munich
  Tel: (089) 4521-3360
  Fax: (089) 4521-33630
  Website: http://www.fokussprachen.com or http://www.fokus-deutschkurse.de

- Forumdeutsch, Kreiller Strasse 52, 81673 Munich
  Tel: (089) 341-450
  Fax: (089) 341-945

TRYING TO BE A LOCAL

The most common greeting in a Bavarian street is '*Grüss Gott*', roughly translated as 'God's greetings.' Though not as many people attend the Catholic Church nowadays, Bavaria is still a Catholic state, and traditions live on. '*Servus*' is the truly Bavarian greeting for 'hello' and 'goodbye.' Many people just say '*Morgen*', an abbreviation of '*Guten Morgen*' or 'good morning'. Several people living in our street whom I passed every day were greeting me after a few weeks, though that was where the conversation began and ended, even after three years. Some people just give a nod of acknowledgement to each other, though many people never make eye contact.

A Bavarian 'goodbye' is either '*Tschüss*' or '*Servus*', though the High German version '*Auf Wiedersehn*', or just '*Wiedersehn*' is often heard. '*Bitte*' is the word for 'please', and can also be used when pointing to something one wants in a shop. It also means 'you are welcome'. 'I'd like' is '*Ich möchte*' and 'I need', '*Ich Brauche*.' '*Danke*' is more commonly used to thank someone, though '*Danke Schön*' and '*Vielen Dank*' are used too. Having eaten in a restaurant you could sit there all day if you do not ask for the bill—'*Bezahlen bitte*'—and you do not always get a receipt unless you ask for a '*Quittung*.'

An English friend who is fluent in German told me that to join in a Bavarian conversation, only three words are necessary. These are '*Genau*' meaning 'exactly, precisely or quite,' '*Echt*' meaning 'really,' and '*Stimmt*' meaning 'that's right.'

It must be remembered that all German nouns are written with a capital letter, and the active verb is the last word in a sentence.

When two vowels are strung together, whatever word they are part of, the sound remains the same, unlike English where 'ough' can be pronounced in seven ways. Think of cough, bough and enough. The vowel *ei* sounds like a long *i*, and *ie* is like a long *e*. Umlauts over vowels—*ä, ö, ü*—are like placing an *e* after the vowel, and more often in the international business world, they are written with the *e*.

Pronunciation Guide

Several letters are pronounced differently from those in the English language. For instance:

- A letter that looks rather like a capital B is in fact double *s*
- *ch* as in Scottish loch
- *j* as y
- *qu* as k
- *r* is almost the hardest to pronounce as it is rolled in the throat, almost like ch in Scotland.
- *v* as f
- *w* as v
- *x* as ks
- *z* as ts

  Names with *e* and *i* sound like the opposite. An *e* at the end of a word is always pronounced more like *u*.

There are several German words that are so similar to English that we often presume them to have the same meaning. Sometimes they do, as in *Ironie, Psychologie, Sommer, Winter* and *Wind*. But there are others that my teacher called 'false friends'. Several of the words sound similar, such as *Wann* meaning 'when'; however, *Wenn* means 'if'. *Wer* does not mean where, but 'who'. 'Where' on the other hand is *wo*.

The strangest difference I have come across is the word 'gift'. In German, gift is poison! I have heard of one family of German children being given 'gifts' by their oblivious foreign grandparents and not wanting to open them! And there are so many more similar sounding, misleading words! The confusing initials RAF are used for the Royal Air Force in Britain but stand for the left-wing Red Army Faction in Germany!

'Am liabsn bin I do, wo scho garbad, awa no ned gessn is.'
'I like being there best when the work is done
and it is lunchtime.'
Socialising is better than working in the eyes of many
Bavarians, so it is great to arrive at work when someone
else has completed it.
—A popular German saying

WORK PERMITS

Many *Auslanders* who come to work in Munich have been transferred to the city by their companies back home. Numerous cultural adjustments need to be made for those concerned, but all the larger companies have human resource departments that are usually helpful. Many of those arriving to live here speak their own native language and often English as well, as English is rapidly becoming the international language for business. I know of Japanese and Korean men who could only speak their own languages and English and yet performed well for their companies in Munich.

When a company transfers its employees to Munich, the employer will arrange for work permits or Green Cards, from the *Arbeitsamt München* or labour exchange. But gaining one of these is not easy for non-EU citizens. Issued by the Federal Government, Green Cards allow the holder five years of residency before renewal. Officially, EU citizens have the same rights to work, study and social security as Germans. In addition, they can be trade union members anywhere within the EU, and they are allowed to bring their families and close dependants to Germany.

The exception to the Green Card ruling is if the person is an IT expert. As IT professionals are in great demand, a work permit can be acquired quickly. The same privilege applies to anyone who has skills that are much needed in Munich. In such a case, the Blue Card is issued. This card is specific to Bavaria and allows for the temporary employment of foreigners who have a specific contract with a company. However, the work permit becomes void once an employee leaves the company. A pre-requisite to obtaining this card is that the employee must earn a minimum annual salary of € 50,000 (though there is a lobby to get this lowered) or be in possession of a college or university degree. An explanation for the Blue Card's introduction in July 2000 was made by the Bavarian Interior Minister Günther Beckstein. He stated that it was 'to prevent foreign experts, who do not fulfil the expectations set for them, or who do not get along with their employers, from becoming a burden on the Welfare System.'

The Bundesministerium für Arbeit und Sozialordnung (Federal Ministry of Labour and Social Affairs) and the Bayerische Innenministerium (Bavarian Department of the Interior) can provide answers to frequently asked questions concerning the Blue Card. IT specialists from abroad can register by email with Germany's Zentralstelle für Arbeitsvermittlung (ZAV) or central labour exchange, in Bonn if they are looking for work with companies in the Munich area.

A useful booklet to have is the *Das IT-Sofortprogramm der Bundesregierung—Informationen für ausländische IT-Fachkräfte und Unternehmen* which translates to *The German Government's Emergency IT Programme—Information for Foreign IT Specialists and Companies.* More help for IT specialists can also be found via the Bundesanstalt für Arbeit or the Federal Employment Office, which has forms that can be downloaded from their website.

JOB HUNTING

If you wish to find employment in Munich, there are many more job opportunities for those who can speak German. Needless to say, having a knowledge of German would also make it easier to read the job advertisements. I know of a Russian couple who came and spent almost all their money on intensive German lessons for their first six months here, before searching for work. Some companies want their prospective employees to have a language diploma to prove their competence before employing them.

The three most usual places to look for jobs are the newspapers, the employment office and a job agency. Advertisements for job openings are usually found towards the back of the papers under the heading *Stellenmarket, Stellenangebote* or *Stellenanzeigen,* and the best day to look is Saturday. The broadsheets, for example the *Süddeutsche Zeitung* and *Die Welt,* usually advertise more executive positions.

The *Arbeitsamt* (employment office) is at Kapuzinerstrasse 26, Munich. For general information call tel: (089) 5154-3333, but depending on your area of expertise, such as hotel work, electronics, or secretarial work, there are different numbers to ring. These can be found on the telephone book under *Agentur für Arbeit München.* Email: Muenchen@arbeitsagentur.de; website: http://www.arbeitsagentur.de.

The final place most people go to is a job agency. You can locate these in the *Yellow Pages* listed under *Seitarbeit* or *Personalvermittlung.* Information on job agencies can also be gathered from advertisements on the U-Bahn or in the local papers. One such department is the Manpower Agency, which has seven offices in central Munich. Call their office at Lindwurm Strasse 79 on tel: (089) 5170-1930.

Here are a couple of useful websites, although the information is mostly in German:

- http://www.monster.de
- http://www.job-office.com (this website has English subtitles).

The EURES network (European Employment Services) was established as a partnership between all the employment services in the European Union. Its purpose is to facilitate free movement of workers in the European Economic Area. The work is co-ordinated by the European Commission. Their website is in English, German and French and contains useful information on living, working, equal opportunities, studying, job seeking, travelling and buying goods within the EU. It can be found at http://www.europa.eu.int/jobs/eures.

Most job applications require a *Lebenslauf* (curriculum vitae or resumé) enclosed with the letter of application, which should preferably be written in perfect German, and a recent photograph of the applicant. References or testimonials should also be made available, preferably with a translation, either before or at a *Vorstellungsgespräch* (job interview).

TAXATION

I can only give a very general impression, as the system is so complex. Everyone who is employed in Germany or is paid via the German 'public purse' is liable to a *Lohnsteuer* or a wage tax. An exception is a person with no permanent residence in Germany and with earnings of less than € 4,000 a year.

Everyone must have a tax card issued at the start of each calendar year to present to their employer. In Germany, the tax year is January until the following January. The local registry office, the *Einwohnermeldeamt*, which is usually located in the local *Rathaus* issues the tax card, and the card is given only after showing the *Aufenhaltserlaubnis* (resident's permit). The tax group is indicated on the card, according to the employee's status. Tax is assessed and deducted by the employer and sent directly to the *Finanzamt* or the tax office. If the employer gets the assessment wrong, they can be liable for the extra tax payments. On the other hand, if an employee is over-taxed, he will only be reimbursed at the end of the financial year.

There are six categories used for assessing individual tax levels:

1. Single or separated, with no children, and not widowed.
2. Single or separated with a child, therefore able to claim child allowance, known as *Kindergeld*.
3. Married, or those who have been widowed less than a year.
4. Married, with both partners earning.
5. As in 4 but the spouse falls under group 3.
6. Individuals who work for more than one employer, or who have several tax cards.

There is a sliding scale of taxation, with a tax-free allowance of approximately € 7,664 for a single tax payer and € 15,328 for a married couple. Employees have 19 per cent of their wage deducted for the lowest earners and up to 45 per cent for those in the highest wage bracket, plus a 'solidarity' tax of 5.5 per cent, which is meant to be used to ease the high cost of German reunification.

There can be income tax relief in some individual cases, for such things as moving expenses, life and accident insurance and for expenses incurred due to illness or disability. However, the relief must be applied for in advance.

If the tax payer is a member of a Christian church, they are also subject to a church tax. The standard rate of Value Added Tax (VAT on most purchased goods is 19 per cent but less on items such as food and books. Information sheets in English about taxes can be found on the following websites:

- http://www.london.diplo.de/Vertretung/london/en/ Startseite.html
- http://www.germany.info/relaunch/business/taxes/ german_tax_rates.html

As foreigners confronted with incomprehensible tax forms, we found it worthwhile to pay a *Steuerberater* (tax consultant) to fill in our forms. The tax consultants advised us to save all our travel tickets and stationery expenses to offset against tax and with their help, we were able to reclaim some tax (though in our case, not quite the cost of their bill). There are many tax advisors in the city with skills in several languages. John's company recommended ours but it is best to have a recommendation rather than pick one at random from the 12 pages of names listed under *Steuerberatung* in the *Yellow Pages*.

For British skilled workers with a trade and who are self-employed, there are many criteria to be fulfilled. They are often asked to prove that they have been employed in their trade for six years and they have to register with a *Handwerkskammer* or Handicraft Chamber, and a *Gewerbemeldestelle,* which is the Local Trades Registration Office. It can be a catch-22 situation as before a contract is agreed upon, a German employer may ask for the form E101, which provides exemption from paying German national insurance contributions. However, in England, this form is only issued by the Department of Social Security (Pensions and Overseas Benefits Directorate), Newcastle upon Tyne, NE98 1BA, tel: (0044) O191 218 7777, when they have the employer's details and the contract's starting date.

Pension and social security insurance—*Rentenversicherung* (19.1 per cent)—and unemployment insurance—*Arbeitslosenversicherung* (6.5 per cent)—are charged on the first € 4,350 of each month's wage.

INSURANCE

Everyone who is employed must pay state health insurance and nursing care insurance, unless they hold private health insurance. Many also pay the state accident insurance scheme, known as the *Unfallversicherung.* It is possible to have additional private accident insurance that pays a one-off sum according to the severity of an accidental injury. Another insurance that is advisable, though not compulsory to hold, is *Berufsunfähigkeitsversicherung,* the incapacity insurance, which pays a pension each month if a person is medically unfit to work.

Contributions to the state pension insurance— *Rentenversicherung*, are also compulsory. This provides old-age pensions and payments to those who cannot work for medical reasons.

Another insurance, which most people hold in Germany, is for personal liability. Known as *Haftpflichtversicherung,* it is not very expensive and covers damage to others and their property caused by the insurer, a partner, a child, or a cat. It is wise for people renting a property to purchase this insurance plan. Be aware that horses and dogs need separate cover.

There are two main types of *Lebensversicherung* or life insurance schemes, which provides security to partners and families. *Risikolebensversicherung* pays only if the insured person dies within a specified period, whereas *Kapitallebensversicherung,* which costs much more, will pay dependants if the insured person outlives the specified duration of insurance.

If a property is owned, the building should be covered by a *Wohngebäudeversicherung* but the contents need a *Hausratversicherung* (household insurance). The latter pays the replacement value of an object in the event of theft, or damage by water, fire or a thief.

LABOUR RIGHTS

If a company employs more than five people, the workers are allowed to have a representative on a *Betriebsrat* (workers' council). If there are between 50 and 200 employees, they are allowed two representatives chosen from amongst themselves. These representatives inform the workers of their rights, collect information and liaise between the company and the workers.

If someone has been working for a company for over six months and that company has more than 16 people on its payroll, the employees of the company have a right to opt for part-time work. The request for part-time work must be made in writing to the employer at least three months in advance of the change and the employer can only refuse the request if there are valid business reasons. If a person works part-time for a company, and they wish to return to full-time work, they will be given priority over outsiders if a position becomes available.

Both fathers and mothers are now entitled to take leave for up to three years to look after their new baby under a scheme called *Erzieküngsürlaüb*. They can return to their former jobs after the three years are up. The parents are also entitled to work part-time, if their company has over 16 employees, for up to 30 hours a week throughout this period. They are also entitled to take an extra year from work when the child is between the ages of three and eight. Of course the company does not pay for the time off.

CHILD BENEFITS

In Germany if a parent is working, they are entitled to claim benefits for their children. Though taxes are higher than in many countries, the child benefits are also generous. *Kindergeld* is paid to all families with children under the age of 18, or under 27 if they are still in full-time education. This applies regardless of whether the children are their own, or if they are in the parents' long-term care. The benefit is also

THERE WAS AN OLD WOMAN WHO LIVED IN A SHOE, SHE HAD SO MUCH KINDERGELD SHE DID NOT KNOW WHAT TO DO.

paid for children between the ages of 18 and 21, if he or she is unemployed and actively looking for work.

Payments are made on a sliding scale. Approximately € 135 was paid for each of the first two children, € 150 for the third child and € 175 for each subsequent child. This amount is deposited directly into the parents' bank account every month. It is also paid if the child is on a voluntary social or environmental year, which is often taken by some German 18-year-olds after they have finished school, instead of doing military service. It is, however, not paid if the parents' income exceeds € 6,000 a month.

Families who live in Munich and who qualify for *Kindergeld* should apply to the Familienkasse des Arbeitsamtes Deggendorf, 94454 Deggendorf. For family surnames starting from A to K, they should apply via fax: (0991) 310-1206. For surnames from L to Z, the applications should reach Familienkasse des Arbeitsames Passau, 94030 Passau; fax: (0851) 508-440.

There are also tax exemptions—*Freibetrag*—for child care costs, amounting to approximately € 2,000. Be aware that you need to make a claim as it is not given automatically.

TRADE UNIONS

German trade unions are invested with a lot of power and it used to be said that if you had a German work contract you had a job for life. This is not really true these days, although individual unions still strike annual agreements with the Bavarian government to get the best possible deals for their members.

In 1996, the Bavarian State Government and all the Bavarian trade unions and trade union associations agreed on an employment pact to stem job losses and increase job opportunities by establishing new companies. There were also agreements on time flexibility and on increasing part-time jobs. This worked well as the unions made moderate wage demands and construction work was in demand in the area. Over the last few years, Bavaria has not been spared from the world-wide recession, though it is hard to believe, seeing the number of cranes lining the skyline and the incessant construction and renovation works on homes and offices.

CHAMBER OF TRADE AND INDUSTRY—IHK

The huge advances among the 'clean' industries in Munich in the last 20 years have been accompanied by an influx of foreign professionals, many in top positions in their companies. The Chamber of Trade and Industry—Industrie-und Handelskammer (IHK)—promotes Munich as a business centre for foreign companies and aims to help established companies develop. The IHK is the expert on German corporate law and has the ear of the government, who in turn has given them responsibility over numerous functions. The leaders of every company in Bavaria, whether German or international, are members of IHK. As such, there are linguistic specialists in every department of the IHK, resolving problems for the international business community. The chamber can be contacted at tel: (089) 51160; website: http://www.muenchen.ihk.de. Of course, it is all in German.

CORPORATE CULTURES

John spotted a job for me with a language school that was advertised over the Internet. As I had been an English teacher in England (native speakers are at a premium), I was put on their books and sent to many different German companies. The culture of each company varied as much as the individual personalities. However, the companies did share certain common traits.

Generally, the older and more senior members of the companies are addressed as *Herr* or *Frau*, followed by their surname. *Sie*, the formal 'you' was also used in conversations with them. It appeared that only the younger staff, or those who worked in the media or in foreign companies, especially American companies, used the given or Christian name at all levels. Certainly, respect for senior management and for their qualifications was noticeably shown by the subordinates. A company I know of has a canteen that caters to all the workers (most large companies do) but the senior management's table was the only one with a tablecloth.

Smoking is not permitted on the premises of many of the larger companies. However, many do have a smoking room set aside. The non-smoking practice does not always apply to smaller private companies where computer screens sometimes glow through the fog.

In the legal and financial centres, attire is business-like and the clothes are as smart and sophisticated as in the business districts of Paris, London or New York. Elsewhere, the smart/casual theme is more prevalent. Most women wear trousers, even in summer, and men usually only wear suits or smart jackets to meet clients or important people within their companies. It really is a smart city!

FAST FACTS ABOUT MUNICH

CHAPTER 10

'Alles hat ein Ende, nur die Wurst hat zwei.'
'Everything has an end. Only the sausage has two.'
—A common German saying

Official Name
München

Flag
Munich has two city flags, one that shows two horizontal stripes of black over yellow, and the other has black and yellow lozenges.

National Anthem
'*Für Bayern*' (For Bavaria) was derived from a poem by Michael Öchsner and composed by Konrad Max Kunz.

Time
Central European Time (CET)

Telephone Country Code
Country code for Germany: (00) 49
City code for Munich: (0) 89

Climate
Munich summers are generally sunny and warm with a few wet or cloudy days. Temperatures range between 11°C and 23°C (51°F and 74°F). During the winter months, temperatures can drop below freezing (between -3°C and 5°C (23°F and 38°F) often with some snowfall.

Land Area
310 sq km

Population
1,273,186 million (2004 est.)

Official language
German

Government Structure
The 80 members and three mayors of the City Council collectively make decisions on and supervise the city's administration but have no legislative functions.

Currency
Euro

Gross Domestic Product (GDP)
65 billion (2002 est)

Industries
Munich is a major centre for film production and book publishing and has one of Europe's largest wholesale produce markets. The Bavarian capital is also home to two leading high-tech companies—both Siemens and BMW are based in Munich. Innovation is a byword in the city, which has ties to some 20 companies that have filed for the most patents at the German Patent Office.

Munich also has a reputation for being the city of banks and insurance companies. It is the leading centre for insurance companies in Germany. After Frankfurt, Munich is Germany's most important banking centre. Over a hundred banks have their headquarters, a branch or representative office in Munich. Many foreign credit institutions also have their principal German headquarters in the city.

Airports
Munich International Airport

FAMOUS PEOPLE FROM MUNICH
Elizabeth of Bavaria (1837–1898)

Born in Munich, she became the Empress consort of Austria and Queen consort of Hungary by her marriage to Emperor Franz Joseph. Her father was Maximilian Joseph, Duke in Bavaria, and her mother was Ludovika, Royal Princess of Bavaria.

Richard Strauss (1864–1949)

Richard Strauss was the son of a well-respected German musician, Franz Joseph. Best known for his tone poems and operas such as *Salome*, he embarked on a long career of conducting and composing, which took him all over Europe and the United States.

Lion Feuchtwanger (1884–1958)

The German novelist and playwright Lion Feuchtwanger was born in Munich on 7 July 1884 as the eldest of the nine children. His historical novel *Die hässliche Herzogin (The Ugly Duchess)*, which was published in 1923, enjoyed critical acclaim. But it was his second historical novel, *Jud Süss [Jew Süss]*, that cemented his reputation as a novelist when it became an international bestseller and was subsequently translated into numerous languages.

Eugen Roth (1895–1976)

A German lyricist and poet, Roth was the son of the well-known Munich writer, Hermann Roth. From 1927 to 1933 he worked at the *Münchner Neuesten Nachrichten (Newest Munich News)* in the capacity of an editor. His humorous poems enjoyed great popularity and are still considered relevant today.

Heinrich Himmler (1900–1945)

The son of a Roman Catholic schoolmaster, Himmler eventually became a German Nazi police administrator, and enjoyed great power in the Third Reich. He joined the Nazi Party in 1925 and rose rapidly through the ranks. He was eventually put in charge of most German police units after

1933, followed by the Gestapo in 1934. The Third Reich's first concentration camp at Dachau was established by Himmler. By 1936 he commanded all the Third Reich's police forces. In World War II he expanded the Waffen-SS (Armed SS) so that it rivaled even the army; after 1941, he took charge of organising the death camps in eastern Europe.

Feodor Lynen (1911–1979)

A German biochemist, he began teaching at the Max Planck Institute for Cell Chemistry in Munich in 1947. His research and contribution to greater knowledge on the mechanism and regulation of cholesterol and fatty-acid metabolism was recognised when he was awarded the 1964 Nobel Prize in Physiology or Medicine, which he shared with K. E. Bloch.

Eva Braun (1912–45)

Famed for being the mistress of Nazi leader Adolf Hitler whom she met in 1929 whilst working as a photographer's assistant, she later joined Hitler in his bunker in Berlin in April 1945. They were married in the bunker on 29 April 1945, one day before they committed suicide together. Eva swallowed cyanide and Hitler shot himself with a pistol.

Charlotte Knobloch (1932–)

She was elected President of Zentralrat der Juden in Deutschland (Central Council of Jews in Germany) in 2006. She is also Vice-President of the European Jewish Congress and the World Jewish Congress. One of the most prominent leaders of the Jewish community in Munich, she has served as President of the Israelitische Kultusgemeinde München und Oberbayern since 1985.

Rudolph Moshammer (1940–2005)

A German fashion designer, his luxury pieces are fashioned primarily out of furs, cashmere and silk—and his exclusive clientele include prominent male figures such as Governor Arnold Schwarzenegger, Prince Johannes von Thurn und Taxis, actor Richard Chamberlain, King Carl XVI Gustaf of

Sweden, tenor José Carreras, magicians Siegfried and Roy and German media personality Thomas Gottschalk.

Percy Adlon (1935–)

A German film and television director, writer, and producer, Percy Adlon is best known for his film *Bagdad Café aka Out of Rosenheim*. He was also awarded the Officer's Cross of the Federal Republic of Germany, and is a voting member of the Academy of Motion Picture Arts and Sciences.

Werner Herzog (1942–)

A German filmmaker, he won two awards for his first feature film, *Signs of Life* (1967). This was later followed by *Aguirre, the Wrath of God* (1972), *Nosferatu* (1979) and *Fitzcarraldo* (1982). His film, *My Best Fiend* (1999), was a recounting of his turbulent relationship with close friend, Klaus Kinski. His films are regarded as some of the best examples of postwar West German cinema.

Willy Bogner, Jr. (1942–)

A renowned fashion designer, he is the heir to the Bogner clothing brand, originally set up as 'Willy-Bogner-Skivertrieb' by his father, Willy Bogner Snr. Willy Bogner Jr worked as a stuntman in a few James Bond films and later became a film maker in his own right.

Harold Faltermeyer (1952–)

A German musician, composer and record producer, he is best known for his film music for *The Running Man* and *Beverly Hills Cop*. He has won two Grammy Awards: the first in 1986 for Best Album of Original Score Written for a Motion Picture or Television special, as a co-writer of the *Beverly Hills Cop* soundtrack; and the second in 1987 for Best Pop Instrumental Performance with guitarist Steve Stevens for 'Top Gun Anthem' from the soundtrack to *Top Gun*.

Moritz Bleibtreu (1971–)

A German actor, he is best known for starring in *Knockin' On Heaven's Door* (1997), *Run Lola Run* (1998), *Im Juli*

(2000), *Lammbock* (2001), *Das Experiment* (2001), *Solino* (2002), *Agnes and His Brothers* (2004), *Munich* (2005) and *Elementarteilchen* (2006).

Philipp Lahm (1983–)

A German footballer who plays for Bayern Munich, he was part of the German team at Euro 2004. He scored the opening goal of the 2006 FIFA World Cup and is considered one of the best young fullbacks in the world. He was also part of the Mastercard All-Star team.

Andreas Ottl (1985–)

A German footballer who currently plays for Bayern Munich. He signed his first professional contract on 1 July 2005. He is also a member of the U20 German Team.

CULTURE QUIZ

SITUATION 1
The beer garden looks quite full. Do you:

A Search for an empty table.
B Stand in a strategic position and wait until a table is vacated.
C Ask if you can join a party with some room left on their table.
D Go and find a quieter beer garden?

Comments
The correct response is **C**. In beer gardens, it is usual to ask to join others if there is space available on their table.

SITUATION 2
When you order a beer in a Munich beer garden, do you ask for a:

A Pint?
B Stein?
C Krug?
D Mass?

Comments
The answer is **D**. A *Mass,* or measure, which is equivalent to a litre, is the usual quantity of beer per serving in beer gardens.

SITUATION 3
Which beer garden is not in the Englischer Garten?

A The Chinese Tower
B The Seehaus
C The Hirschgarten
D The Aumeister

Comments
The answer is **C**. Hirschgarten, or 'deer garden', is west of the city. Take trams 16 or 17 to Steubenplatz or bus 183.

SITUATION 4
You have enjoyed a delicious meal in a local restaurant. The bill is a reasonable € 43 for two. You

A Tell the waiter to take € 50.
B Accept the change and leave a good tip under the side plate.
C Tell the waiter to take € 45.
D Pay the set price and leave.

Comments
The correct response is **C**. It is usual after a meal to round up the bill to the nearest € 5, though in international hotels it is usual to tip 10 per cent or 15 per cent.

SITUATION 5
You have been invited round to a Bavarian home for the afternoon. What are you most likely to be served?

A White sausage and sweet mustard
B Coffee and cake
C Pork and dumplings
D Muesli

Comments
The answer is **B**. Coffee and cake is the usual afternoon fare.

SITUATION 6
When does Oktoberfest begin?

A October
B September
C November
D August

Comments

The answer is **B**. Okoberfest begins on the third Sunday in September. It is warmer than 17 October, when the wedding that is commemorated originally took place.

SITUATION 7

You are introduced to your boss' wife for the first time at a formal function. Do you

A Click your heels together and bow
B Kiss her on both cheeks
C Smile and say "Hi, good to see you"
D Wait until she extends her hand, then shake hands?

Comments

The correct reponse is **D**. Smile and wait until she extends her hand to shake. If she doesn't, it is better that you do than for nothing to happen.

SITUATION 8

It is your birthday. Do you

A Take cakes in to work for your colleagues
B Take in beer and wine for your colleagues
C Ignore the fact that you're getting older
D Invite the department round to the local hostelry after work?

Comments

The correct response is **A**. Take in cakes, and you can decide whether to have them in the morning, after lunch or in the afternoon.

SITUATION 9

You have just put new batteries in your radio. What do you do with the old ones?

A Take them back to the shop where you bought them.
B Put them in the general rubbish bin.

● Take them to a collection point for poisonous substances.

● Put them in a bin for waste metals.

Comments

● or **●**. The shop where you bought batteries must dispose of the used ones, but if that is inconvenient, they can be taken to a depot at a set time when dangerous substances are collected.

SITUATION 10

The week after you bought it the handle fell off your new briefcase. You have the receipt, do you:

● Go back to the shop and demand a refund

● Take it back to the shop and ask for a repair or replacement

● Take it to a leather shop to be repaired

● Use an old belt as a handle? You need to use it everyday.

Comments

The answer is **●** and **●**. You can ask for a refund and some of the larger shops may give one but they are not obliged to. However they must repair faulty goods or replace them.

SITUATION 11

You have an appointment with a company manager at 8:30 am on Monday morning. You

● Leave five minutes earlier than you would for the same journey by car on Sunday afternoon.

● Take a train that would get you there with two minutes to spare.

● Go by bike, it is only 8 km.

● Go for the train that gets you there 22 minutes early.

Comments

The answer is **●**. There are sometimes line repairs at weekends, and Monday morning trains, especially in winter, are not quite as reliable, and the roads can be a nightmare at this time. So riding your bike down would be the safest (and healthiest!) choice.

SITUATION 12

You want tickets for an opera at the Nationaltheater. Do you buy them from:

Ⓐ A petrol station
Ⓑ The local news agent
Ⓒ The tourist office
Ⓓ The booth in Pasing station

Comments

All except **Ⓑ**. Several Aral petrol stations sell theatre tickets in Munich, as does the tourist office and a ticket booth in Pasing station.

SITUATION 13

The most usual size for a family apartment to rent in Munich is around

Ⓐ 60 square metres
Ⓑ 80 square metres
Ⓒ 110 square metres
Ⓓ 130 square metres
Ⓔ 150 square metres

Comments

Ⓑ. Looking through the newspapers, the most usual size for a family apartment in Munich is 80 square metres.

SITUATION 14

Your landlord says that by next month you must vacate the flat that you have lived in for over five years, as he has found a new tenant who will pay more. He offers to return you deposit. Do you:

O Insist that he gives you two months' notice.

B Pack up and leave the next month, cash in hand.

C Ask for three months' notice.

D Ask for six months' notice.

Comments

The answer is **D**. If you have lived in a rented place for over five years, the landlord must give you six months' notice to vacate the place, as he has no right to throw you out to get more money. There are set amounts by which rents can be increased and you must be given the option first. If he wants to renovate the place, however, that is a valid reason for asking you to leave.

SITUATION 15

Bavarian children are brought presents by the Christ Child on

O December 6

B December 24

C December 25

D January 6

Comments

The correct answer is **B**. The Christ Child visits Bavarian homes on the evening of December 24.

SITUATION 17

Which famous couple is closely associated with Munich?

O Wassily Kandinsky and Gabriele Münter

B Romeo and Juliet

C Benjamin Britten and Peter Pears

D Napoleon Bonaparte and Josephine

Comments

A. Wassily Kandinsky and his mistress and former pupil, Gabriele Münter, were founders of the Blue Rider group of modern painters, along with Franz Marc and Paul Klee. The group's first exhibition was held at the Thannhauser Gallery in Munich in 1911.

SITUATION 18
Which church was not within the old city walls?

Ⓐ St Peter's
Ⓑ Matthäuskirche
Ⓒ St Michael's
Ⓓ The Frauenkirche

Comments
The answer is Ⓑ. Matthäukirche is just beyond Sendlinger Tor Platz on Lindwurmstrasse.

SITUATION 19
Which political party holds the power in Munich?
Ⓐ The CSU
Ⓑ The SPD
Ⓒ The VFW
Ⓓ The Greens

Comments
The correct answer is Ⓑ. The SPD (Social Democratic Party) holds power in Munich, but the CSU (Christian-Social Union) holds power in Bavaria.

SITUATION 20
Which part of old Munich didn't have a gate-Tor?

Ⓐ Frauen
Ⓑ Isar
Ⓒ Sendlinger
Ⓓ Karls

Comments
The answer is Ⓐ. Frauenplatz is the centre of the old city, the others were all gates in the old walls.

SITUATION 21

Which initials means that no swim wear is required?

Ⓐ FKK Freikorperkultur
Ⓑ DRR Deutsche Demokratische Republik
Ⓒ TUV Technischer Uberwachungs-Verein
Ⓓ Lkw Lastkraftwagen

Comments

The answer is **Ⓐ**. The free body culture is prevalent on sunny days along the banks of the Isar and in some swimming pool areas.

SITUATION 23

You've just started living and working in Munich. You haven't got much spare money to spend on German lessons, do you

Ⓐ Invest in a few private lessons
Ⓑ Go round to a local bar and listen hard to everything said
Ⓒ Enrol at the local *Volkschochschule* for group lessons
Ⓓ Buy a self-help book

Comments

All of the above. The more you are exposed to the German language, the easier it is to assimilate.

DO'S AND DON'TS

DO'S

- Take lots of walks around your local area and you'll feel more at home.
- Learn German. Speaking the language is the magic formula for enjoying every aspect of living here.
- Understand that the gruff tone used by Bavarians isn't hostility.
- Talk to other people in the beer garden. Even if your German is poor it may turn out that they speak English, which they often want to practise.
- Go to the Bavarian festivals, as everyone is really relaxed there.
- Try the Bavarian food, most of it is delicious.
- Join clubs and meet people you have something in common with.
- Take some flowers or a plant for the host/hostess when you are invited to another home, especially for birthdays. Chocolates or wine are welcome additions.
- Offer to take your shoes off when you arrive at someone else's home. Most family members and children do so in their own and friends' houses.
- Invite people in to your home if you want to be good friends.
- Dress appropriately to the area you're visiting. Some Bavarians dress quite formally (though not on the river's pebble beaches, when they may undress completely!).
- Buy warm clothes and boots for the winter then you may never feel the cold.
- Always carry an umbrella, the weather is unpredictable!
- Bring king-sized bedding with you as it is virtually impossible to buy here. Double beds have two single mattresses and usually two single quilts to cover the occupants.
- Understand that rented homes are painted white everywhere, and if you change the colour it must be returned to white when you leave.

- Acknowledge that children are expected to work, not play when they go to a German state school, but they usually have every afternoon off!
- Accept that German children and teenagers have more freedom. They are left alone younger and are allowed out later than in some other western cultures.
- Realise that it is not unusual for people to be students until they are 30, and live with their parents until that age too. It's cheaper.
- Do leave yourself plenty of time to reach a destination, especially during the rush hours and holiday periods as the road congestion can be horrendous then. (I'm told that Monday morning trains are unreliable after weekend work on them, but I have never experienced this.)
- Observe the quiet times, 12 noon to 3:00 pm, then between 7:00 pm and 7:00 am.
- Remain positive and optimistic.

DON'TS
- Stay at home and expect people to come to you. They won't.
- Be late for appointments as Germans are always punctual.
- Greet your new Bavarian colleague with a "Hi there Hans...". He may want to be addressed as Herr Müller.
- Get carried away with small talk at the start of a meeting. Germans in business like to come to the point quickly.
- Wash the car on a Sunday—it is still a day of rest in Munich and could offend the neighbours.
- Play loud music for hours on end as it may offend the neighbours.
- Get upset by poor service in shops and restaurants—everyone is treated the same whatever nationality.
- Become impatient in queues—everyone else is waiting.
- Argue with policemen, they are always right. (World-wide!)
- Talk about the two World Wars, the German nation has moved on and most regard that part of their history with horror.

- Be offended by nudity, it is perfectly acceptable here, in an appropriate setting.
- Mock any aspect of the Bavarian culture, we are all guests here and must integrate and accept any differences.

GLOSSARY

Common German Phrases and Expressions

Do you speak English?	*Sprechen Sie Englisch?*
Yes/no	*Ja/Nein*
Hello	*Grüss Gott*
Hallo!	*Servus*
Goodbye/Bye	*Auf Wiedersehn/Tschüs*
Good morning	*Guten Morgen/Morgen*
Good evening	*Guten Abends/Abends*
Good night (at bedtime)	*Guten Nacht*
Please/You are welcome	*Bitte*
Thank you	*Danke/ Vielen Dank*
How are you?	*Wie geht es Ihnen?*
Fine, thanks	*Gut danke*
See you soon	*Bis bald*
I don't understand	*Ich verstehe nicht*
Where are the toilets?	*Wo sind die Toiletten?*
Excuse me/Sorry	*entschuldigen*
I would like...	*Ich hätte gern...*
How much does that cost?	*Wieviel kostet das?*
Is it expensive/cheap?	*Ist es teuer/billig?*
Have you anything bigger/ smaller?	*Haben Sie etwas Grösseres/ Kleiners?*
We are looking for...	*Wir suchen...*
Where do I buy a ticket?	*Wo kann ich eine Fahrkarte kaufen?*
Does this train/bus go to...	*Fährt dieser Zug/Bus nach?*

Days

Monday	*Montag*
Tuesday	*Dienstag*
Wednesday	*Mittwoch*

Days	
Thursday	*Donnerstag*
Friday	*Freitag*
Saturday	*Samstag*
Sunday	*Sonntag*

Months	
January	*Januar*
February	*Februar*
March	*März*
April	*April*
May	*Mai*
June	*Juni*
July	*Juli*
August	*August*
September	*September*
October	*Oktober*
November	*November*
December	*Dezember*

Numbers	
one	*eins*
two	*zwei*
three	*drei*
four	*vier*
five	*fünf*
six	*sechs*
seven	*sieben*
eight	*acht*
nine	*neun*
ten	*zehn*
eleven	*elf*
twelve	*zwolf*

Numbers

thirteen, fourteen, fifteen....	*dreizehn, vierzehn, fünfzehn.......*
twenty, twenty one, twenty two	*zwanzig, einund zwanzig, zwei und zwanzig.*
Thirty, forty, fifty, sixty, seventy, eighty, ninety	*dreizig, vierzig, fünfzig, sechzig, siebzig, achtzig, nuenzig*
Hundred, thousand	*hundert, tausand*
A pair	*Ein Paar*

Food and Drink

A table for four please	*Einen Tisch für vier Personen, bitte*
I would like a beer please	*Ich möchte ein Helles, bitte*
May we have some tea please?	*Könnten wir bitte Tee haben?*
Coffee with milk/cream	*Kaffee mit Milch/Sahne*
Biscuits	*Keks*
Cake, gateau	*Kuchen, Torte*
Meat	*Fleisch*
Beef, steak	*Rindfleisch, Steak*
Pork, roast pork	*Schweine, Schweinebraten*
Lamb, lamb chop	*Lamm, Lammkotelett*
Chicken	*Hähnchen*
Duck	*Ente*
Turkey	*Puten*
Sausage	*Würst*
Ham	*Schinken*
Meat in paprika sauce	*Gulasch*
Veal escolope	*Wiener Schnitzel*
Fish	*Fisch*
Perch	*Zander*
Trout	*Forelle*

Food and Drink	
Potato	*Kartoffel*
Crisp (Brit) chip (US)	*Kartoffelchip*
Chips, french fries	*Pommes*
Lettuce	*Salat*
Mixed salad	*Bunte Salat*
Cheese	*Käse*
Egg	*Ei*
Bread	*Brot*

RESOURCE GUIDE

EMERGENCY TELEPHONE NUMBERS

- Police   110
- Fire and emergency medical care   112
- Home medical service   (089) 551-771
- Emergency Pharmacy   (089) 594-475
- AIDS Hotline   (089) 19411
- Alcoholics Anonymous   (089) 19295
- Poison Control Centre   (089) 19240
- Emergency Dental Service   (089) 19243
- To block credit cards   (089) 116-116
- Helpline for children and youths (freecall)   (0800) 111-0333
- Helpline for parents (freecall)   (0800) 111-0550

HOSPITALS
Central Munich
- **Kinderklinik (Children's hospital)**
  Lindwurmstrasse 4, 80337 Munich
  Tel: (089) 5160-0
- **Zahnklinik (Dental Clinic)**
  Goethestrasse 70, 80337 Munich
  Tel: (089) 5160-0

South Munich
- **Grosshadern Klinikum**
  Marchioninistrasse 15, 81377 Munich
  Tel: (089) 7095-1
- **Harlaching Krankenhaus**
  Sanatoriumsplatz 2, 81545 Munich
  Tel: (089) 6210-1

West Munich
- **Kreiskrankenhaus Pasing**
  Steinerweg 5, 81241 Munich
  Tel: (089) 8892-0

North Munich

- **Schwabinger Krankenhaus**
  Kölner Platz 1, 80804 Munich
  Tel: (089) 3068-1

East Munich

- **Bogenhausener Krankenhaus**
  Engelschalkingerstrasse 77, 81925 Munich
  Tel: (089) 9270-0
- **Städtisches Krankenhaus München Neuperlach**
  Oskar-Maria-Graf-Ring 51, 81737 Munich
  Tel: (089) 6794-1
- **Rechts der Isar Klinikum**
  Ismaningerstrasse 22, 81675
  Tel: (089) 4140-0

TOURISM AUTHORITY

- **Munich Tourist Authority**
  Tel: (089) 233-0300

CONSULATES

- **British Consulate-General**
  Bürkleinstrasse 10, 80538 Munich
  Tel: (089) 211-090
- **Canadian Consulate**
  Im Tal 29, 80331 Munich
  Tel: (089) 219-9570
- **American Consulate**
  Königinstrasse 5, 80539 Munich
  Tel: (089) 2888-0

TRANSPORTATION

- **Hauptbahnhof (main train station)**
  Tel: (089) 2333-0257
- **Munich Airport Information**
  Tel: (089) 9752-1313
- **MVV service centre (public transport inquiries)**
  Tel: (089) 4142-4344

BANKS

- **HypoVereinsbank**
  Website: http://www.hvb.de
- **Deutsche Bank**
  Website: http://www.deutsche-bank.de
- **CitiBank**
  Website: http://www.citibank.de
- **Stadtsparkasse**
  Website: http://www.sskm.de
- **Kreissparkasse**
  Website: http://www.kskms.de
- **Münchener Bank**
  Website: http://www.muenchner-bank.de
- **Volksbank**
  Website: http://www.volksbank.de
- **Raiffeisenbank**
  Website: http://www.raiffeisen.ch

INTERNET CAFES

- **easyInternetCafe GmbH**
  Bahnhofplatz 1, 80335
  Tel: (089) 559-9969
- **Internet-Cafe Hossain**
  Amer Schleissheimer Strasse 51, 80797 Munich
  Tel: (089) 1202-7070
- **Internet Cafe SAEB**
  Schleissheimer Strasse 188, 80797 Munich
  Tel: (089) 3266-7444
- **Internet Cafes in München**
  Nymphenburger Strasse 145, 80636
  Tel: (089) 129-1120
- **Kaufhof Rotkreutplatz Internet-cafe**
  Tel: (089) 1307-7170
- **Munich Internet Service Center**
  Tal 31, 80331 Munich
  Tel: (089) 2070-2737
- Pasinger Internet Cafe und Computerschule
  Landsbergerstrasse 511, 81241 Munich
  Tel: (089) 8899-8100

ENGLISH PUBLICATIONS

Most of the main English and American newspapers are available at the airport and at the International Presse at the two main railway stations, Hauptbahnhof and Ostbahnhof. *Munich Found,* an invaluable resource for all English speaking newcomers is also available at these locations, at the international schools and at the Museum Lichtspiele cinema near Isartor S-bahn station.

INTERNATIONAL SCHOOLS

- **Bavarian International School**
  Schloss Haimhausen
  Hauptstrasse 1, 85778 Haimhausen
  Tel: (08133) 9170
  Fax: (08133) 917-135
  Email: admission@bis-school.com
  Website: http://www.bis-school.com
- **Munich International School**
  Schloss Buchhof, 82319 Starnberg
  Tel: (08151) 366-120
  Fax: (08151) 366-129
  Email: admissions@mis-munich.de
  Website: http://www.mis-munich.de
- **European School**
  Elise-Aulinger-Strasse 21, 81739 München
  Tel: (089) 630-2290
  Fax: (089) 6302-2968
  Email: berth@eursc.org
  Website: http://www.eursc.org
- **Lycée Francais Jean Renoir**
  Berlepschstrasse 3, 81273 München
  Tel: (089) 721-0070
  Fax: (089) 7210-0730
  Email: contact@j-renoir.m.by.schule.de
- **Japanese International School**
  Bleyerstrasse 4, 81371 München
  Tel: (089) 748-5730
  Fax: (089) 789-263
  Email: info@jism.de

Website: http://www.jism.de
- **Greek Lyceum München**
  Ungsteiner Strasse 46, 81539 München
  Tel: (089) 6880-0395
  Fax: (089) 6880-0995
- **Islamische Schule**
  Freisinger Landstrasse 40/40a, 80939 München
  Tel: (089) 322-6245
  Fax: (089) 324-1766
- **Jüdische Volksschule München 'Sinai'**
  Möhlstrasse 44, 81675 München
  Tel: (089) 475-992
  Fax: (089) 470-8245

Useful email addresses and website for Munich	
Tourist Information	www.muenchen-tourist.de
Coping with aspects of German life	www.howtogermany.com
Information site	www.expats-in-bavaria.de
Online magazine for English speakers in Germany	www.expatica.com/germany.asp
American Embassy's site for Germany	www.germany-info.org
Weather	www.wetter.de
Free maps	www.de.map24.com/www.viamichelin.de
Tickets for theatre and events	www.muenchenticket.de
Oktoberfest	www.oktoberfest.de/en/index.php
On a budget	www.MunichLowCost.de
Newcomers	www.newcomers-festival.de/bavaria
To find craftsmen/decorators	www.handwerk-und-wohnen.de

Useful email addresses and website for Munich

English-speaking nannies	www.felicity-nannies.de
Magazine listing what's happening + clubs	www.munichfound.de
English lifestyle shop	pomeroy-winterbottom.de
English Comedy Club	englishcomedyclub.de
Theatre Group	www.entitytheatre.com
German English Association	www.gea-muc.de
German Canadian Club	team@dkg-oberbayern.de, www.DKG-online.de
International Women's Club	internationalwomensclub.org
Women of Color	Women-of-color.de
Munich Ladies Choir	www.munichladieschoir.de
Munich Dining Club	www.MunichDiningClub.com
Democrats Abroad	www.munich4america.com
Association of American University and Professional Women	www.aaupw.de
English-speaking chat line and information	www.toytowngermany.com/munich
English Speaking Union	www.esu-bavaria.de
Scottish Club	www.munichscottish.de
Cinema	www.cinemaspider.com/munich.html
Bike routes	www.tour-de-radl.de
Gay parade	www.csd-munich.de
Outdoor Classical music concerts	www.klassik-am-odeonsplatz.de
Munich Fun Run	filiale_muenchen@sportscheck.com
English Golf Society	www.egsmunich.de

Useful email addresses and website for Munich

Munich Rugby Football Club	www.munich-rugby.de
Munich Hiking Club	www.munichwanderers.de
Munich Writers' Club	www.munichwriters.de
In-line skating nights	www.muenchen-blade-night.de
English Speaking Playgroups	cheekymonkeys26@hotmail.com www.stickyfingers-munich.com www.munichmommies.com/ mumstots@web.de
Children's summer clubs	info@pinguincamp.de

Public Holidays in Munich

1 January	New Year's Day
6 January	Three Kings Day
February or March	Fasching, only a few companies
March or April	Good Friday Easter Monday
1 May	May Day
May or June	Ascension Day Whit-Monday Corpus Christi
1 August	Federal holiday
15 August	Mary's ascension
3 October	German Reunification Day
1 November	All Souls Day
November (Third Wednesday)	Buss-und Bettag, day of prayer and penance. Schools on holiday, and some firms
25 December	Christmas Day
26 December	Boxing Day, the 2nd day of Christmas

FURTHER READING

BOOKS

Bentley, James. *Travellers Munich and Bavaria*. Hampshire, United Kingdom: AA Publishing, 2003.

Gelbe Seiten (Yellow Pages). Germany: Deutsche Telekom.

HarperCollins German Concise Dictionary. New York City, USA: HarperResource (HarperCollins).

Marcellino's—München Restaurant Report 2003. Munich, Germany: Heyne Verlag.

München-Handbuch 2000. Munich, Germany: Landeshauptstadt München.

Munich and the Royal Castles of Bavaria (Michelin: In Your Pocket guides). France: Michelin Travel Publications, 2000.

Munich Insight Guides. Edited by Susann Rick. Washington DC, USA: APA Publications, 2006.

Schacherl, Lillian, and Joseph H. Biller. *Munich—Prestel Guide*. Munich, Germany: Prestel Verlag, 1987.

Tenberg, Reinhard, and Susan Ainslie. *Deutsch Plus*. London, England: BBC Books, 1996.

Themen neu. Frankfurt, Germany: Hueber Verlag.

OTHER PUBLICATIONS

Abendzeitung: Daily newspaper.

Bayerischer Behördenwegweiser: Leaflet published by the Bavarian Ministry of State with useful information on bureaucratic matters for living and working in Bavaria.

Bild: Tabloid daily newspaper.

Bogenhausener Anzeiger: Weekly Munich newspaper.

Deutschland Journal: Official magazine of the German government available in 13 languages, including English, and found in Goethe Institutes and German embassies abroad.

Hallo Landkreis Nordost: Local Munich newspaper.

Infopool—Young People's Guide: Published by the City of Munich.

Lufthansa Magazin: Inflight magazine of Lufthansa Airlines with articles in English published six times a year.

Münchner Mieter Magazin: Useful information when looking for a place to rent in Munich. Also available online at http://www. mieterverein-muenchen.de/tenants/engl_info.htm

Münchner Wochenblatt: Weekly Munich newspaper.

Munich Found: Monthly magazine for the expatriate community in Germany. Also available online at http://www. munichfound.de

TZ: General information and news magazine. Also available online at http://www.te-online.de

INTERNET
http://dict.leo.org/: Online English–German, German–Englishdictionary.

www.expatica.com/germany.asp: Online magazine for the English-speaking community in Germany, includes local news, shopping, entertainment and travel information.

www.expats-in-bavaria.de/: Useful site with information on relocating to and starting your own business in Bavaria.

www.germany-info.org: Official site of the German embassy in the United States, with general information on Germany and news articles.

ABOUT THE AUTHOR

Born in Yorkshire, Liz Smith fled the nest to study in the 'wicked' city of London. She spent a happy cloistered life teaching and raising a family in the small Hertfordshire town of Harpenden. Then her husband John was relocated to Munich and the family scattered to Sydney, London and Munich. Liz and her youngest daughter followed John to Munich in 1999, unable to speak the language and knowing no one. Through volunteering in her daughter's school, Liz had the opportunity to build a network of friends and work snowballed. She became a supply teacher in an international school, final editor of a glossy magazine and English teacher to business people in a diverse array of companies.

Naturally gregarious, Liz made several close friends, first with expats (though within the next two years many of them left the country) but also with others in this high-tech, cosmopolitan city. She got to know several native Bavarians who introduced her to the finer points of Munich culture— the wonderful array of museums, many different types of music, Oktoberfest, Christmas markets, street festivals and traditional costumes.

Intrinsic to the way of life was sport and the family started to cycle and swim. On a clear day the magnificent Alps would coax them away from the city to explore the beauty of the surrounding countryside.

308

INDEX

Titles in the CULTURESHOCK! series:

Argentina	Hawaii	Paris
Australia	Hong Kong	Philippines
Austria	Hungary	Russia
Bahrain	India	San Francisco
Barcelona	Indonesia	Saudi Arabia
Beijing	Iran	Scotland
Belgium	Ireland	Sri Lanka
Bolivia	Israel	Shanghai
Borneo	Italy	Singapore
Brazil	Jakarta	South Africa
Britain	Japan	Spain
Cambodia	Korea	Sweden
Canada	Laos	Switzerland
Chicago	London	Syria
Chile	Malaysia	Taiwan
China	Mauritius	Thailand
Costa Rica	Mexico	Tokyo
Cuba	Morocco	Turkey
Czech Republic	Munich	Ukraine
Denmark	Myanmar	United Arab
Ecuador	Nepal	Emirates
Egypt	Netherlands	USA
Finland	New York	Vancouver
France	New Zealand	Venezuela
Germany	Norway	Vietnam
Greece	Pakistan	

For more information about any of these titles, please contact any of our Marshall Cavendish offices around the world (listed on page ii) or visit our website at:

www.marshallcavendish.com/genref